Yuthasak Chatkaewnapanon

A Tourism History of Koh Samui, Thailand

ABSTRACT

A Tourism History of Koh Samui, Thailand

This thesis proposes an analytic framework of tourism history and discusses its value for a tourist destination's analysis. Employing a tourism history perspective, the thesis focuses on Koh Samui case study as a reference. This is done to illustrate specific points of the thesis's argument, such as demonstrating the validity of the analytic tool, which in this thesis links history philosophy (and their perspectives) with tourism studies. Focusing on the case study the thesis examines the influences of tourism development on Koh Samui society, an island in the Southern part of Thailand. In response to the growth of global tourism, Koh Samui has changed significantly from having an agricultural livelihood to a tourism economy. The thesis argues that the present society is the product of wider historical processes that have not been addressed yet. The focus of the thesis goes beyond the account of the interaction between Koh Samui and its tourism development as it is argued that the present society of Koh Samui is the product of reinforcement between global tourism and the islands' historical and cultural legacy.

Regarding the history of Koh Samui, the island has been significantly influenced by Thailand's central history, particularly in relation to the effects of the Thailand modernization process and also, more recently, Thailand tourism system. The process of Thailand's modernization as the result of the pressure from the nineteenth century Western colonial power provided the basis for the cultural traditions of Koh Samui society, which in turn prepared the next generations for their encounters with global tourism development. The present examination emphasizes the importance of recognizing the constitution of the national history and cultural in relation to the island's distinctive cultural traditions and its significant economic and social progress in modern time.

Through analysis of empirical data, the thesis suggests that Koh Samui's socialization in its tourism period has been characterized by significant tourism-related experiences. However, this work also shows that by including issues of national politics and 'traditional culture' it is possible to gain a deeper understanding of Koh Samui society in its tourism development period. Consequently, the thesis argues that the tourism history framework provides the understanding of the transformation of traditional agriculture and

i

A TOURISM HISTORY OF KOH SAMUI, THAILAND

YUTHASAK CHATKAEWNAPANON

Impressum/Imprint (nur für Deutschland/only for Germany)
Bibliografische Information der Deutschen Nationalbibliothek: Die Deutsche
Nationalbibliothek verzeichnet diese Publikation in der Deutschen Nationalbibliografie;
detaillierte bibliografische Daten sind im Internet über http://dnb.d-nb.de abrufbar.
Alle in diesem Buch genannten Marken und Produktnamen unterliegen warenzeichen-,
marken- oder patentrechtlichem Schutz bzw. sind Warenzeichen oder eingetragene
Warenzeichen der jeweiligen Inhaber. Die Wiedergabe von Marken, Produktnamen,
Gebrauchsnamen, Handelsnamen, Warenbezeichnungen u.s.w. in diesem Werk berechtigt
auch ohne besondere Kennzeichnung nicht zu der Annahme, dass solche Namen im Sinne
der Warenzeichen- und Markenschutzgesetzgebung als frei zu betrachten wären und
daher von jedermann benutzt werden dürften.

Coverbild: www.ingimage.com

Verlag: LAP LAMBERT Academic Publishing GmbH & Co. KG
Heinrich-Böcking-Str. 6-8, 66121 Saarbrücken, Deutschland
Telefon +49 681 3720-310, Telefax +49 681 3720-3109
Email: info@lap-publishing.com

Herstellung in Deutschland:
Schaltungsdienst Lange o.H.G., Berlin
Books on Demand GmbH, Norderstedt
Reha GmbH, Saarbrücken
Amazon Distribution GmbH, Leipzig
ISBN: 978-3-8484-2387-3

Imprint (only for USA, GB)
Bibliographic information published by the Deutsche Nationalbibliothek: The Deutsche
Nationalbibliothek lists this publication in the Deutsche Nationalbibliografie; detailed
bibliographic data are available in the Internet at http://dnb.d-nb.de.
Any brand names and product names mentioned in this book are subject to trademark,
brand or patent protection and are trademarks or registered trademarks of their respective
holders. The use of brand names, product names, common names, trade names, product
descriptions etc. even without a particular marking in this works is in no way to be
construed to mean that such names may be regarded as unrestricted in respect of
trademark and brand protection legislation and could thus be used by anyone.

Cover image: www.ingimage.com

Publisher: LAP LAMBERT Academic Publishing GmbH & Co. KG
Heinrich-Böcking-Str. 6-8, 66121 Saarbrücken, Germany
Phone +49 681 3720-310, Fax +49 681 3720-3109
Email: info@lap-publishing.com

Printed in the U.S.A.
Printed in the U.K. by (see last page)
ISBN: 978-3-8484-2387-3

Yuthasak Chatkaewnapanon

A Tourism History of Koh Samui, Thailand

Change and Adaptation in the Tourism Period

LAP LAMBERT Academic Publishing

the process of the assimilation of tourism development which present the most important mechanisms and conditions for Koh Samui modernity. The tourism history approach advances understanding of tourism and social change as well as the meaning of culture, livelihood, landscape and development on the island during its tourism development period.

Acknowledgements

First of all, I would like to thank my parents for their financial and emotional support and encouragement. My greatest debt is to all of my family, Mae, R-Pa, J-Nooch, J-Nong, Hea-Go, Hea-Chet, P-Tui, Charp, Pakkad, Nonggun and Mongmuk for their patience and willingness to come along on my long journey. They have always been extremely supportive and encouraging throughout the suffering years and understand that this time of my life is critical and have put my study as their priority. I own them for the rest of my life. To Hea-Cha, my uncle, to whom I am grateful for his support and hospitality during my time on Koh Samui. I am indebted to the many people on Koh Samui, whose contribution allowed this thesis to continue and who were willing to contribute their stories to my work. Very special thanks to them for their trust and openness. Their willingness to share their personal stories and observations of their lifestyle are highly appreciated.

I own special thanks to Dr Hazel Tucker and Dr Anna Thompson, my supervisors, for their continuous encouragements, support and enthusiasm. I especially want to thank Dr Hazel Tucker for her genuine interest in the topic. The friendly manner of her supervision has greatly helped to establish an excellent working relationship throughout the years. For Dr Anna Thompson, I cannot thank you her enough for her closely supervision on the final submission. Thank you also to Teresa Leopold and Andrea Valentin, who very graciously helped me by proof-reading. Their assistance played an invaluable role on both a personal and an academic level. Chawan, who was my assistance during my research on Koh Samui contributed valuable figures and photos, which greatly assisted the success of the thesis.

In Dunedin, I gratefully acknowledge the assistance and support provided by the administrative staff at the Department of Tourism, University of Otago. I would like to thank the participants in the department seminars for their invaluable ideas and comments throughout the years. As colleagues and friends at the department, I would like to thank everyone, particularly Paolo, Julia and Andrea for their great conversations over coffees and beers. I am also very grateful to P'Ann, Kay, Misuk, Hanim and Edi for their friendship and support. In Bangkok, I am indebted to the Department of History,

Srinakharinwirot University in Bangkok, Thailand, and especially to R-Jan Sawitri and R-Jan Pubblung. I am very grateful for their encouragement to pursue an academic career.

I am especially indebted to the Thai temple (Meditation Centre) in Dunedin and the fellows there. Their spiritual support has pointed me in the right direction throughout my critical times. I also owe special thanks to Na Pat, P' Keaw, P' Noy, P' Nui, who's support and kind hospitality was invaluable to my time in Dunedin. I especially want to thank Na Pat for generosity: her Thai cooking played an important part in the process of this work! Linn, Tui and Joob, our friendships over years in New Zealand will last forever. P'Ake in Sydney, Ying, Good, Nee, Aey and Ford in Bangkok, Wat and P'Pad in Chiangmai, even though they are in Australia and Thailand, their support and friendliness is here with me all the time. I am very grateful.

Table of Contents

LIST OF TABLE

LIST OF FIGURES

LIST OF PLATES

LIST OF APPENDICES

GLOSSARY

Baan	Village
Caroen	Progress
Chon chan klang	Middle Class
Farang	Foreigner, westerner
Haad	Beach
Hlung-kou	Behind the mountain (under develop area)
Hua-muang	Principle provincial towns
Kalahom	Ministry of the South
Khlang	Ministry of Finance
Koh	Island
Kon chon	Poverty
Mahat Thai	Ministry of the North
Monthon	Group of circles small provinces/regional
Muang	City
Muang khun	Thailand subordinate settlement
Muang pratetsarat	Vassal states
Ngoen suai	Money
Pa	Forest
Phatthana	Develop
Rai	Measurement of land equivalent to 1.6 square hectors
Rong Rean	School
Sakdina	Feudal
Sangha	Assemble of monks
Siwilia	Civilized/civilization
Talad	Market
Tambon	Sub-district
Thanon	Road/street
Thansamai	Civilized/Civilization
Wat	Temple

CHRONOLOGY

1238	Foundation of the Sukhothai Kingdom
1351	Foundation of the Ayutthaya Kingdom
1569	First fall of Ayutthaya to Burnese
1767	Second fall of Ayutthaya
1767	King Taksin establishes new royal center in Thonburi
1782	Foundation of Chakri Dynasty (Bangkok as the capital)
1851	Accession of King Mongkut (Rama IV)
1855	Bowring Treaty singed with Great Britain
1868	Accession of King CHulalongkorn (Rama V)
1892	Creation of royal cabinet and start of administrative centralization
1897	Rama V's first tour of Europe
1902	Sangha Act institutionalizes the monastic order
1907	Rama V's second visit to Europe
1908	Implementation of the Lay for the Prevention of Venereal Disease
1910	Accession of King Wachirawuth (Rama VI)
1925	Accession of King Prachathipok (Rama VII)
1928	Implementation of the Trafficking of Women and Children Act
1932	End of the absolute monarchy (24 June); promulgation of constitution
1935	King Anatha Mahidon proclaimed successor (Rama VIII)
1939	Siam is renamed Thailand
1941	Japanese army lands in Thailand
1941	Accession of King Phumiphon (Rama IX)
1959	Creation of Tourist Organization of Thailand
1960	Declaration of illegalization of prostitution
1961	Implementation of first five-year national plan
1962	Vietnam War; Massive development of a commercial foreign-oriented sex service infrastructure
1970s	Tourism started on Koh Samui
1975	End of Vietnam War
1987	Visit Thailand Year Campaign
1988-1989	Thailand Arts and Crafts Year Campaign

CHAPTER 1

INTRODUCTION

1.1 Introduction

This thesis employs the perspective of history to the understanding of tourism. The research is aimed at contributing a new approach to studying 'tourism history' (Walton 2005; 2009). Tourism history as understood in this thesis implies not only issues of the history of tourist activities or the history of the tourism industry at a destination – but rather, it is the analysis of a location which has become a tourist destination through the influences of its cultural and historical legacies over time. Despite the importance of the relation of a locality and tourism in space and time, there are only a few studies that employ the paradigm that provides the 'depth of tourism's influence on a community' (Macleod 2004). In other words, the influence of local historic legacies and tourism development into a tourism destination is as yet an insufficiently theorized concept. Some previous research, such as Cohen (1996), Hall (1997), Stonich (2000), Timothy and Boyd (2003), and Tucker (2003) have similar research foci in that they were centered on the process of tourism development over time and its implications on a destination's social, cultural and physical environments. Overall, however, the existing literature on tourist destination development, despite being very useful, mostly addresses historical and cultural legacies in a piece-meal, add-hoc manner. Therefore, this thesis addresses the importance of including a place's historical and cultural legacies into the study of tourist destination development.

The thesis argues that to understand any change and adaptation of a place as a tourist destination, it is necessary to go deeper in order to understand the 'tourism history' of a place. In essence, to present the process of tourist destination development and its implications on a destination society, it is important to take its history, culture, society, economy and environment into consideration. The thesis therefore addresses the role of local cultural conditions that reinforce the process of tourist destination development over time. The thesis follows the promotion of a relatively new field – tourism history (Walton

1

2005, 2009) by developing a theoretical framework and fieldwork methodologies. This thesis proposes an analytic framework of tourism history and discusses its value for a tourist destination's analysis. The thesis develops a framework, approach and concept for tourism history by using existing literature, particularly from the history discipline (see Chapter 2). Thus, the aim of this thesis is to develop and apply the concept of tourism history research by examining a tourist destination's changes and adaptation over time. To develop the framework, approach and theoretical conception in the field of tourism history, the thesis employs a case study approach. Examining a given locale provides a better understanding of that approach, the concept and the methodological issues of tourism history. Consequently, Koh Samui has been chosen to serve as the case study to this tourism history concept that has been developed for this thesis. The main objective of the thesis is to develop the framework, approach and theoretical conception of tourism history research to examine Koh Samui society. With the case study, and by considering the implications of tourism development within a tourism history concept, the thesis examines Koh Samui society change and adaptation during its tourism period. The case study facilitates a clearer understanding of the process of a place's development into a tourist destination demonstrating the importance of considering the relationship between tourism development and a place's historical and cultural legacies. In this respect, the thesis's objectives are focused on the interactions between tourism development and Koh Samui society over time. Table 1.1 outlines the aim and the objectives of the thesis.

Table 1.1: Aim and Objective

Aims	To develop and apply the concept of tourism history research by examining a tourist destination's change and adaptation over time
Objectives	1. To develop the framework, approach and theoretical conception of tourism history analysis to examine Koh Samui society,
	2. To assess the influence of Thailand's historical and cultural legacies on Koh Samui society during the island tourism development period,
	3. To explore the character and process of change of Koh Samui society, its people, its inherited structures (physical, social, economic and gender issues) during its tourism development period.

1.2 Research Approach

The approach and theoretical conception of tourism history developed in this thesis emerge from the importance of incorporating all aspects of a destination's tourism development process. This includes its cultural, social, economic, political and environmental landscape, which changes over time, without losing sight of the destination's historical and cultural legacies in the analysis of its tourist destination development. To address this approach, the thesis develops a concept based on a three-pronged approach:

1) The 'touristification of culture (Picard 1996) – the concept recognizes that tourism needs to be understood in terms of *how* it becomes part of local culture;

2) The 'touristic transition' (Cohen 2001) – the concept refers to the process of transformation of destinations after going through the pressure of rapid and heavy tourism development; and

3) The 'touristization' of a tourist destination landscape (Young 1983) – the concept emphasizes that tourism development is a process that links a place, people and tourism system together.

These three approaches are discussed in more detail in Chapter 3.

In line with this three-pronged approach, the thesis is constructed under a concept called the 'touristization of society'. This is the examination of the process of tourism expansion and the effects of tourism upon a particular population, traced over an extended period of time (the tourism history approach). This not only results in a destination's changing socio-cultural aspects, but also changes of land use, landscape, geographical and occupational distribution of population and their economic activities, that ultimately affect their livelihood. At the same time, under the concept of 'touristization of society', the thesis recognizes the process of local community's change and adaptation towards tourism development expansion in association with its historical and cultural legacies. As such, the thesis develops and applies the concept of tourism history research by examining a tourist destination's change and adaptation over time. This tourism history approach suggests that the history of a society is a process of continuous and mutable progressing of a society as a

3

tourist destination that is reinforced by a combination of the global tourism process and local cultural heritages. The thesis examines Koh Samui as a case study of a process of interaction and interplay between a place and its tourism development. According to Duval (2004: 58), 'one needs to be conscious of the larger historical processes that have shaped the very performance, culture or attribute under scrutiny'. Therefore, the tourism history approach explains how tourism emerged and blossomed on the island along with the consequences of tourism on Koh Samui society, considering its historical and cultural legacies in accordance with the national history of Thailand. Thus, the thesis proposes that Koh Samui's tourism history needs to be discussed within Thailand's general historical context in order to provide deeper insights on local societal change.

Figure 1.1 illustrates the conceptual framework of the thesis, and provides an overview of how the concepts work together. The thesis is conceptualized through the linking of the fundamentally historical perspective with tourism studies, tourist destination development theory, and the concept of the tourism period (see Chapter 2). The case study of Koh Samui provides a clearer understanding of the implications of tourism development on the process of a place that has become a tourist destination. Under the realm of 'tourism history', the historical approach is used to examine tourism development. Data collection for reaching the objectives included observation and participation techniques, in-depth interviews and oral history, as well as map survey (see Chapter 4). Thus, the research accounts are based on interviews, involvements and discussions concerning tourism practices and experiences on Koh Samui over time. Specifically, historical and cultural legacies of Koh Samui were examined through the experiences of the island's transformation during its tourism development period, as well as the experiences of people on the island and their everyday practice. These are included in the account of constructing the production of tourism history research on Koh Samui (Law 2000). Importantly, the thesis constructs the history of Koh Samui through its tourism development in order to understand the relationship between place, people, culture, tourism and the dynamics of time. However, with Koh Samui merely being the case study illustrating the approach of tourism history research, the practice of examining tourism development through historical approach can be applied to other tourist destinations.

Figure 1.1: Tourism History, A Conceptual Framework

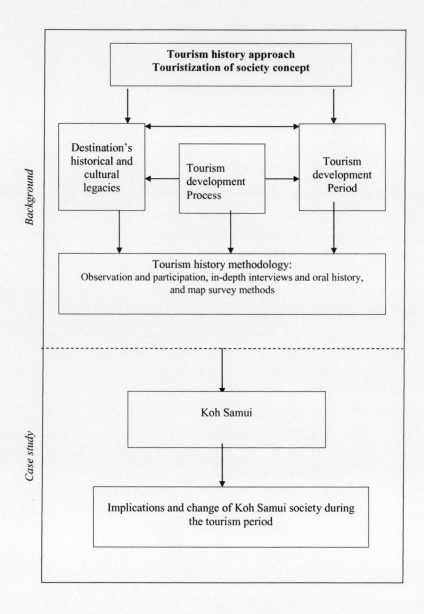

1.3 Background of the study

This section provides a brief context to studying tourism history and explains why it serves as a useful concept to study the process of a tourist destination's development. When studying 'tourism history', it is important to make a link between different perspectives – tourism studies, history philosophy, and tourist destination development concepts. In the case of Koh Samui, tourism is recognized as a process of interaction on the island. As tourism is continuing to grow, there is an increasing awareness of the overwhelming success and growth of international tourism on Koh Samui. Although tourism development is relatively in its 'infancy' compared to some other Thai destinations such as Pattaya and Phuket (further explained in Chapter 5), there have been various academic research studies conducted that address the 'impacts of tourism' on the island. Koh Samui was chosen as the case study in this thesis because it is considered as a relatively new destination and it is representative of change and adaptation of a rural area towards a tourist destination due to its tourism development (the choice of Koh Samui as a case study is discussed further in Chapter 4 of this thesis). This next section provides linkages between tourism and history, tourism and tourist destination, and Koh Samui as a case study in order to provide a foundation of the thesis setting.

1.3.1   Tourism and history

Tourism, due to its position as the world's largest and most dynamic industry, has drawn contributions from diverse disciplines in social science. Academic fields such as anthropology, sociology and geography have only recently begun to focus on the field of tourism history (Walton 2005). Although tourism is a relatively new field for history study, there is an increase in tourism studies from a historical perspective. Such an increase in historians' interest has also had the effect that journals such as the long-established Journal of Transport History now increasingly deal with issues of travel and tourism (Walton 2005). Moreover, the growing interest in tourism within the discipline of history has resulted in the establishment of a new academic journal entitled 'The Journal of Tourism History', with the first issue having been launched in 2009 (Walton 2009). With this regard, this thesis contributes to the new and growing body of tourism history literature.

Walton (2005) comments that historical studies with a focus on tourism offer a particularly interesting field of study as the historical analysis provides an in-depth understanding of changes associated with tourism. Moreover, there is a deeper need for integrating tourism into the historical subject. Walton (2009: 115) argues that any study of tourism 'cannot be understood without reference to what has gone before; nor ... to predict or preempt the future without achieving some understanding of where we and others have come from'. Despite this argument, tourism is commonly concerned with *current* processes rather than *past* processes. Interestingly, apart from the recent emergence of tourism studies within the area of history (Walton 2005), historical perspectives have long been applied within tourism studies. Thus, history has been a relatively common component of tourism studies, rather than vice-versa. According to Walton (2005, 2009), a general review of past tourism historical research has led to the first three perspectives of this thesis: 1) history of tourism; 2) history represents tourism; and 3) history for tourism commodities. Firstly, the concept of *history of tourism* covers areas such as the history of tourist activities and the history of a tourism industry at a destination. Thus, the relationship between history and tourism, specifically from the point of view of tourism studies, relates to 'the evolution of tourism in specific localities' (Towner and Wall 1991: 74). However, the relationship should not be limited to simply understanding tourism development in any location (see e.g. Engerman 1994; Towner 1996; Walton 1997; Walton ed. 2005). Rather, the analysis of the history of tourism in a location should provide an understanding of the place (destination) in relation to its contemporary culture, society, economy and environment over time. This, however, is rarely emphasized. The second concept is that of *history representing tourism*. In line with Walton's (2009: 118) observation that 'a key role of history in tourism studies is to challenge or complicate disarmingly simple stories about the past through detailed and carefully documented research in archives as well as published texts', the element of history in tourism studies appears in the form of statistical records or a linear chronology of tourism development. The essential practice within history using sources of historical data is also found in tourism research, not only in the form of statistical records, but also in the form of personal documents and oral narratives (Towner 1988). Tourism research can be presented in different forms such as government reports or travel writing (Walton 2009). Finally, there is the conceptualization of *history being used as a commodity* within the tourism industry. Walton (2009: 116) argues that with this perspective 'history tends to be reduced to a scattering of attractive tales, traditions and vignettes'. Walton (2009: 116) further explains

7

that history is used 'for the purpose, as part of systematic projects in the creation of national or regional identity and distinctiveness'. Thus, historical commodities in the form of cultural identities, historical events and historical heritages have functioned to promote and to develop tourism industry (Cohen 1996; McKercher and du Cros 2002; Richter 1999; Robinson, Evans and Callaghan 1996; Ryan and Aicken 2005; Timothy and Boyd 2003; Tucker 2003). Within this thesis this aspect is named *history for tourism commodities*, in that historical legacy has often become a mechanism for economic regeneration in tourist destinations.

As discussed above, the role of history in tourism studies or vice versa has been addressed by several authors (e.g. Cohen 1996; Hall 1997; Picard 1996; Stonich 2000; Timothy and Boyd 2003: Tucker 2003; Walton 2005). However there are only few studies relating to the influence of local historic legacies and tourism development into a tourism destination (e.g. Picard 1996; Stonich 2000). For example, as will be elaborated in Chapter 3, Picard (1996) discusses the historical processes of Bali becoming a tourist destination, including aspects of how tourism has developed, the circumstances, constraints and cultural conditions that defined the process. Picard illustrates how the tourism industry, destination development and cultural conditions all need to be considered from a historical perspective. However, it does not address the core concern of this thesis. Rather than focusing only on the implication of tourism development on local cultural conditions, the thesis addresses the role of local *cultural condition* that reinforces the process of tourist destination development over time. In other words, this thesis is not only about the process of tourism development over time and its implications on a destination's social, cultural and physical environments. Additionally it argues that a place's historical and cultural legacies strengthen the process of a place becoming a tourist destination.

1.3.2 Tourism and tourist destinations

Tourism is a well-established part of urban development, particularly, in rural and remote areas (World Tourism Organization 2004). Specifically, tourism is a major cause of the urbanization process in previously non-tourist settings, generally in areas with outstanding scenic, natural and/or cultural resources (Green 2005; Stonich 2000). For example, the transition of the Goreme community in Central Turkey from a largely

8

agricultural-based community to a contemporary tourism-based society is a major structural change reflecting the response to the process of tourism development (Tucker 2003). In this respect, the area in question is faced with structural change and differentiation, which is manifested by a shifting of occupations, roles, powers and social standing among various social groups (Tucker 2003). This process of tourist-related urban development results in commercial activity by creating a demand for accommodations, goods and services (Butler 1980; Smith 1991). In Thailand for example, tourism has resulted in urbanizing many places such as Pattaya and Phuket, stimulating their local economies, and creating a wide range of areas. Furthermore, a major portion of the national income is derived from the tourism industry (Tourism Authority of Thailand 2001).

In recent years, however, major concerns have arisen about the potentially disastrous effects of tourism on the social and cultural aspects of the affected areas as well as on their natural and man-made environments. These concerns focus on an increasing awareness of the dynamics, development processes and consequences for tourist destinations and their populations (Butler 1980; Cohen 1996; Cole 2008; Smith 1991; Stonich 2000; Tosun 2002; Tucker 2003). In addition, since tourism can create tourism-related business communities (Tucker 2003; Young 1983), there is little doubt that tourism involves various aspects of a destination's economy, politics and culture (Macleod 2004; Singh 1989; Tucker 2003). A series of tourism development processes influences the social structure and the historical sequences of development in a destination. Particularly, tourism can create changes in values and system, traditional lifestyles, individual behavior and community structure (Singh 1989). Many research studies, particularly those concerned with the issues of sustainable management and tourism planning, have focused on the adverse effects of tourism on community development (Abbott 1995; Nash 1996). Nash, in particular, summarizes:

> [F]or example McKean (1976) in Bali, Cohen (1979a) in Thailand, Boissevain (1978) in Malta and Hermans (1981) on the Costa Brave, who found tourism to be a benign and possibly beneficial agent of change. Others [argue] that tourism could have a range of consequences ranging from good to bad, such as impact assessments by Pye and Lin for Asia (1983), Preister (1987) for and American ski resort, and the World Tourism

Organization for Bhutan (see Smith 1981). Proper intervention, however, has turned out to be a highly problematic thing.

There is the idea that tourism is responsible for the uncontrollable changes to traditions and morals, individual behaviour and lifestyle (Harrison 1992; Jamal and Getz 1995). Additionally, social problems such as increased crime rates, prostitution and drug addiction have been emphasized in many research studies (Jamal and Getz 1995; Tosun 2002). In spite of arguments that attempt to depict tourism-driven development as either singularly good or bad, it is impossible to categorize the phenomenon as purely positive or negative. Specifically, looking analytically at tourist destinations, their environment and the cause of their transformation, 'we will see a very broad set of influences, which may be regarded as positive or negative according to the position of different observers' (Macleod 2004: 9).

In general, if the notion of social inequality is repudiated, then discussion of the practical response to the current issue of tourism-driven development will become more beneficial. Particularly, given the impact that tourism has upon tourism stakeholders, 'both the tourists and the villagers need to develop a liking for the serendipity in their circumstances, because it seems clear that much of the complexity of contemporary tourism is given to chance and thus requires sagacity from all involved' (Tucker 1999: 241). In other words, if tourism is to continue to provide wealth to a destination and at the same time to effect environmental, cultural and social changes, the effects associated with the results of increased tourism activities must be identified and understood. In addition, Green (2005: 38) further concedes that 'local residents can be involved in such efforts [...] about the types of environmental changes they consider appropriate (or inappropriate) and by providing insights into how future changes might be made compatible with existing environmental conditions and social values'. This includes the mechanisms and systems for managing the effects, which must be examined to ensure that they are effective in protecting the interests of a local community (Butler 1980; Green 2005; Stonich 2000; Tosun 2002). Consequently, this has called into focus the need to study tourism processes and tourist destinations, including the issues of new social relations that arise through tourism processes. The research study of tourism processes and tourist locales leads to the recognition of the fundamental importance of socio-cultural studies to the practice of tourism (Tucker 2003).

1.3.3 Koh Samui as a case study

Tourism is an important economic activity that plays a vital role in Thailand's socio-economic development. As a result, the Thai Government recognizes the great potential of tourism and encourages the creation of tourism in rural and provincial destinations (Tourism Authority of Thailand 1998). Furthermore, the government seeks to facilitate an extensive development process at national, provincial and local levels in response to the growth of tourism. The Tourism Authority of Thailand (TAT), a government body, plays an important role in tourism development. Through the support of TAT the tourism industry in Thailand is becoming internationally competitive (Tourism Authority of Thailand 1998). With the overwhelming success and growth of international tourism in Thailand, places like Koh Samui have been placed by the Tourism Authority of Thailand (1998) into one of the principal regions of the tourism industry. While this strategy promotes economic growth bringing more income to the island, it also leads to increasing pressure on the local community (Wangpaichit 1996). There are various research studies that suggest that tourism impacts negatively upon the island, its resources and its population (e.g. Boonsirichai 2002; Green 2005; Pongponrat 2007; Wisansing 2004). Also according to the Action Plan Formulation for Rehabilitation of Tourism Attractions Final Report 1998 (Tourism Authority of Thailand 1998), the sudden growth of tourism on Koh Samui had negatively affected its natural environment. There is much evidence that validates the claims of these studies. For example, tourism related activities have caused the degradation of the water system, which includes a shortage of potable water, lack of proper drainage, and wastewater management. In addition, Cohen's study (1996) demonstrates how the impact of the excessive water demand on Koh Samui created by tourism forces the local people to compete for the available water supply. There are many other tourism impacts on the island as well, such as traffic congestion, air and noise pollution, and flooding after rains because of inadequate sewers (Swarbrooke 1999). Moreover, tourism has caused the conversion of land use on the island from agricultural to commercial in order to accommodate hotels, resorts, pubs, bars and other tourist facilities (see Chapter 6).

While the local community is facing serious environmental problems and agricultural land scarcity, there are positive aspects as well - people on the island are

11

gaining economic benefit from tourism-related endeavors such as working in restaurants, hotels and resorts and selling products, for example. Furthermore, Jarujitiphan (1993) notes that the consequences of tourism include the opportunity of people on Koh Samui to access a quality education. Overall it can be said that rapid tourism development is likely to be held responsible for the livelihood change on the island (Jarujitiphan 1993; Kontogeorgopoulos 1998). Discussion about tourism on Koh Samui comes at a time of strong interest in the concept of sustainability and its application in many sectors (Pongponrat 2007; The Tourism Authority of Thailand 1998). In the development of a strategy for sustainable tourism, there is a need to pay close attention to the relative roles and responsibilities of the government agencies, tourism businesses, local communities, and the relationships between them (Apostolopoulos and Gayle 2002; Richards and Hall 2000; Vivian 1992). However, the Koh Samui Tambon Municipality's Five Year Plan (2002-2006) claims that there is a lack of community participation in the tourism planning process, particularly limiting the cooperation among the various sectors when it comes to the achievement of local development goals. Furthermore, the tourism study by Pongponrat (2007) shows that the barriers to participation of local people come from a low level of local education, a lack of knowledge and skill and also interest in participation of local people (Pongponrat 2007).

As tourism continues to expand unabated, the future of the island is unclear – it can either go the way of rejuvenation and restoration or further decline (Butler's Model of Tourist Lifecycle is further discussed in Chapter 3). While Conlin and Baum (1995) claim that the small scale of an island's physical resources puts it in a defenseless position against the negative effects of mass development, Maiava (2001) argues that locals are not always passive victims to development projects. In other words, while Conlin and Baum (1995) state that small islands are somewhat challenged in their capacity to control the diverse impacts of tourism, Maiava (2001: 19) believes that locals are becoming well aware of their situation and have begun defining their own problems and needs. Therefore, the question arises as to whether it is appropriate to focus on the consequences of tourism on the island as 'impact of tourism'. The wider issues surrounding the consequences of tourism development on Koh Samui as discussed throughout this thesis include locals' abilities to change and adapt to tourism development. In the Koh Samui context, the development of tourism is salient to the daily life of local people. However, to efficiently examine Koh Samui and its tourism development, it is important to understand how Koh

Samui, both in geography and population, changed and adapted under the influences of tourism. It is also important to understand the island's economic interest and social predisposition. Therefore, the thesis discusses the tourism history of Koh Samui society, including how tourism emerged and blossomed as well as the effects of tourism on Koh Samui society in light of its historical and cultural legacies. By taking the tourism history approach, the thesis sheds light on the historical, cultural and economic transformation processes on Koh Samui. This is achieved by asking what the development is and how it took place, what tourism has brought and how it brought change. In other words, the thesis addresses the issue of shifting communities through the process of tourism development of Koh Samui, starting in the 1970s (Cohen 1996; Schultz 2003). The role development has played in the transformation of the island is addressed, both physically and socially. Consequently, the thesis explores the changes in Koh Samui society during its period of tourism development, going beyond previous studies of 'impact of tourism' on a local community.

1.4 Contribution to knowledge

This thesis contributes to the growing concern that the tourism history perspective, and tourism studies from a historical perspective in particular, has been a neglected area of research. In this respect, the thesis suggests a historical approach – the touristization of society – to tourism history studies. The thesis develops methods to show *how* history and tourism are mutually intertwined. Specifically, it sets out to highlight tourism as significant events, and historical impact. Therefore, the contribution of applying tourism history in this research is the examination of how tourism is viewed in itself, in addition to discussing the specific features of historical and cultural legacies, behaviors, and cultural practices at both local and national level (Koh Samui and the Thailand modernization process). The study therefore contributes to the growing field of 'tourism history' literature. The case study of Koh Samui contributes to the knowledge on tourism development and the effects of societal change on local communities. The relations of a locality and tourism in a space and time paradigm '... enable[s] the researcher to appreciate the breadth and depth of tourism's influence on a community' (Macleod 2004: viii). The thesis further adds to an understanding of social change through tourism development in a rural area by drawing and building upon concepts relating to the role of tourism in societies in general. Thus this study addresses the lack of historical knowledge and depth on the relationship between tourism and Koh Samui societal development by contributing to the general socio-cultural tourism studies literature on Thailand, from a Thai perspective.

The thesis discusses recent changes on Koh Samui in response to growing concerns on the issues of global tourism processes and rural tourism development. By focusing on the touristization of society concept, the thesis addresses the social, cultural and physical landscape of Koh Samui and how they are related to tourism development on the island and its historical and cultural legacies. The study adds to the continuous concerns within tourism studies by addressing cultural change and the issue of host-guest relationships. The ethnographic study of Koh Samui society with a portrayal of the lives of those who 'live with tourism' (Tucker 2003) can contribute significantly to this concern. To address this, the thesis focuses on how life at home in relation to the family and the neighborhood has changed and how those who are directly associated to tourism have learned to live with it. Indeed, it is about the social integration and cultural changes of those who have lived on the island during the time of tourism development. Understanding how a tourist destination society changes because of tourism, how it adapts to tourism, and how this relates to its wider historic legacy adds to knowledge on tourism history. As an attempt to promote this relatively new field – tourism history (Walton 2005; 2009), the thesis, based on my own experiences of having lived on the island since 1989 and seventeen months of ethnographic research undertaken on the island between March 2005 to March 2006 and March 2007 to July 2007 (further discussed in Chapter 4), contributes to existing knowledge on;

a) The levels of conception and methodological issues of tourism history;

b) The 'tourism history' approach and the 'touristization of society concept' as applied to the process of a tourist destination, with specific focus on Koh Samui;

c) How Koh Samui society changed and adapted during its tourism development period in accordance to its historical and cultural legacies.

The thesis emphasizes the new approach of tourism history with the concept of touristization of society in order to link historical approach to tourism studies. However, the thesis is not arguing for it as the dominant approach or concept. Rather, it is an

14

alternative to the variety of approaches and concepts that are available. The potential of understanding the wider implications of tourism history to a tourist destination is not restricted to only Koh Samui society. In fact, this approach could be applied to other destinations.

1.5 Outline of research

The thesis consists of nine chapters. Chapter 2, 'Tourism History: the Approach and Theoretical Conception' discusses the approach and theoretical conception of tourism history. The chapter emphasizes the relationship between history and tourism, and proposes the approach, theoretical conceptual framework and fieldwork methodology in order to achieve the aim of the thesis. It develops the framework, approach and theoretical conception within which knowledge of history and tourism emerge. Chapter 3, 'Tourism, Destinations, and Rural Development' is a review of literature relating to tourism and destination development. This chapter examines the issue of tourism and analysis of change, after which the concept of destination development through life-cycle theories is discussed. Previous research on Koh Samui is reviewed in order to provide a balanced view on tourism destination development. Chapter 4 identifies the research methodology used in the study. There are three research methods: semi-constructed interviews; participant observation; and mapping surveys. The semi-constructed interviews and observations were conducted with key persons whose occupations were tourism related. The mapping surveys were used to illustrate the historical geographical development of Lamai Beach in order to explain the evolution of the beach into a tourism related business area. Background on research limitations and data analysis is also provided in this chapter. Chapter 5, 'Locating Koh Samui: Understanding the Island in the Context of Thailand', examines the foundation of Koh Samui society. This chapter discusses general issues about Koh Samui, reviews existing studies on Koh Samui, before it explains how Thai history, including the Thai modernization process, have influenced Koh Samui society until today. It explains how domestic Thai tourism affects the development process of tourism on Koh Samui. By discussing the shifting of Koh Samui's historical periods between pre-tourism period and tourism period, the chapter reveals the connection between tourism and development on Koh Samui over time.

Chapter 6, Touristization of Koh Samui: 'Geography in Transition', looks at the continuous change and adaptation of the island's geography in response to tourism development. The chapter discusses tourism related issues at a specific location – Lamai Beach – by demonstrating how local traditions and practices were reinforced by tourism growth, having resulted in transformations of space. The chapter presents the results of the mapping surveys by explaining how the process illustrates the history of Lamai Beach's geography. Chapter 7, 'Tourism Economy and Koh Samui's Social Landscape', focuses on tourism as an economic space on Koh Samui. The chapter is concerned with how tourism development plays a critical structural role in recreating the social positions of Koh Samui society. It discusses tourism and the continual process of change of the island's population as a continuing part of how people organize and give meaning to their lives, creating a sense of new identity. Chapter 8, 'Tourism Implication for the Koh Samui Gender Landscape', examines the issue of tourism and Thai gender by reviewing their interrelations within Thailand, where tourism is overwhelmingly a field dominated by women. The chapter focuses on how tourism has influenced the changing roles and representatives of Thai genders on Koh Samui over time. It discusses sex tourism in particular as it has drawn large numbers of women into contact. The chapter sets out to present stories of women working in the sex tourism industry on Koh Samui to reveal their positions and perspectives. The chapter demonstrates how the sex tourism industry on Koh Samui was reinforced by values and practices of Thai genders through women's stories of working in the sex industry there. In other words, the chapter reveals how cultural legacy of Thai genders influenced the growth of the sex businesses of Koh Samui. Chapter 9, the concluding chapter, 'Positioning History, Tourism and Koh Samui', summarizes and re-emphasizes the thesis's approach and perspective before discussing the findings critically. Taking Koh Samui as a reference point of tourism history analysis, the chapter concludes on the validity of the analytic tool.

CHAPTER 2

TOURISM HISTORY: THE APPROACH AND THEORETICAL CONCEPTION

2.1 Introduction

In order to achieve the aim of the thesis – to contribute a recent approach of 'tourism history' – it is important to emphasize the relationship between history and tourism. This thesis proposes an approach, a theoretical conceptual framework and a variety of fieldwork methodologies to refer to how history as a discipline can look at tourism as a significant historical event, focusing on the case study of Koh Samui. To address the aim of the thesis, this chapter develops the framework, approach and theoretical conception within which knowledge of history and tourism emerge. Figure 2.1 is a model that was developed to emphasize the relationship between history and tourism in order to understand the historical aspects of a tourist destination. In the model (Figure 2.1), the historical time line of a tourist destination is divided into 2 periods (pre-tourism period and tourism period). The breaking point is the early time of tourism development at the destination. A study of a destination during its tourism period is constructive to understand the deeper implications of the destination's tourism history. The tourism history of the destination is, arguably, influenced by global tourism, national and local governments' tourism strategies, and historical and cultural legacies of the destination's society. These factors are reinforced, which result in change and adaptation of the destination's society to cope with its tourism development. Consequently, tourism changes a destination's society through continuous period of tourism development and thus becomes a historical event.

Figure 2.1 Tourism history model

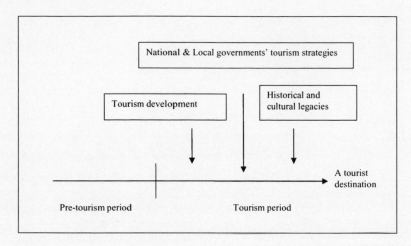

In order to achieve the aim of the thesis, this chapter provides the central theoretical discussion of the thesis, a critical examination of 'tourism history'. An understanding of the wider relationship between history and tourism is essential to make sense of the tourism history approach. Specifically, a clear understanding of the historical perspective of tourism is essential in the context of understanding the tourism influence on the societies' change and adaptation over time. Consequently, to address the tourism history approach with the 'touristization of society' concept, this chapter begins by linking the fundamentally historical perspective with tourism studies. The touristization of society concept involves fieldwork to construct tourism experiences and tourism practices of locals (Young 1983). By seeking to understand the role of tourism as significant events or a cause of the history, the role of tourism to historical writing needs to be discussed. Following on these concerns, therefore, the ensuing sections discuss the narrative in tourism history; the need of oral history and ethnography methods for the research fieldwork; the role of tourism to historical approach; and the importance of the tourism period. Overall, these discussions have the potential to explain how to view tourism in a historical perspective. It has the potential to critique tourism in addition to analyze the specific features of behaviors, and cultural practices.

2.2 Local historical perspective

Schwartz (1997) notes that tourism provides an understanding of a tourist destination over time. In this respect, it is similar to the notion of local history, a way of understanding local society over a period of time (Dymond 1982). Walton (2009: 115) emphasizes that tourism studies;

> '[C]annot be understood without reference to what has gone before: nor can we attempt to predict or preempt the future without achieving some understanding of where we, and others, have come from, or of how relevant interested parties understand and appreciate their versions of the past'.

As tourism studies mostly focus on a place as its tourist destination (see Crick 1994; Cohen 1996; Macleod 2004; Picard 1995; 1996; Stonich 2000; Tucker 2003; Waldren 1996), the local history of the place is the subject of tourism history research's attention. This chapter argues that to understand the philosophy of tourism history is in the same way to understand the philosophy of local history. In other words, this section discusses a local history philosophy to identify the keys concepts and the significance of local history in order to provide the framework of the 'tourism history'.

Conventionally, a national history attempts to reconstruct the national attitude and national identity of the particular nation. Thus, traditionally, historians concern themselves with issues or events that have or had significant impacts and/or lead to considerable changes in societies. One example of these is Bunnag (1977) who focuses on the provincial administration of Siam during the country's modernization process. His study emphasizes on the provincial administration as an event for 'a period of great reforms in the history of the Kingdom of Siam' (Bunnag 1977: 1). Phongpaichit and Baker (1995) are an example of following the traditional historical writing by focusing on the central history, viewing the process of Thai modernization as keys factors that have shaped the development of the country. The study of Bangkok by Askew (2002) also centers on issue of the Thai modernity process as a main aspect of the Bangkok transformation process. This is socially organized around kinship and is politically managed by feudal and monarchical rule. Consequently, subjects of national historiography are centered on political events and elite groups that thus present historical state symbols. The stories of ordinary people or a location that is less connected to the national history is ignored (Burke

1991; Carr 2001; Evans 2001; 2002; Kanjanaphan 2000; Thompson 1978), whilst this history might go further back than the national history (Kanjanaphan 2000; Thompson 1978).

It is important to note that every place has its own history, which combines all values and experiences of its society. History is, clearly, an interpretation of past events from different sources, which renders every life experience as important regarding its uniqueness within different historians' interests (Barnes 1962; Burke 1991; Carr 2001; Collingwood 1959; Evans 2001; 2002; Kanjanaphan 2000; Meyerhoff 1959). Therefore, material and evidence that a historian uses are somewhat 'perceptible to him [historian]' (Collingwood 1959: 82). Consequently, there is a growing literature that focuses on other aspects within national history formation (ranging from economic, social, labor, women, and local issues) with the aim to provide a more complete picture of history. This is reflected in the growing concerns with Thompson's (1978: 4) statement: 'Once the life experience of people of all kinds can be used as its raw material, a new dimension is given to history'. Nevertheless, this does not mean that local history is in competition with traditional history. Rather that local history is a part or sub-area of traditional history, which gives more aspect to history as a discipline as well as contributing to the history of a whole nation. The recognition of this leads to an essential shift in emphasis from conventional to local history, rather than an abandonment of the classical historical themes (i.e. the national attitude and identity). With this local history approach emerges an understanding of changes over time, how they are reflected in the present of the locale, and ultimately contribute to the wider picture of a national history (Dymond 1982; Evans 2001; 2002; Towner 1988; Towner and Wall 1991).

Importantly, when writing about history, some of the essential points in producing local history need to be discussed. According to Dymond (1982), when thinking of local history the aspects of 'time' – a period of historical writing; 'place' – a location of historical writing and 'theme' – a cause of historical writing; need to be recognized. Thus, local historians need to identify the most significant issues in the history of a given location. Additionally, an awareness of the uniqueness of events, and not only the notion of development and succession over time but also the notion that each period has a specific character with its own values and standards, are characteristic of a historical concern (Barnes 1962; Burke 1991; Carr 2001; Collingwood 1959; Dymond 1982; Evans 2001;

2002 Kanjanaphan 2000; Meyerhoff 1959). In essence, in relation to defining a significant subject for the research, the issues of place, time, and theme for writing a local history need to be identified. In addition, the contribution of history to understanding a locale has certain distinctive characteristics. Thus, local history relies largely on local documents and encourages local amateurs or knowledgeable people to produce a 'within' local history (Dymond 1982; Iredale 1974; Kanjanaphan 2000). The ideology of within local history is to reflect on a study subject or particular event that has a significant influence on every life in the area. The event might have no effect on people outside the setting, but is unique and significant to the studied location. Therefore, to understand local history is to understand what drives and forms local history from inside a community (Soonthornwanit 1996). The scope of time is an important aspect within historical writing as its central concern is the documentation of change over time. However, a timeframe varies depending on the theme of the research and of the historian's interest (Barnes 1962; Burke 1991; Carr 2001; Collingwood 1959; Evans 2001; 2002; Kanjanaphan 2000; Meyerhoff 1959). Thus, historians should identify a significant issue and discuss its general characteristics within a particular period of time, with local chronology providing a good tool to frame the work (Dymond 1982). But as local history is a notion of history, it is important that it provides a link to the national history, regardless of its limited autonomous history. This emphasizes the essential need to link the local history to the traditional notion of history, rather than abandoning classical historical themes. This shift in position and awareness of local history would lead to its continuous presence within the discipline of history and the society at large (Evans 2001; 2002; Jordanova 2000).

2.3 Tourism history perspective

In the case of tourism, history holds many different images and ideas. Indeed, it involves various aspects of a destination's economy, politics and culture. Thus, tourism is clearly perceived as a significant cause of many changes as a tourist destination (Cohen 2001; Crick 1994). In this view then tourism becomes a 'theme' – a cause of historical writing in this thesis. In the light of this idea, tourism causes changes in the social structure and the historical sequences of development (Stonich 2000: Tucker 2003; further discussed in Chapter 3 – in Section 3.2). To respond to the process of tourism development, destinations are faced with structural change or differentiation, which is manifested in forms of shifting occupations, powers, roles and statuses among various social groups (Tucker 2003). Then issue of 'place' in a tourism historical writing of this thesis is referred to a tourist destination. Overall, it is imperative to recognize that the place as a tourist destination is the negotiations of the place's society and the global process of tourism. In the case of Koh Samui, it is a process of transformation from a traditional livelihood (pre-industrial, rural, agrarian or agriculturally organized) to a tourism livelihood (service industrial, capitalist, urban, business oriented). This shift from traditional livelihood to contemporary tourism livelihood is a major structural change and consequently becomes a part of the restructuring process of a society and its value system. Therefore, in the aspect of 'time' of tourism historical writing, the period of contemporary development of a destination's society is a corresponding to a specific historical stage of development. In this thesis it is referred to as 'the tourism period' (further discussed in this chapter). In particular, when research concerns locals' roles and relations that emerge from everyday life, historians generally adopt an anthropological approach to construct the research study (Goodman 1997). Nevertheless, this type of research is not anthropological research per se. Rather, it borrows an anthropological perspective in order to conduct local history, generally known as 'historical anthropology' (Jordanova 2000) or 'ethnographic history' (Gentilcore 2005; Goodman 1997)[1]. In other words, 'historical anthropology' or 'ethnographic history' simply refers to the process of conducting a historical study in an ethnographic manner (Gentilcore 2005). Therefore, the following sections discuss the narrative in tourism history; and the importance of ethnography and oral history as the centrality of local history research.

2.4 Narrative in tourism history

In common usage, historical narrative is used to 'describe a situation, analyze a historical process, or tell a story' (White 1990: 26-27), particularly that associated with the contemporary national attitude, national identity, and/or life of those elite groups (Carr 2001, Evans 2001). In this sense, historical discourses are characterized by such political events and elite groups. Historical discourses also represent issues or events that have/had significant influences leading to substantial changes in societies (Phongpaichit and Baker

---

[1] Please refer to Gentilcore (2005) and Goodman (1997) for more detail on the discussion of anthropological approaches in writing of history.

1995). In terms of local historical discourse, the significance of the past reflects in the present of the locale and ultimately contributes to the wider picture of a national history (Dymond 1982; Evans 2001; Towner and Wall 1991). To establish what narrative in tourism history discourse means, it is important to discuss the context of local history. Local history discourse is concerned with an awareness of the uniqueness of events, the notion of development and succession over time and the recognition of specific character of its historical period (Burke 1991, Car 2001, Evans 2001; 2002). In turn, tourism history discourse is to reflect on the historical sequences of tourism development that causes changes in a destination's economy, politics and culture. The framework for narrating tourism historical discourse is therefore a necessity to understand tourism studies from a historical perspective. In other words, the framing of issues of narrative in the (re)construction of local history through its tourism development is the focus in this section.

During the tourism period, tourism developments and activities are the historical events. These historical events, from which the tourism history emerged, are crucial to comprehending changes and adaptations of the destination's society. In this respect, based on tourism development and its implications on a tourist destination, tourism history of a destination is an account that holds meanings fundamental to the understanding of, if not only, the constitutive elements of the society during its tourism period. Therefore, it is discussed how tourism history accounts deal with its narrative representation within the role of tourism development and the process of a destination's socialization. According to White (1981: 1), representation in narrative is 'to invite reflection on the very nature of culture and, possibly, even on the nature of humanity itself'. Relating this statement to the tourism history context, representation in tourism history is to invite reflection on the nature of the *implications of tourism*. Thus, narratives in tourism history represent tourism experiences and practices of the locals in the tourist destination. This kind of narrative refers to the presence of particular institutional structures that exist in many tourism researches, particularly to those focuses on socio-cultural changes at tourist destinations (see Crick 1994; Cohen 1996; Picard 1996; Stonich 2000; Tucker 2003). Within this instance of narrative, the representation of tourism history accounts should not be limited to simply understanding tourism development in linear form of any location (Engerman 1994; Towner 1996; Walton 2005). In other words, the representation of tourism history discourse should go beyond the history of tourist activities and/or the history of a tourism industry in a destination. In fact, the analysis of the historical accounts in tourism history need to be presented as a *complex narrative* through the discussions of the location's contemporary culture, society, economy and environment over its tourism period. To reflect on White (1990), as a framework it moves beyond an emphasis on the chronological description of tourism development in representing tourism history. Instead White (1990) proposed that implications of tourism are organized and analyzed through complex collective representations of a tourist destination. Including the issues such as the representation of tourism landscape, social configuration and gender pattern are presented throughout this thesis.

In addition, as local history reflects the locale and ultimately contributes to the wider picture of its national history (Dymond 1982; Towner and Wall 1991), a historical discourse of tourism history needs to be discussed through a textual analysis of the destination by connecting the text to broader societal issues (Fairclough 1989) that influence the process of becoming a tourist destination. Duval (2004: 58) notes that 'one needs to be conscious of the larger historical processes that have shaped the very performance, culture or attribute under scrutiny'. Therefore, at the 'macro-level' (Fairclough 1989) the linking to socio-historical accounts at national level is essential. Additionally, national tourism development strategies are used to connect the broader analytical examination of tourism history at a destination level. Narrative in tourism history in this thesis is the representation of the implications of tourism on a location by connecting both national history and national tourism development strategies by the central government. Tourism history narrative, then, deals with tourism development data both governmental and industrial information, the analysis of experiences and the practices of the locals, and the story telling of those who live with tourism. In this sense with the case study of Koh Samui, tourism historical narratives represent particular processes of change in socio-cultural and physical environments that tourism is bringing about. More importantly, throughout the thesis, the focus is on people at the local level especially on how they perceive and respond to tourism opportunity.

2.5 Tourism history: making a history with ethnography and oral history

As mentioned above, 'ethnographic history' attempts to understand societal and physical changes over time and how they are present within a given location (Dymond 1982; Evans 2001; 2002; Gentilcore 2005; Jordanova 2000). Fieldwork and oral testimonies play significant roles in order to achieve a mutually constitutive research study, where documents are mainly seen as 'living history' Ladkin 1999, 2004). Within this context, it is necessary to address some issues of oral history and ethnography. Oral history and ethnography share similar characteristics in terms of carrying out fieldwork and interviewing people about their life experiences. On the one hand, oral history aims to understand its subject in a particular historical aspect of a wider chronological framework. It reconstructs the experiences of local life in the passing of time and builds self-presenting collections of locals' events through interviews. Thus, it is a transformation of life experience into public statements (Huen, Morrison and Guan 1998; Morrison 1998; Prins 1991; Thompson 1978; Vansina 1961; 1985). On the other hand, ethnography is the study of a culture at a certain point in time, namely the time of observation (Herbert 2000; Inglis 1993; Kearns 2000), and is seen as an intensive study of people through observation and participation (e.g. Kearns 2000). Thus, the ethnographic approach is an important key within anthropology as it allows a researcher to be able to have a 'close-up' glimpse of a community (Tucker 2003: 15). Furthermore, it provides the possibility to make 'a detailed account of directly observed behaviour' (Jordanova 2000: xv-xvi), based on an in-depth understanding of the local perspective of a community.

While oral history interprets the evidence of the past through the experiences of the locals, ethnography interprets a society through the observation of local behaviors. Therefore, it is important to highlight the incompatible nature of the two terms 'experience' and 'behavior' (Bruner 1986). According to Bruner (1986: 6) the concept of 'behavior' refers to the description of someone's actions by the observer, while 'experience' refers to 'an active self … which include[s] not only actions and feelings but also reflections about those actions and feelings'. Through an interview process, which is a main tool in oral history and an ethnographical instrument, the attempt is made to portray the life of locals and to allow the informants to reflect on the beliefs and norms of the society in which they live and function within their own cultural context. Bruner (1986: 6-7) further notes that the limitation to capture the complexity of lived experiences is important to acknowledge as they derive from first, the reality of something significant happening and second, the experience of the significant happening. The final limitation is the memories of the significant happening and how such experience is presented. Within the thesis's objectives, the limitation of examining local life experiences to tourism development is the accuracy and the abilities of remembering the significant happening of tourism development. It includes the reaction of the local to the tourism as well as the interpretation of the researcher's representation to both local's reaction and to tourism development itself. Despite the differences, both fieldwork methods – ethnography and oral history – offer 'rich and deep cultural and historical insights' (End 1998: 101) and thus produce significant results within a local context. Therefore, in tourism history research, oral history and ethnography methods are employed to undertake the fieldwork. The research accounts are based on interviews, involvement and discussions concerning tourism practices and locals experiences of a tourist destination society. People experiences over time (through oral history method) and their everyday practice (through ethnography method) are included in the construction of tourism historical research. In this regard, tourism history approaches in local historical perspective should receive increased academic interest in their respective discipline.

2.6 Tourism history: tourism and its implications for historical writing

At a practical level, tourism holds many different images and ideas. It involves various aspects of a destination's economy, politics and culture. Specifically, tourism is centered on the study of tourist destination change, cope and adapt physically and socially with the increased cultural and social exchange (Crick 1994; Cohen 1996; Mecleod 2004; Stonich 2000). Furthermore, tourism studies are also focused on shifting identity or identity alienation at tourist destinations (Picard 1996; Tucker 2003; Waldren 1996). For example, Crick (1994) focuses on how tourism affects the Kandy community in Sri Lanka. The expansion of tourism creates positive and negative impacts on the host community. However, Crick suggests that with the encounters between locals and tourists and tourist activities, locals react to the encounters differently depending on their social status. Green (2005) is another example of a research study on tourism with a case study of Koh Samui. The development of tourism has generally had a wide range of effects on the environment. Some examples include the destruction of coastal areas, air pollution, water pollution and

26

waste water management from the tourism infrastructure and facilities noise pollution, traffic congestion and an over loading of the infrastructure. Green's research portrays the rapid negative change and damage of the island's natural systems due to tourism development.

While tourism is claimed to generate potential revenue and other economic benefits to the host communities (Ioannides 2003), it also contribute to cultural revival (Fagence 2003). In many instances the development of tourism industrialization and urbanization transforms traditions, customs and aspects of culture. At the same time it can also stimulate the cultural and environmental preservations and helps to encourage local people to show more concern towards their communities (Cohen 1996; Hall 1997; Jenkins 1997; Tucker 2003). For example, in the case of Koh Samui, the awareness of the potentially negative impacts of tourism resulted in establishing the 'Samui Eco-Tourism Club' in the year 2002. The club is a local organization which plans to protect and preserve the delicate marine environment. Its target is to help monitor and minimize the negative impact on the island's natural resources. Furthermore, in 2006, a committee consisting of business professionals, resort owners, education specialists, and senior government officials set up a group called 'Spirit of Samui. They place high hopes on the abilities of Koh Samui's residents to respond to local community development issues. Their aim is to support the island through finding alternative solutions to some of the problems facing Koh Samui (fieldwork notes).

Thus, tourism development is, if not to all, conventionally perceived as a negative social change, also illustrated by the usage of the word 'impact', which contains a negative connotation. Although tourism initiates many changes at a tourist destination, it is impossible to depict social changes caused by tourism development as purely negative or positive (the idea in relation to impact/negative approach will be discussed in-depth in Chapter 3). As Macleod (2004: 10) concedes:

> The difference between the ways a business speculator, a tourist and a fisherman will see a beach – their various 'gaze' – gives us a clue as to the importance of experience, cultural background and current activity in relation to their interaction with the environment.

Therefore, looking at tourist destinations, their environment and the cause of their transformation analytically, 'we will see a very broad set of influences, which may be regarded as positive or negative according to the position of different observers' (Macleod 2004: 9). The thesis argues that changes in the destination's society and hence the historical sequences of development have been caused by tourism and are manifested in a series of tourism development processes. To respond to the process of tourism development, destinations are viewed in this thesis as changes and adaptations rather than impacts. Thus, destinations are faced with structural change or differentiation, which is manifested in forms of shifting occupations, powers, roles and statuses among various social groups (Tucker 2003). Furthermore, the shift from traditional livelihood to contemporary tourism livelihood is a major structural change and consequently becomes a part of the restructuring process of a society and its value system. Therefore, to examine a tourist destination and its tourism development efficiently, it is important to understand how the destination, both socio-cultural and physical environment change and how they adapt under the influences of tourism. Consequently, looking at tourism and its implications for historical writing in this thesis is to explore the change and adaptation of a tourist destination during its tourism development by going beyond the study of 'impact of tourism'.

2.7 Tourism history and tourism periodization

A review of tourism period is important to include as it represents the aspect of 'time' of historical writing. As mentioned earlier in this chapter, the scope of time is an important aspect within this thesis, as its central concern is the documentation of change over time. As tourism is the focus of this research, the timeframe is referred to as the 'tourism period'. Examining the 'tourism period' is to consider the period of contemporary development of a destination's society – a specific historical stage of a society's development. Therefore, this section reviews the general concept of historical periodization in order to apply it to a tourism context.

According to Marwick (2001), when a particular period shares common features of unity of change in attitudes, values and social hierarchies, this concerned epoch is represented as an historic 'periodization' for historians to focus in particular chronology.

Marwick (2001) further states that an interpretation of periodization is unique within different historians' interests. The specific term of 'periodization' in historical writing is therefore varying according to the perception of historians. Consequently, a variety of historical and methodological approaches has influenced the institutionalization of the term historical 'periodization'. Putting modern history of Thailand into the historical periodization concept, for example, is to explain Western colonization as one of the major historical events influencing the remaking of the history of Thailand (Baker and Phongpaichit 2005; Krongkaew 1995; Panya 1995; Phongpaichit and Baker 1996; Reynolds 1991(b); Tanabe and Keyes 2002a;; Van Esterik 2000; Wyatt 1994). Particularly, in the study of Thailand, it is customary to begin 'modern' Thailand at the country's reformation in the late nineteenth century. This approach is informed by an implicit assumption that the historical event of Western colonialism and imperialism in nineteenth-century Thailand represented a shift from the declining feudal order to the modernizing influences of the West. In addition, as this period is simultaneously institutionalized in the modern historical profession of Thailand (Baker and Phongpaichit 2005; Girling 1981; Krongkaew 1995; Panya 1995; Phongpaichit and Baker 1996; Reynolds 1991(b); Tanabe and Keyes 2002a; Wyatt 1994), this 'period' of modernity transformation represents the preoccupation with the role of the West in Thailand. In particular, the period forms the privileging of institutional history and the cultural view of the elite. Therefore, the period of Western colonization in the late nineteenth century in Thailand historical chronology can be viewed within Marwick's (2001) periodization concept as a 'Western periodization'.

Accordingly, in the thesis of tourism history, tourism is introduced as a means of change. Koh Samui, before exposure to the West through tourism, had been in 'change' by being penetrated by the country's influences, but had not itself been capable of generating transformative energies (see Chapter 5). In fact, change in Koh Samui's history has been opened through the island's *reactions* to tourism (see Chapter 5). More precisely, a series of reactions is perceived through the interlinking of tourism growth and the island's physical and social change – a history of Koh Samui society in the tourism period (see Chapters 5, 6, 7 and 8). Furthermore, this thesis shows that the modernization of Koh Samui is mainly the result of the presence and persistence of tourism. Tourism, as this study argues, is the historical periodization by which to analyze Koh Samui and the modernizing influences on the island.

2.8 Summary

By analyzing the literature relating to tourism studies and history it was observed that studying the role of history in tourism studies is an alternative approach to understand the *processes of change* in socio-cultural and physical environments (Walton 2005). It has also shown that in particular, the discussion on tourism history needs to consider the local historical perspective. It has clarified the importance of this thesis' tourism historical research being undertaken thorough ethnographic research through focusing on people and their socio-cultural and physical environments at the local level. Overall, tourism history discourse focuses on how locals change and their adaptation toward tourism development at the tourist destination. However, to reflect on Duval's (2004), tourism historical discourse is not only related to the local area but is also influenced by national history and the country's tourism development strategies. This research study recognizes tourism as a significant event in historical writing, thus, this chapter provides the background of history philosophy and tourism practice. This allows for an understanding of the processes of change and adaptation of a tourist destination's society and geography within its tourism development period. Before applying the tourism history model to the Koh Samui case study, in order to achieve the objectives of the thesis (see Table 1.1), the following chapter reviews the issues of tourism as a catalyst of change, destination development theories, and relevant case study in tourism.

CHAPTER 3

TOURISM, DESTINATIONS AND RURAL DEVELOPMENT: A REVIEW OF LITERATURE

3.1 Introduction

The aim of this thesis is to develop and apply the concept of tourism history research by examining a tourist destination's change and adaptation over time, with Koh Samui being the case study. By considering the implications of tourism development within the tourism history concept, the objectives of the thesis are to examine how the island's historical and cultural legacies influenced the production of Koh Samui society during its tourism period. The main concern is, therefore, the ways in which local experiences, socio-spatial and socio-culture have changed as a result of both Koh Samui's historical and cultural legacies and rapid tourism growth on the island. Thus, in order to achieve the objectives of the thesis, this chapter provides a review of existing literature and research on tourism and tourist destination changes which includes a review of tourism studies of Koh Samui. The thesis intends to provide an understanding of the discussion of destination development through the tourism history concept with specific focus on Koh Samui. While Thailand's historical and cultural processes of change that influenced Koh Samui society are discussed in Chapter 5, this chapter provides the discussion on tourism as a catalyst of change. Thus, the chapter begins with a discussion of destination development in relationship to destination life-cycle theories. This section addresses the general problem of applying the tourist area lifecycle model (Butler 1980) in order to form a foundation for the discussion of changes of Koh Samui society. Section 3.3 reviews existing case studies on tourism and local development in order to provide a link between tourism development and the changes to local communities. Section 3.4 reviews tourism studies of Koh Samui. This section discusses tourism and previous research undertaken on Koh Samui. The purpose of this section is to provide background information on already existing tourism research that is concerned with society, culture, environment and economics and their implications for tourism development of Koh Samui. These three sections are important as they highlight the role of tourism in rural community development. Particularly they provide an essential understanding for the implications of tourism on Koh Samui society.

3.2 Destination development: debates surrounding destination lifecycle theories

Destination development may be defined as the transfer of general processes of economic, social and environmental changes at a local level (Agarwal 1997; Cooper and Jackson 1989). In examining the destination development origins of tourist destination lifecycle theory, it may be argued that it was broadly based on Butler's concept of the tourist cycle of evolution concept (1980). This theory led to a paradigm of destination development projects that provide 'an analytical framework by which to examine the evolution of tourist destinations within their complex economic, social, and cultural environments' (Cooper and Jackson 1989: 382). In this respect, the destination life cycle model provides a framework for analysis of tourism studies because tourism brings about varying effects on the destination.

According to Butler (1980), the lifecycle of tourist destinations begins with the development of tourist numbers and infrastructure as an evolutionary model. Exclusively, the model defines the development of destinations as having six stages each of which has its own identifiable features (see figure 3.1). It begins with the exploration stage and moves on to the involvement, development, consolidation, stagnation, and decline stages. Base on Butler's tourist area lifecycle model (1980), at the *exploration stage*, a tourist destination is still fresh and non-commercialized. There is small numbers of visitors but a high degree of contact between locals and tourists. In the *involvement stage*, locals see the potential of tourism and start to provide tourism facilities along with advertising the destination. At this stage, a destination receives increased and regular numbers of visitors. At the *development stage*, a destination is being heavily advertised and marketed resulting in large numbers of visitors. At the same time, the destination receives foreign investments where too often than not, the real power and income remains in the hands of the foreign investors (Priestley and Mundet 1998). In the *consolidation stage*, a destination becomes dependent on the tourism economy. Although visitation levels continue to increase, the actual rate of increase has declined. Usually, marketing and advertising are heavily

32

invested in hope of extending the tourism season and attracting tourists that are more distant.

The *stagnation stage* is a critical point when a destination reaches its capacity. The destination experiences economic, social and environmental problems and is no longer fashionable. In the *decline stage* (first part of stage six), tourists move to newer destinations and leave the destination to those weekend visitors or day trips. In the second part of the stage six – the *rejuvenation stage*, indicates changes in tourism resources in order to bring up the popularity of the destination. These changes are either establishing new sets of artificial attractions as in the case of Atlantic City's gambling casinos (Butler 2006b) or introducing new unexploited natural resources. The first four stages signify growth in most aspects such as tourist products, marketing and local economy while the last two stages, the stagnation and decline stage, indicate a gradual decline of the tourist destination. According to Butler (1980) this usually happens as the result of an oversupply of tourist facilities which in turn causes environmental, social and economic problems.

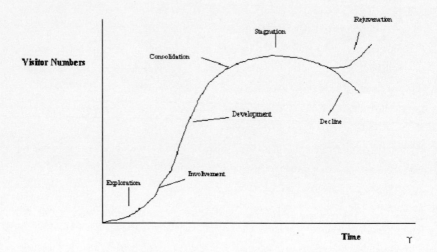

Figure 3.1: Butler's the destination life cycle model (1980)

Butler's destination lifecycle model has stimulated a widely discussion and empirical testing around the globe (see Butler 2006a; 2006b; Foster and Murphy 1991; Haywood 1986; Papatheodorou 2004; Priestley and Mundet 1998). In offering up this model, the tourist area life cycle further suggests that;

> [R]esorts evolve over a logistic curve, consisting of six stages; exploration, involvement, development, consolidation, stagnation, and post-stagnation. Over these distinct periods, there are notable changes in the tourism groups, the available infrastructure, the natural and built environment, and the local community attitude towards tourism. The cumulative effect of these changes is apparent in the alternative scenarios of the post-stagnation stage. If growth is left unplanned, resorts are likely to become victims of their own success and eventually decay. Conversely, appropriate policy measures may not only sustain tourism flows over time but also rejuvenate resorts initiating a new lifecycle...   (Papatheodorou, 2004: 220)

The destination lifecycle paradigm, however, was proposed with the assumption that tourist destinations are social *free* and/or social *neutral* in the host community and did not take into account the 'lack of standardization' of destinations (Agarwal 1997). In fact, a destination is unique in terms of its social, culture, politic and environment that influences the growth within the locality (Haywood 1986). Furthermore, the potential of Butler's lifecycle model is complicated as tourism consists of activities in various forms and sizes (Tooman 1997). This complication includes the issue of emerging of significant new attractions and expansion of other elements of tourism in addition to (or in replacing of) the principal attraction during the exploration, involvement, and development stages of a destination (Hovinen 2002). There are also the issues of 'complex relationship, in which factors such as the intensity of tourism demand, the fragility of the environment, and the influence of initial tourism development' (Priestley and Mundet 1998: 107) that need to be taken into consideration. As such Butler (2006a: 10) comments on the 'reflecting variations in such factors as rate of development, numbers of visitors, accessibility, government policies and numbers of similar competing areas' all of these have influenced the evolution of tourist areas.

34

Nevertheless, the assumption of social neutrality in the tourist area lifecycle concept (Butler 1980) is examined for its applicability and validity in different locations. For example, Cooper and Jackson (1989) apply the theory to a case study of the Isle of Man. They agree that while the concept has significant value in analyzing the development of destinations and the evolution of their market, it is difficult to operationalize. Moreover, Ioannides (1992) identifies fundamental characteristics of Butler's resort cycle in the Cypriot tourism industry and stresses that different agents have a different degree of influence on the island's tourism developmental patterns. Accordingly, Haywood (1986; 2006) argues that as the change takes place at a destination, the characteristics that determine suitability also change. Furthermore, the issue of the difficulties of assembling sufficient and suitable data to test the model coupled with the operational problems associated with defining and distinguishing between each stage is another aspect of the limitation of the lifecycle model (Haywood 1986; 2006). This is particularly applicable to the aspect of the post-stagnation phase of the lifecycle (Priestley and Mundet 1998). In addition to the specific characteristic of the tourist area lifecycle, 'a destination as being made up of a single product' (Agarwal 1997: 67) Agarwal (1994) argues that a destination is a product comprised of different elements such as hotels, local businesses or other tourist facilities in which different elements of tourism products at the destination exhibit separate lifecycles. Priestley and Mundet (1998: 108) point out that 'the pattern of the process of change of the natural and built environments and of tourism growth [is] depicted separately'. In this respect, Ateljevic and Doorne (2000) emphasize that one destination can consist of various tourist area lifecycle patterns. In essence, Agarwal (1994) further emphasizes the importance of the unit of analysis, or geographical scale. Agarwal (1994) argues that each unit within a destination exhibits its own lifecycle in which some may prove growth and other may show signs of decline. In other words, the diversity of the destination is, possibly, for one sector of tourism industry to be declining or showing signs of 'stagnation' in Butler's model, while others experience significant growth.

Another criticism of the destination lifecycle model is that the evolutionary pattern is not inevitably due to the application of the identification of the various phases of the model (Ioannides 1992). According to Di Benedetto and Bojanic (1993) it is important 'to recognize internal and external events that affect the lifecycle of a tourism attraction and assess their impact on the attendance or visitation.' For example, Butler (2006a) points out

35

that the issues of accessibility, government policies, and the competitiveness of similar patterns of tourist products affect the lifecycle of a tourist destination. Papatheodorou (2004) further notes that other factors such as natural disaster or political conflicts can affect destination evolution not moving accordingly to the Butler's lifecycle model. There are various factors in creating the conditions for a destination shifting form one stage in the lifecycle model to another. Therefore, specific analysis is required at any stage for a better understanding of the destination lifecycle. While the first three stages of exploration, involvement and development generally follow to the lifecycle model, the consolidation, stagnation, decline and rejuvenation phases are more complicated (Hovinen 2002). For instance, Hovinen (2002: 227) proposes the recognition of the 'maturity stage which is characterized by multiple products, each with its own lifecycle. During this stage, growth, stagnation, decline, and rejuvenation may coexist.' Furthermore, Ateljevic and Doorne's research suggests that when focusing on the conceptualization of economic analysis in New Zealand tourism, the rejection of massive growth in mass tourism does not mean the development of the 'stagnation' stage of the destination but rather that the destination is at the 'development' stage as defined in Butler's tourist area lifecycle. In fact, the destination is at the 'reproductive stage' of the new market, the niche market products (Ateljevic and Doorne 2000). In addition, Agarwal (1994) proposes the introduction of the theoretical reformulation of the post-stagnation phase in which a 're-orientation' phase between stagnation and post-stagnation. At the re-orientation phase, '[g]reater emphasis is placed on encouraging growth and market maturity, rather than on accepting decline (Agarwal 1994: 206).

Priestley and Mundet (1998: 87) summarized several researches on the issues of the possibility that the lifecycle in general can be revitalized and rejuvenated as 'tourism life cycles can be extended or revitalized as a result of conscious, deliberate decision-making on the part of management.' Di Benedetto and Bojanic (1993) argue that lifecycle in tourism can be extended or revitalized with a 'strategic' life cycle extension (internal factor) through the introduction and promotion of a new attraction at the destination. In this context Cooper (1992: 62) notes that 'a good strategy is to look at new users and increased use among current visitors; modify the product through improvements in quality, features and style; and modify elements of the marketing mix'. Besides a strategic life cycle, a tourist destination lifecycle can be extended and revitalized also with an 'environmental' life cycle extension (external factor) such as, for instance, falling gas

36

prices and in turn, cheaper travel. Likewise, the progress of a destination lifecycle is influenced by 'the rate of development, access, government policy, and competing destinations – each of which can delay or accelerate progress through various stages' (Di Benedetto and Bojanic 1993: 558). Although Butler's tourist area lifecycle is widely accepted as the universal evolutionary model and is used as a guide for much research, it is important to remember that each tourist destination is unique and that accordingly each stage of its lifecycle will vary in length and have differing shapes and patterns (Agarwal 1997). In other words, while 'the development life cycle indicates a temporal phasing of growth and development, reflecting the responses of tourism entrepreneurs, agencies, tourists and local communities to the availability of tourism resources [...], the challenge occurs after consolidation, with the destination needing to determine what will happen next – stagnation, decline or rejuvenation' (Fagence 2003: 60). Therefore, strategic destination managers have become increasingly aware of the lifecycle.

As a criticism of this concept, Fagence (2003: 60) notes that 'at each phase are environmental, economic, political, social and cultural implications'. Therefore, it can be argued that all the components of society at a destination, such as the economy, political system, social structure, culture, local people, and different agents in tourism businesses and not to forget the multiplicity of internal and external factors that are interacting to stabilize tourist destination development or its decline (Agarwal 1997). Respectively, all the components of a destination are a package which cannot be evaluated by taking only one aspect of the package into consideration (Agarwal 1997). In essence, if it is possible to isolate and predict the forces driving of a destination, then the predictive power of the lifecycle should not be underestimated for destination forecasting (Di Benedetto and Bojanic 1993). While the tourist area lifecycle concept provides a tool by which the tourist stage of any destination can be evaluated, the concept has mellowed in its stated expectations of a destination's change. Its latent force is explained in a single pattern of destination development. As the notion of development of tourism is the progress over time, the implications of tourism hold different meanings to each of the elements of the society[2]. Particularly, implications of tourism represent tourism experiences and practices of the locals in a tourist destination (Cohen 2001; Picard 1996; Young 1983). Essentially, the prediction of a tourist's destination development, combined with different aspect of

---

[2] See section 3.5 for instance to explain that at the same location – Koh Samui – different research examines and analyses the implications of tourism differently.

implications, should not be limited to simply understanding the destination lifecycle in *one linear form.*

In fact, the analysis of a tourist destination development needs to be discussed in various forms of Butler's lifecycle model. This is particularly applicable regarding its tourism implications on different aspects such as contemporary culture, society, economy, and environment. Then the reflection on Butler's model as a framework will go beyond an emphasis on the one single linear description of tourist destination development. Instead this research stresses the *complex collective representations* of Butler's model. Furthermore, 'if the model is seen ... as a flexible framework or a hypothetical development path, not as an independent mechanical process' (Ioannides 1992: 714), then applying the lifecycle concept in individual case study can add to the formulation of more generally applicable conclusions. Much social and economic change has occurred along the lines of prediction, however, the tourist area lifecycle did not bring about the multiple development patterns that were envisaged. Rather, it later came to be suggested as mostly having a negative image or indicated the decline of the destination. Therefore, Butler's early lifecycle model (1980) has always been perceived within a notion of decline, because ultimately the destination is bound to fail. Much has been written on the advantages and limitations of the tourist area lifecycle model (Agarwal 1997; Cooper and Jackson 1989; Hovinen 2002; Rapatheodorou 2004; Priestley and Mundet 1998; Russo and Segre 2009). Appropriate planning and adequate implementation are the key components of lifecycle extension (Butler 1980; 2006b) and, arguably, tourism planning can be prepared to control changes if any future changes can be predicted (Cooper and Jackson 1989; Getz 1992; Hovinen 2002; Ioannides 1992; Papatheodorou 2004). In the case of Koh Samui, the boom of tourism on the island politically resulted in the central government in Bangkok starting to reorganize the island's local government administrative procedures and to manage and oversee what was becoming a substantial influx of capital (Tambon Municipality of Koh Samui 2003). Along with massive investments from both national and local governments for tourist infrastructures, multi-million corporations for tourist facilities have been instrumental in the introduction of a new market 'development' stage of mass tourism on the island. The empirical analysis of the evolution of tourism on Koh Samui throughout this thesis therefore helps to identify the applicability and the validity of the Butler's destination lifecycle model. Again, 'if the model is seen, as Butler (1980) intended, as a flexible framework or a hypothetical development path, not as an independent mechanical process' (Ioannides 1992: 712), then the study of the implications of the evolution of tourism on the island 'can contribute to the formulation of more generally applicable conclusions' (Ioannides 1992: 712) for the tourist area lifecycle model on Koh Samui.

3.3 Tourism and local development: reviewing of existing case studies

Many research studies on tourism focus on how tourist destinations change, cope and adapt physically and socially with the increased cultural and social exchange as a result of tourism (see Crick 1992; Cohen 1996; Macleod 2004; Picard 1995; 1996; Stonich 2000; Tucker 2003; Waldren 1996). In these investigations several common themes have emerged. For example massive tourism development encourages a shifting of identity, even up to identity alienation (e.g. Picard 1996; Tucker 2003; Waldren 1996). Another theme refers to the struggle of tourist destinations due to the tourism development processes; these studies depict locals' lives and adaptation to tourism as complicated and difficult (e.g. Crick 1994; Cohen 1996; 2001; Macleod 2004; Tucker 2003).

Crick's (1994) study on tourism in Sri Lanka is an example of a study where a researcher applied ethnographic fieldwork within a case study setting. His ethnographic monograph discussed the process of tourism development and its implications on the tourist destination of Kandy. Through the possibility of active participation of the local people and the reconstruction of tourism in academic writing, Crick's (1994) research provides views of locals from various social groups about their encounters with tourists and tourist activities in order 'to suggest that a community can display quite a marked variation in response depending on their social status' (Crick 1994: 115). Crick's research is significant for tourism research as it presents a reconstruction of a tourist site through the active participation of local people. However, from a historical perspective, the work lacks an explanation of the influence of the place's social and cultural background on the process of becoming a culturally complex tourism community. Although he includes a section on the history of Kandy, it mainly emphasizes on the history of tourism of Kandy rather than focusing on how history and cultural legacies influenced the process of it becoming a tourist destination.

Tucker's (2003) ethnographic monograph entitled 'Living with Tourism' is a research study focusing on the implications of tourism development in the village of

Goreme in Central Turkey. Her work is on Goreme's identity in the context of local community and the negotiation of tourism cultures in Central Turkey. The issue of identity representation and transformation and the role of the country's tourism development strategies in cultural and social processes are stressed by Tucker (2003), including the actions and reactions of both local community and tourists in the area. Through her observations and participation analysis, Tucker (2003) examines tourism in Goreme from various aspects, including the locals' activities, businesses and relationships with tourists and the national tourism context. The village is placed within the tourism context in a way that it portrays the interaction of tourists, locals and other tourism-related agents. The main focus of Tucker's (2003) work is to discuss the reinforcement between the village and tourism development, which resulted in the community moving from being an agriculturally-based society to being heavily linked with and increasingly dependent on national and international tourism processes and policies. Particularly she emphasizes that local responses to tourism development may not only be placed into passive victims but they may also take advantage of opportunities presented in the promotion of the tourism industry and successfully live with tourism. Indeed, she takes up the story of the 'traditional' and the past; the role of different genders and the experiences of social change as a means of understanding tourist-local relationship. In her historical point of view, research suggests that an individual's past and social experience reflects upon the ability to cope and negotiate global tourism development (Tucker 2003).

In response to growing concerns regarding the influence of tourism development upon local communities, Stonich (2000) discussed such issues and their linkages in the Bay of Islands, Honduras by focusing on the reconciliation between tourism development and environmental conservation strategies. Stonich's research suggests that to be able to understand the current impact of tourism upon the population and natural resources of the Bay of Islands, one has to take the historical legacies of the place into the research account. In addition, Stonich (2000: 177) states '[c]onsidering the islands' fascinating history leads to a comprehension of its current social, cultural, economic, and political complexity – the context in which contemporary tourism is taking place'. Certainly, there are new conceptual grounds that affect for tourism planners, or perhaps more accurately tourist destination planners. Stonich (2000) presents relatively broad issues of tourism development in its potential and constraints, and discusses in a straightforward way the concerns of managers of tourism, sustainability, conservation, preservation, and manageable and local participation. She acknowledges that to manage tourist destinations efficiently for the benefit of a local community is to recognize the complexity of the historical context of the place.

Cole's study (2008) on the emergent cultural tourism which focuses on tourism, culture and development in East Indonesia is another important work. The aim of the research is to add yet another perspective to the conflicts of tourism both between actors and because of tourism processes. Cole undertook longitudinal research at the site over sixteen years of visits from 1989-2005. Using the longitudinal study on Wogo, a village in the East Indonesia, Cole has focused on different stakeholders that influence tourism development in the local community by examining their values, attitudes and priorities. The areas of discussion include 'how tradition, ethnicity and culture are strategically articulated, moulded, manipulated and used, to serve the different actors' purposes' (Cole 2008: 4-5). In other words, with the longitudinal study, the work portrays the picture of tourism development and cultural change at the micro level over time. Cole (2008) further notes that with the improvement of tourist infrastructure and transportation, the travel patterns of the tourists have changed. It moves from only group travelling with a tour guide to independent backpackers and cruise tourists. Furthermore, along with tourism development in the village, experiences of 'conflicts of acculturation' are discussed. In this respect, to maintain the attractiveness of tourism products, the villages must remain 'primitive, traditional and exotic' whilst the notions of tourism development is to bring in wealth and modernization (Cole 2008: 37). The issue of tourism and local identity, Cole (2008: 246) argues that the 'process of commodification of the villagers' identity is bringing them pride and a self-conscious awareness of their traditional culture'. With this argument, Cole's discussion goes beyond the analysis of culture commoditization process as a result of the loss of authenticity and cultural distinction. Rather, it has examined 'how tourism can be used, as a force to be mobilized and the resultant affirmation of identity, increased pride and empowerment that can follow' (Cole 2008: 37). Indeed, Cole (2008) proposes that it is important to examine tourism development internally in order to understand the interaction between culture and tourism.

Within this context, it is important to note that through their case studies, these researchers draft out certain positions. Thus, they focus on questions about how locals handle tourism and how locals' culture and identity, for example, are produced/reproduced or challenged in everyday life. Then it is important to take the influence of the history of a destination upon a destination's tourism development into consideration. Consequently, for a better understanding of the present condition of a tourist destination, it is important to understand the history of tourism development of a place along with the history of a destination. For example, Cole (2008: 225-226) provides a discussion on tourism development as an adding force to the historical legacies forces; the way of the ancestors, the Catholic Church, and the Indonesian state; which 'compete for authority in the villagers' lives'. MacCannell (1992) and Walton (2005) have provided other portrayals of tourism in the context of the historical and cultural legacy of tourist destinations. Their research which deals with the concern of history and tourism concludes with the following:

> ...[acknowledging] important aspects of the history of tourism in its own right, as something worth understanding for its own sake in terms of process and impact ... adds depth and comparative grasp to our understanding of the present and its potentialities and discontents, without falling into the trap of present-mindedness or forgetting the need to try to understand past societies on their own terms. (Walton 2005: 5)

MacCannell (1992) also concurs with this argument pointing out that:

> [T]ourism is not just an aggregate of merely commercial activities; it is also an ideological framing of history, nature, and tradition; a framing that has the power to reshape culture and nature to its own needs. (MacCannell 1992: 1)

In addition, the research work of Picard (1996) dealing with tourism in Bali is significant as it presents another angle of research of tourism and the history of a tourist destination. The Picard study essentially discusses the historical processes of Bali becoming a tourist destination, including aspects of how tourism has developed and the circumstances, constraints and cultural conditions that defined the process. By focusing on a deep, grounded and sustained historical analysis to discuss essential historical processes of Bali becoming a tourist destination, Picard (1996) suggests that the process of Balinese tourism transformation is the internalization of tourism in Balinese culture and its 'touristification' of the Balinese society. Picard (1996: 199) emphasizes that:

[I]nternational tourism, far from being foreign to Balinese culture, is an integral part of a process of cultural invention. ... [T]his process must be seen in the context of the opening-up of the Balinese world following the island's integration into, first, the Netherlands East Indies, then into the Republic of Indonesia. In short, the touristification of the Balinese culture cannot be dissociated from Bali's colonization and its subsequent Indonesianization.

Furthermore, Picard (1996) states that rather than viewing tourism as an external force influencing the Balinese society, instead Bali's transformation is based on its society's internal factors of tourism experiences over time. In this respect, Bali society is the process of reinforcement of tourism, its demands and interests, local definitions and expressions of culture and how they transform the touristification of Balinese society. Accordingly, Walton (2005) notes that to understand a tourist destination, it is important to take various aspects of the destination into consideration. Walton (2005: 6) states:

A problem in tourism studies has been a prevailing present-mindedness and superficiality, refusing deep, grounded or sustained historical analysis even when dealing with essentially historical processes [...], which is about change over time but usually treated schematically and without reference to how the product has developed, under what circumstances, constraints and cultural conditions and how that might affect its present prospects.

Therefore, these reviews clearly highlight the importance of incorporating all aspects of a destination's tourism development process, which include its culture, social, economic and political changes over time, without losing sight of the destination's historical and cultural legacies in the analysis of its tourist destination development. To address this concern, this thesis takes a three-pronged approach, as one way of examining tourism development to the analysis of the tourist development process: 'touristification of tourism' (Picard 1996) and the 'touristic transition' (Cohen 2001) and the 'touristization' by Young (1983). In other words, the findings of this thesis are significantly shaped by this three-pronged approach. The concept of the 'touristification' (Picard 1996) of a culture recognizes that tourism needs to be understood in terms of *how* it becomes part of local culture. In order to understand the 'actual cultural implications of the touristification of societies' (Picard 1996: 8), the transformation of a society must be examined by taking into account its local values, concerns and practices rather than focusing solely on the impact of tourism on the culture. The second approach, touristic transition (Cohen 2001), refers to the process of integration between a society and its tourist culture. Touristic transition is a process of transformation of destinations 'in order to either adapt them to tourist demand or to prevent their progressive destruction' after going through the pressure of rapid and heavy tourism development (Cohen 2001: 295). Cohen (2001: 171) notes that the main characteristic of 'touristic transition is the increase in the relative number, size and significance of contrived attractions ... [both] ... a nation-wide and ... a localized process.' Therefore, the touristic transition concept examines the development process with tourism as a major factor. The final approach, touristization (Young 1983), is based on the process of change, particularly changes to the landscape as a result of tourism development. In Young's (1983) research, a general model of touristization of traditional Maltese fishing-farming villages is presented in six sequential growth phases or stages. The dynamic processes from one stage to another stage are influenced by the growth of tourism development. He looks at the stages of landscape transformation in the village over time and analyzes this transformation in accordance with the tourist destination development. In Young's (1983) concept of 'touristization', tourism development is a process that links a place, people and tourism system together. However, Young does not conclude that 'at any particular stage of touristization the impacts are bad or negative ... [rather] ... if all traditional villages were to be transformed into resorts, reaching Stage 6 [Butler's 'Consolidation stage (Young 1983: p. 40)] in the model, then the tourist product on the island would be seriously weakened or diminished (1983: p. 35).

3.4 Tourism and local development: reviewing of tourism studies of Koh Samui

Because of the growing awareness of the overwhelming success and growth of international tourism on Koh Samui, the Tourism Authority of Thailand initiated different surveys examining the impact of tourism on the island with the hope of making the island a more sustainable tourism destination (such as Tourism Authority of Thailand 1985). In corresponding to the central government, Koh Samui Municipality also issues local development and monitoring plans in order to formulate plans and policies for public services and development. In addition, various academic research studies, each influenced by the different researchers' backgrounds and perspectives, have been conducted about tourism on Koh Samui.

Eric Cohen authored a number of articles on tourism on Koh Samui in the 1980s, collectively published in his book 'Collected Articles' (Cohen 1996). In this collection, Cohen provides an overview of the work that he had undertaken on Thailand particularly on trends and transformations of Thai tourism. In his work on beach-resort tourism on Phuket and Koh Samui, he makes important remarks on the processes of tourism development on both islands. Cohen provides convenient means of comparing and contrasting the tourism experiences of both places. For Koh Samui's experience, he points out that most of the early tourism products were a source of additional income to coconut production. Furthermore, he notes that those early tourism products were established by elite-local residents with the initial ideas that 'came from the visitors, rather than the locals' (Cohen 1996: p.190). In this respect, those elite-local residents converted their own properties to create tourism facilities. As tourism continued to grow, the process of the rapid tourism expansion and the accompanying infrastructure resulted in an increase in the diversity of international tourists and most importantly, a diversification of the facilities and amenities to serve the tourism industry. Although Cohen relates the growth of tourism mainly to a process of economic development, he emphasizes that 'the impact of tourism on mainstream Thai culture has had some creative as well as debasing consequences' (Cohen 1996: 26). Tourism in Thailand, as with tourism on Koh Samui, is 'a highly diversified, complex, and changing phenomenon, the impact and consequences of which have to be gauged within the wider process of economic development and social change' (Cohen 1996: 28). Indeed, Cohen's remarks and observations about tourism developmental processes serve a useful starting point for studying the role of tourism development in Thailand, and on Koh Samui in particular. It simply illustrates where, when and how tourism started to play a major role to Koh Samui society. It provides the very first descriptions and discussions of tourism development on the island. In other words, Cohen's research on Koh Samui was a first and important step in raising important tourism implication issues and presenting more detailed empirical material on such matter as, in his own words, 'touristic transition' (Cohen 2001).

Westerhausen (2002) published an ethnographic work based on interviews with long-term travelers and a personal observation entitled 'Beyond the Beach: an

Ethnography of Modern Travelers in Asia'. The book presents tourism development on Koh Samui as a transformation from a backpacker paradise to a mass tourist attraction. Westerhausen (2002) discusses and presents the different stages of tourism development on Koh Samui and categorizes tourists to the island into different types, which are all based on his perceptions and understanding of the interviews. In terms of tourism development, Westerhausen (2002) proposes that the 1990s were the beginning of investment in tourism development from people outside of the island, including a number of partnership arrangements among local elites and outside tourism developers. Massive investments facilitated the construction of larger, more modern accommodations and better dining and leisure facilities for an increasing number of tourists. This phenomenon is reflected in the boom period of Koh Samui in the 1990s, a period that clearly reflected the economic turnover along with the significant expansion of international tourism on the island. While tourism facilities were generally improved, competition among tourism businesses also increased. The situation went from gentle to severe. Westerhausen (2002) illustrates the change of the situation:

> [The] competition between the operators of these resorts remained subdued … Many of the owners were related to each other and usually came from the dominant families in the local village society' (p. 189)

> … [and] …

> Competition among locals increased because people from different parts of the island were attracted to the centres of the tourism boom. There, they competed with each other, with outsiders from the mainland, and with Westerners who had set up businesses in partnership with local Thais. Traditional values that had prevented conflict from arising in individual villages did not apply under these conditions (p.195).

Reviewing Westerhausen's (2002) work, the book examines the general matter of tourism development on Koh Samui, placing tourism on Koh Samui in an ethnographical perspective. This research examined the historical dimensions of tourism development on the island, social and cultural issues, and host-guest interactions. Although his work is one of very few informative reference works on more general tourism development on Koh Samui, the focus of the work is directed primarily to address the transformation of visitor types who visit the island. With the emphasis on social and cultural change and the implications of host-guest interactions on local business competitiveness, there are important connections with the interests and approach of this thesis. In particular, in the aspects of the tourism economy and the island's social landscape (Chapter 7) that play an important role in the research approach of this thesis.

Jarujitiphan (1993), a Thai doctoral candidate from Srinakharinwirot University in Bangkok, Thailand, studied the impact of tourism development on Koh Samui's economy and education using a quantitative method approach. Her research examines the 'positive' aspect of tourism development on Koh Samui. Particularly, her research focuses on the consequences of tourism on the local people, particularly on the opportunity of the local people to access a quality education. The research concludes that tourism positively influences the island's overall economic situation and consequently improves the quality of the locals' education. However, according to the study, the enhancement in the quality of education not only comes from the improved financial situation, but also from the improved patterns of education of local schools, such as more emphasis on English language and tourism studies in an effort to prepare the students to enter the tourism industry upon completion of their education. The examination of the relationships between tourism and educational opportunities by Jarujitiphan (1993) placed an optimistic perspective to the present research study. Her work that not only discusses how tourism improved individual financial positions to allow better education opportunities but its enhancement of local education indicates that the implications of tourism are complex. This thesis therefore, in considering the economic benefits tourism brings to women on Koh Samui, will discuss how it allows them to redefine their identities (Chapters 6,7 and 8). More specifically, it examines women and the sex industry on Koh Samui (Chapter 8). While touching on the political economy and political struggle against sex tourism, it will discuss the opportunities and optimistic views of those engaged in the industry that have not yet been considered (Chapter 8).

Green (2005) is another example of a research study on Koh Samui tourism. He portrays that the development of tourism has generally had a wide range of effects on the island's environment, including the destruction of coastal areas, air, water and noise pollutions, traffic congestion and over development of the infrastructure. Although his research describes the rapid negative change and damage of the island's natural systems due to tourism development, the research mainly focuses on community perceptions of environmental and social change and tourism's development on the island. He uses a projective mapping technique to identify a range of rapidly changing local environmental settings within the context of tourism and its associated development. In his study, respondents are asked to define which environmental features are suitable and which are unsuitable for Koh Samui. The study concludes that locals recognize the rapid negative change or damage of the island's natural systems due to tourism development. In addition, Boonsirichai (2002) conducts a master's thesis on tourists' perceptions of Koh Samui. Her study examines the perceptions of both Thai and foreign tourists towards the overall image of the island. In particular, her research focuses on problems within the infrastructure services and the environment on Koh Samui. Through questionnaire surveys at the Moom Thong, one of the Koh Samui's downtown restaurants, the researcher observes that the island needs to improve the quality of its infrastructure services and environment in order to create a good image of Koh Samui. Both Green (2005) and Boonsirichai (2002) point out that to increase numbers of tourist arrivals to Koh Samui, improvements in the tourist facilities and infrastructure to facilitate both tourists and locals satisfaction and not to mention to facilitate sustainable tourism development need to be implemented. However, the effects of uncontrolled tourism development are witnessed across the island. Boonsirichai (2002) states that too much and the low quality of tourism development, particularly to those tourist facilities, amenities, and infrastructure, presently damages tourist appreciation of the island. She emphasizes the significance of the improvement of the quality of the island's infrastructure services and environment. In fact, the studies by Green on the locals' perceptions of effects of tourism on the island' environment both natural and man-made, and Boonsirichai on the tourist perceptions to the tourism development and development of tourist facilities and infrastructure, are both particularly valuable contributions to overall studies of tourism development on Koh Samui.

Finally, Pongponrat (2007), a doctoral researcher, studies community participation in the local tourism development planning on Koh Samui. The goal of her research is to develop a community participatory planning framework for local tourism development on Koh Samui by using questionnaire surveys, informant interviews and focus group discussions with a case study approach to collect data. Pongponrat states that local economic development, environmental conservation, the preservation of local culture and tradition, the cost of living, income distribution, and of the stability of land prices, have a great impact on community participation and the need to design and implement local tourism planning. She further notes that to promote sustainable tourism, it is important to emphasize the implementation of local tourism planning by applying a participatory approach as sustainable destination management mechanisms. In addition, Pongponrat's (2007) research shows that the level of participation of local people depends on their social and economic background. Her research indicates that women participate in the community-based group more actively, while men are more into activities of the Tambon Municipality and private sectors. She concludes that barriers to participation are: a low level of education, lack of knowledge and skill, and no interest in participation. In addition, as community participation responds to local people's problems and needs, to improve the quality of formulation and implementation of the local participatory process is needed for the sustainability of the Koh Samui tourism development. However, she emphasizes that there were no clear directions on participatory techniques and practices for the Koh Samui local government to apply in the tourism planning process. Hence, there were no binding structures to make such plans active and able to solicit greater voluntary and effective participation among the local people (Pongponrat 2007). It is therefore suggested that much of destination management is more theoretical, rather than realistically implemented on the ground.

Indeed, the above research studies present various aspects and empirical overviews of major areas of tourism development, initial development, policy and local government, tourism participation and planning, the encounter of host-guest, potential and constraints, organization and infrastructure on the island, including the issue of locals and tourists satisfactions. Although all these research projects provide an understanding of tourism development's effect on the island from multidisciplinary perspectives, there is an absence of the engagement between tourism and Koh Samui society within tourism history conception and analysis. This is precisely the gap that this thesis attempts to address.

3.5 Tourism as a catalyst of change

Various researches have focused on the social and cultural changes in association with tourism development (Cohen 1996; Cole 2008; Crick 1994; Stonich 2000; Tucker 2003). Although tourism is the business that brings 'contact between cultures and directly or indirectly the cause of change particularly in less developed regions of the world' (Nash 1989: 37), it is important not to overlook other causes of cultural changes at a destination, particularly the process of globalization. Although 'tourism is very much part of the globalization process' (Macleod 2004; 4), the subject of tourism in association with globalization has not received sufficient attention within the context of Thailand. While the discussion of the processes of globalization and modernization in Thailand that reflect on major social structural features of modernized Thailand and their influence on Koh Samui society is presented in Chapter 5, this section presents the discussion on the issue of tourism as a catalyst of change in Thailand and Koh Samui in particular.

Tourism is a popular topic of study in the Thailand context (Askew 2002; Cohen 1996; 2001; Hall 1994; 1997; Hall and Page 2000; Higham 2000) as it has important consequences for economic, social and culture. Within the aim of this thesis, it is important to examine the concept of tourism as a cause for social change. Therefore, this section discusses the concept of tourism as a catalyst of change in order to explore the fundamental cause of modern Koh Samui history during its tourism period. 'Change' as used within this research study refers to the development process of the 'place' and 'space' of a society and its culture as the result of tourism development. The intention of this section is *not* to identify alterations in social conditions in exact time frames, but instead serves to trace general trends in recent history in order to help understand the process of a society and area becoming a tourist destination through revealing the underlying social development (Walton 2005). In particular, to theorize about the forces which have caused societal growth and/or delay of a particular period (Carr 2001; Evans 2002), a historical view of social development is adopted.

According to Marwick (2001), the central idea is that historical evolution or stages of development are influenced by new tangible social and economic factors, which result in the unity of change in attitudes, values and social hierarchies of the place. Furthermore, such a historical view of development, which is based on qualitative data, portrays new concepts (such as colonization, modernization, industrialization or globalization) rather than new chronologies. This alternative approach to this thesis may lead to the formulation of basic concepts of development which are applicable to a host society in its tourism period. Within this idea, if tourism is a means of change (Crick 1994; Cohen 2001), it is important to define how change occurs and how it reshapes place identification. Since this thesis interlinks tourism growth and the location's physical and social change, there is a need to examine the destination's history mainly from a tourism development perspective. In this context, tourism development, as a series of events and activities, is perceived as a unique social cause occurrence in a tourist destination. A destination which is in the process of a thorough qualitative transformation due to tourism development forms a unique concept, called 'touristization' (Young 1983). The concept of 'touristization', which is adopted from Young (1983), is a process of tourism development that links a place, people and tourism system together. However, as touristization concept by Young (1983) is a relatively old reference, to cope with the means of 'change', this thesis adopts other concepts along with Young, such as 'touristification of tourism' (Picard 1996) and the 'touristic transition' (Cohen 2001). Within this combination of the concepts, the thesis views the process of tourism expansion as a cause of 'change' in a destination's socio-cultural aspects, land use, landscape, geographical and occupational distribution of population and their economic activities. Through this concern, change focuses on tourism development and a society in the process of becoming a tourist destination, which is the intensification of the tourism growth as a process of social change (Crick 1994; Cohen 2001; Nash 1996). The growth of this tourism development leads to an increased focus on the place of culture in the formation of identity and image (Cohen 2001; Nash 1996; Tucker 2003). Therefore, it has been suggested that tourism is, if not a primary factor, it is at least a major driving force for the radical process of social change (Nash 1996). Although the thesis accepts tourism as the primary driving force for destination change on Koh Samui, it does not reject the possibility that there are other mitigating factors such as localization, modernization, socialization, and globalization at work as well. Regarding the latter, the thesis acknowledges tourism as part of the globalization process, as illustrated by Maclead (2004: 6):

> Tourism is regarded as part of the process of globalization ... Just as globalization reaches out to others resulting in the exchange of money, items and information encouraging trade, travel and communication, so does tourism.

Even though tourism can be viewed as part of globalization, its uniqueness is worth examining in more detail. Apostolopoulos (1996:2) notes 'with several aspects of modern life, the development and expansion of the tourism industry has brought both 'blessings'

51

and 'curses' to the socioeconomic and socio-cultural spheres'. Therefore, it is recognizing tourism as a crucial and far-reaching process that occurs over time in all aspects of social life including a society's economical, political and cultural factors. This is also illustrated in Apostolopoulos' (1996: 2) statement;

> In the socioeconomic sphere, tourism has dramatically affected 'foreign exchange, income, employment, prices, the distribution of benefits, ownership and control, development, and government revenue' (Apostolopoulos 1993; Cohen 1984), while in the socio-cultural sphere, tourism has affected 'community involvement in wider frameworks, the nature of interpersonal relations, the bases of social organization, the rhythm of social life, migration, the division of labor, stratification, the distribution of power, deviance, and customs and the arts' (Apostolopoulos 1993: Cohen 1984).

In this regard, tourism development influences how the current society is performing. To illustrate this further, the modern entrepreneur needs to be examined. This is not only due to psychological cultural factors but also to concrete economic forces that influence the social structure that marks the change of a tourist destination. In addition, the tourism period begins through the addition of a new phase of society and economy into the overall social development process of a destination (Marwick 2001). This tourism development increases the complexity of the social structure (Walton 2005). Thus, tourism is a process of change, which is reflected in a variety of social and political manifestations (Cohen 2001). Therefore, the tourism development stage coincides with the rise of new socio-cultural formations that have social, economic and political consequences (Tucker 2003).

3.6 Summary

This thesis raises questions about how history can look at tourism as significant events and how to study their implications on a tourism destination. With a tourism history perspective, this research study is an examination of the practice and effects of tourism development on Koh Samui society during its tourism period. Chapter 2 raised issues significant to the approach and theoretical conception of tourism history. It provided the discussion of tourism development in the important aspect of historical approach in terms of 'time', 'place' and 'theme'. This chapter discussed the issues of tourism and change in order to provide perspectives on how international tourism development (along with the processes of Thailand modernization presented in Chapter 5), the influences and demands of outside cultures, have built upon each other over time and have contributed to change and adaptation of Koh Samui society. This chapter included a discussion on the tourist destination lifecycle theories, and reviewed the relevant case studies of tourism and local development, including tourism studies of Koh Samui. The literature on tourism and local development has helped in an understanding of the implications of tourism from various aspects. It also has helped to form the thesis approach under the concept of 'touristization of society'. This concept being the process of tourism expansion and the effects of tourism upon a particular population, which not only results in a destination's changing socio-cultural aspects, but also in changes of land use, landscape, geographical and occupational distribution of population and their economic activities, ultimately affecting their livelihood. The discussion on tourism studies of Koh Samui has provided an increasing awareness of how tourism development affects the local community. It has formed an understanding that to understand the touristization of society one has to understand the place (destination) as a tourist site. This understanding stems from negotiations of the place's historic legacy and the global process of tourism. It is the process of transformation from a *traditional* livelihood (pre-industrial, rural, agrarian and agriculturally organized) to a *tourism* livelihood (service industrial, capitalist, urban, and business oriented) that is the focus of this research. At the same time, it has shown that the aspect of this thesis – touristization of society – is an unaddressed aspect. The following chapter outlines the research methodologies in order to achieve the aim of this thesis.

CHAPTER 4

RESEARCH METHODOLOGIES: WORKING IN THE FIELD, COPING WITH THE WORK

4.1 Introduction

This thesis adopts qualitative research methods to gather data to meet the main objective of this thesis – to examine the value of the thesis's framework, approach and theoretical conception of tourism history by applying it to the case of Koh Samui. This chapter outlines and discusses the methodological stance and the research, which occurred during seventeen months of ethnographic fieldwork on Koh Samui (between March 2005 to March 2006 and March 2007 to July 2007). Qualitative research is adopted in this thesis as it is seen as more than identifying research questions, observing social phenomena, collecting and analyzing research data and interpreting the data. This chapter includes a reflection of the qualitative researcher's understanding of the world, and particularly the researcher's perception and interpretation of such phenomena (Denzin and Lincoln 2000; Hall 2004; Phillimore and Goodson 2004).

To address the issues of qualitative research and the researcher it 'is to take account of subjectivity, of their ethics, values and politics, and use a range of appropriate interconnected interpretive methods to maximize understanding of the research problem' (Phillimore and Goodson 2004: 34). Therefore, the chapter begins with the issues of the researcher and the research. An overview of the relationship of the researcher to the research site and the selection of case study site are discussed in order to provide the personal background to the research, which include who I am and my relationship with Koh Samui. The data collection sources and methods are discussed in-depth to explain my activities on Koh Samui and how I gathered the data. The chapter continues by providing a discussion on fieldwork experiences, including the shifting of my identity. It then follows with the discussion of ethical consideration and the reflective remarks on the issues that emerged during the research process. The issue of my representation and responsibility relating to research limitation are the final aspects presented in this chapter.

54

4.2 Researcher and the research

Local history attempts to understand societal and physical changes over time and how those changes are present within a given location (Dymond 1982: Evans 2001; Jordonova 2000). Thus, fieldwork plays a significant role in achieving such a constitutive research study. In turn, fieldwork reflects the complexity of research studies, particularly in the issues of 'self' and 'researcher' (Tucker 1999). Belsky (2004) summarizes that the aspects of qualitative research are contextual, interpretative and subjective. He also notes that in qualitative research it is not only the research methods employed that are important, but also the values that influence the choice of topic (Belsky 2004). Hammersley and Atkinson (2007: 16-17) note;

> [...] Research is an active process, in which accounts of the world are produced through selective observation and theoretical interpretation [...] And in this way the image of the researcher is brought into parallel with that of the people studies, as actively making sense of the world.

Taking these statements into consideration, then self-reflection is an important aspect to understand the influence on data collection and analysis of qualitative data (Hall 2004). Thus, the role of my values needs to be addressed and discussed as one aspect of ensuring the dependability of this research study. Situating myself within the context of the research is significant as Collingwood (1959: 82) emphasizes that material and evidence that a historian [I] uses are somewhat 'perceptible to him' [me]. In this respect, my own values provide the key to my understanding of Koh Samui society. Therefore, it is important to discuss my place on Koh Samui and my selection of a case study site as a way of addressing the advantage or disadvantage of qualitative methods used in this research study.

4.2.1 My relationship with Koh Samui

My family has lived and been involved in tourism businesses on Koh Samui since 1989. The first time my father and my uncle went to the island was in 1986 at the invitation of a high ranking policeman in our hometown Kampangphet, who was originally from Koh Samui. At that time, the potential tourism boom on the island was beginning with a large number of hotels and bungalows under construction. At that time, there was a plan to develop Koh Samui's airport (refer to Westerhausen 2002 for a detailed description of the stages of tourism development on Koh Samui). My uncle was already involved in the tourism industry as a hotel and restaurant owner in Nakornsawan, a bigger city near Kampangphet. Thus, he and my father recognized the potential for tourism related businesses on Koh Samui and bought some land on Lamai Beach with the help of their friend the policeman. In the following year, my uncle moved to Koh Samui and opened his business *Galaxy Resort* (he has recently renamed it 'Samui Sense') and my family went on their first visit to the island to see the new property. This was my first visit to the island. During the following two years, my father commuted frequently between Koh Samui and Kampangphet before moving the whole family to the island in 1989 when we opened a restaurant and bungalows called *Lily House*[3]. Our business comprised of bungalows, a restaurant and a very small travel agency that specialized in the organization of transportation tickets, overseas call services as well as running a laundry service. It is important to note that, at this time, my family was among the first outsiders to start a tourism business on Lamai Beach (the issue of Lamai Beach is further discussed in Chapter 6, section 6.6). As my family was introduced to the area by a high-ranking Koh Samui-born policeman, we were able to settle in with dignity and were highly accepted within the local community without experiencing conflict with local elites or suffering any constraints from the local politicians (see Chapter 6).

At the time of my family's move to the island, I was going to school in Northern Thailand. Later I moved to Bangkok for my higher education. During school vacations, I returned to Koh Samui to work in *Lily House*. At this time, both family businesses, *Lily House* and *Galaxy Resort* were encountering problems finding qualified staff as there was a great deal of competition for tourism workers. This situation reflected Kontogeorgopoulos's work in 1993 (Kontogeorgopoulos 1998: 331) that tourism businesses on the island were 'experience high rates of turnover'. He emphasizes that was because 'most employees commonly seem to view tourism jobs as temporary and unreliable' (Kontogeorgopoulos 1998: 331). Therefore, in the 1990s, with the growing number of tourism related businesses, the competition went beyond competing for customers, to competing for qualified workers as well. From the perspective of Butler's

---

[3] In 2005, in addition to the existing business, my family opened a new café named 'Perk & Peck' in the same compound on Lamai Beach.

evolutionary model, my family entered into Koh Samui tourism industry during its 'involvement stage' by providing some basic tourist facilities. However, when tourism significantly developed in the 1990s and the island moved into the 'development stage', high pressure was put on small local businesses, including that of my family. Responding to this situation, and hoping to not only attract more tourists but also qualified workers, the *Galaxy Resort* was upgraded through the addition of a new three-storied hotel with a swimming pool and a beachfront restaurant. My parents planned to upgrade our business as well, expecting me to return home and take over the management of the business. This, however I did not agree with, so when I moved abroad for my higher education, my parents leased out *Lily House* and moved back to the north in 1997[4]. My uncle still lives on Koh Samui. After my family started renting out our property I continued to return to Koh Samui regularly for vacations. Since other people managed the family business premises, I stayed at my uncle's hotel. As I was not staying in *Lily House* and was not helping with any of the work at *Galaxy Resort,* my neighbors viewed me as a tourist to the island. In other words, as my family was no longer living there, my neighbors' perception was that I was coming to Koh Samui on holiday rather than returning home.

4.2.2 Selection of the case study site of Koh Samui

The decision to conduct my research on Koh Samui was as a result of an emerging interest in the island even before beginning the study. Besides the prevalent tourism characteristics of Koh Samui, which enabled me to do research into the changes affecting tourism destinations following the development of tourism, the decision regarding my fieldwork location was made for a combination of reasons. First, as my family had moved to Koh Samui in 1989, I had gained early experiences in operating a tourism business on the island, even before the boom period in the early 1990s. These experiences highlight my familiarity and knowledge of the early development of Koh Samui. The second reason for my choice is based on my educational background. During my undergraduate studies in history, I developed a particularly strong interest in the local history. Thus, my Koh Samui experiences are based on different periods spent on the island since my first visit in 1987.

---

[4] This is similar to Cohen (1996), who points out that with experience in business and limited capitalized resources, the tourism business owners were not willing to take risks by putting more investment in the business to compete with others.

Since then and particularly since my family's permanent move to Koh Samui in 1989, I have returned to spend many periods on the island, which has given me a strong awareness and has provided me with the ability to frame and contextualize the historical research study. Moreover, from the very first stages of the tourism boom in the 1990s to now, I have witnessed Koh Samui's development and observed the changes that tourism has brought to the island. For example, when my family first moved to Koh Samui, our businesses were situated close to the end of the developed part of Lamai Beach. During the 1990s however, tourist activities spread further to the other side of the beach which meant that by the time I began my fieldwork, my family property was almost in the middle of the beach development area. Throughout the time of the island's tourism development, I observed first-hand how Sak and Nee (their stories in Chapter 6) and Som (her story in Chapter 7) for example, had developed their businesses to cope with the growth of tourism on Koh Samui. Indeed, Koh Samui and tourism have been part of my life since a early age, which ultimately underpinned my decision to examine Koh Samui society based on its tourism development using the local history approach, which I have developed into 'tourism history' approach for this thesis. This has affected my understanding of Koh Samui and thus the presentation of the overall thesis.

I selected Lamai Beach in particular as a field site for a number of different reasons: First, my familiarity with the place and prior knowledge of the site were a benefit to the research study. Thus, the strengths of having background experience and the familiarity of the site helped me in dealing with the stresses of getting to know the place, culture and norm (see e.g. Fadzillah 2004; Fordham 1994; Ganguly-Scrase 1994; Hastrup 1987; Hume and Mulcock 2004a; 2004b; Killick 1995). Perhaps this circumstance improved the quality of the observations, participation and the overall work in the field. The second reason for selecting Lamai Beach was to follow up on one of the very first academic writings on tourism development on Koh Samui and Lamai Beach, in particular, which portrayed a picture of the beach as far back as the late 1970s (Cohen 1996). As this thesis intends to provide an overview of the historical development of the beach, with reference also to Cohen's (1996) collected articles entitled *Thai Tourism: Hill Tribes, Islands and Open-ended Prostitution*, the researcher sought an understanding of how the beach came to be a 'touristic' area. The final contributing factor regarding the choice of field site was based on Lamai Beach's rapidly developing economy and its geographical transformation, which were influenced by its tourism development. The area of and the activities on Lamai Beach are characterized by high levels of both 'touristification' (Picard 1996) and 'touristization' (Young 1983) (coming in at 'development stage' of Butler's evolutionary model since the beginning of the 1990s - tourism only started around the 1970s). Furthermore, what should be noted is that in addition to all these factors, Lamai Beach is the second biggest tourist center on the island, which is particularly well known for its nightlife entertainment and deserves to be studied in its own right. As a result, Lamai Beach presented a highly suitable site for my study on changes in landscape and for the observation of people in how they construct and respond to tourism processes (Chapter 6, 7 and 8).

4.3 Data collection sources and methods

One important aspect of history is that, traditionally, historians work with written documents (Jordanova 2000). However, not every place or local society has documented their stories. In some societies, particularly in Asia and Africa, histories have been handed down orally through generations (Huen *et al.* 1998; Morrison 1998). Thus, the lack of written documents and concerns regarding the value of information (as history has been verbally passed on) results in problems of discourse. With regard to this, local history is often seen as politically insignificant due to its historical autonomy and thus receives attention from only a small part of academic historians (Jordanova 2000). The issue of the validity of oral sources is important as the need exists to academically accept and to understand oral narratives as valid historical texts. However, the issue of achieving an academic acceptance of the oral text and of the local history approach as a theoretical concept is challenging. In other words, as discussed in Chapter 2, the contribution of local history as a category within the discipline of history requires some of the other related disciplines such as archaeology, linguistics, and anthropology (Dymond 1982; Goodman 1997; Iredale 1974; Jordanova 2000; Thompson 1978). Consequently, this section focuses on the mechanisms of the present construction of tourism history on Koh Samui. As mentioned in Chapter 2, there is the need to develop a common ground of combining two methodologies (ethnography and oral history) when researching the tourism history of the island in its tourism period. This combined methodological approach aims to bridge the everyday experience of the island's population with the subject matter – tourism development – in a historical way. For the purpose of reconstructing the history of Koh

Samui within the tourism phenomenon, this thesis views documents that represent 'living history' (Ladkin 1999, 2004), and oral testimony of high significance.

Furthermore, tourism history in local history perspective is, accordingly, one place where the historical approach and ethnographic methods meet (discussed in Chapter 2). Both are suitable fieldwork methods, which are based on contact and interaction with informants and participant observation to reconstruct local history. With regard to this, a historical perspective illustrates the multiple realities of contemporary Koh Samui society and the dynamics of its transformation within the island's tourism development period. In turn, ethnography provides an understanding of social practices in tourism contexts (Nash and Smith 1991). Thus, the two types of methodologies are not contradictory, but complementary, as they bridge the gap between 'past' and 'present' subjects by negotiating the methods of collecting, analyzing and interpreting texts in tourism studies. In addition, the research method in this study consists of collecting information from both primary and secondary sources. The secondary data in forms of official reports and existing data both nationally and locally were consulted and collected from government documents, papers, records, and articles from newspapers and statistics. This was coupled with an extensive literature review conducted on an ongoing basis throughout the research process to help support the research scheme and the fieldwork. However, the research was designed to obtain primary information from different aspects in the local community (older generations as well as newer generations of local elites or local businesses) including the owners, managers and workers in tourism businesses on different parts of the island. Moreover, women's life stories, including women working in the sex tourism industry, were explored. The data was collected in such a way as to assist with developing a picture of Koh Samui society during its tourism development. In fact, the points of concern for the research study were related to the issues of history, cultural characteristics and settlements, tourism businesses, landscape transformation and overall changes on Koh Samui over time. Particularly, it is an examination of the ways in which the relationships between social, culture and landscape of Koh Samui has been transformed due to Koh Samui society's historical and cultural legacies and tourism processes on the island (discussed in Chapter 1). Thus, I followed the format of a traditional ethnographic study in the hope that the strengths of ethnography, namely 'an engagement of the researcher's senses and emotions ... its full sensuality – the sights, sounds, smells tastes, and tactile sensations' (Herbert 2000: 552) would add to my understanding of the transformation and

60

tourism processes of Koh Samui society. I used different data collection techniques: observation and participation, in-depth interviews and oral history, and map survey. All were employed in order to reach the research aims.

4.3.1 Observation and participation

Observations, as an intensive study of people through observation and participation (e.g. Kearns 2000), were carried out in order to understand the community's relationship to its tourism development. The technique used was to study the culture at a certain point in time, namely the time of observation (Herbert 2000; Inglis 1993; Kearns 2000). Thus, the observations allowed the researcher to garner a 'close-up' glimpse of a community (Tucker 2003: p.15). Furthermore, it provided the opportunity to make 'a detailed account of directly observed behaviour' (Jordanova 2000: p. xv-xvi) based on an in-depth understanding of the local perspective of a community. The thesis applied the participant observation method of gathering information on the locals' lifestyles as well as their responses to the tourism development of their island. Observations were initiated by the researcher exploring the island by motorbike, which also facilitated the observation of the geography of the island (see Chapter 6. section 6.6). This activity turned out to be a powerful method in helping, as in Sunstein and Chiseri-Strater (2002: p. 223-224)'s words 'to retrieve and record [recall my] own internal landscape'. The purpose of this 'scan' of the island was to register as well as to understand the changes in landscape and land made to serve the tourism industry.

Participant observations were focused mainly on Lamai Beach's tourism businesses and its 'girlie bar' ghetto. The participant's 'girlie bar' ghetto observations were conducted between August 2005 and February 2006. I gained an in-depth understanding of the cycle of the girlie bar and the lifestyle of women engaged in the industry as the research ranged over both the low season (August, September, October and February) and high season (November through January). Furthermore, finding a place that allowed for exclusive observational opportunities of the 'girlie bar culture' was essential. A friend's bar proved to be just such a place to begin to undertake observations. As the owner's friend, I was accepted by the bar women. After becoming familiar with the nightlife and earning the trust of those women, I began to construct a picture of the area; the 'girlie bar' business and the in-depth descriptions of those women (see Chapter 8). Other than the 'girlie bar' ghetto, every day I spent most of my day time moving around from place to place taking photos of the tourism business area in order to construct a picture of the process of tourism development on Koh Samui. Restaurants, hotels, spas, and other tourism enterprises were visited almost daily providing opportunities to observe everyday tourism activities and for in-depth descriptions of tourism businesses. Facilitated by familiarity of the places studied, I was able to observe first-hand the daily activities of businesses on the island and how they take advantage of the different opportunities provided them by tourism. Moreover, this also allowed me to study the tourists and their demands for services. A research diary was kept during the field visits. This diary included detailed information recording business characteristics by listing tourism activities by type as well as general observations made about the people, places and things encountered, including the descriptions of girlie bars (in Chapter 8). Analysis of the data from the observations involved reviewing notes, organizing the data, and looking for patterns. This method proved to be a valuable technique in doing in-depth descriptions of the sex tourism business ('girlie bar' ghetto business) and to understand how sex tourism is embedded in the tourism dynamics of Koh Samui.

4.3.2 In-depth interview and oral history

In-depth interviews and oral history share some similar characteristics such as carrying out fieldwork and interviewing people about their life experiences. However, there are some different aspects between these techniques. On the one hand, oral history aims to understand its subject in a particular historical aspect within a wider chronological framework. It aims to reconstruct the experiences of local life in the passing of time and builds self-presenting collections of locals' events through interviews (Huen et al. 1998; Morrison 1998; Prins 1991; Thompson 1978; Vansina 1985). Oral history is a transformation of life experience into public statements. So while oral history serves as a tool in interpreting the evidence of the past through the experiences of significant happenings of the locals, in-depth interviews, on the other hand, assist in the interpretation of a society through the reality of a significant happening (Bruner 1986). Through the interview process, an attempt is made to portray the lives of locals and to allow the informants to reflect on the beliefs and norms of the society in which they live and function within their own cultural context (Bruner 1986).

In my fieldwork, I used both informal interviews and oral histories with the different people with whom I had developed a variety of relationships on Koh Samui. I started first with casual conversations with the workers at the *Galaxy Resort*. When they felt comfortable with our relationship, participation in the lifestyle of a small working community group was realized and I was able to spend free time with them. The list of informants expanded as I was introduced to other people working in the tourism businesses through those workers. I regularly visited them at their work places and sometimes went out with them to social activities. In the beginning of my research stay on Koh Samui, I contacted a long-time friend of mine who is the daughter of a resort owner there. Upon the introduction of my research project, she generously introduced me to a group of her friends, the sons and daughters of tourism business owners and their families. This provided access to people who represent the new economic blood on Koh Samui (see Chapter 7). This group of upcoming tourism operators (the protégé of current business owners[5]) included me in their social activities and welcomed me into their homes. As a result I was able to discuss, informally, the future of tourism on Koh Samui, benefits to their family businesses, new projects they planned to undertake on succession to the family business. Through this acquaintance, I was also included in formal events such as weddings and religious festivals allowing me access to more senior members of their families. They provided invaluable information on Koh Samui's past (Chapter 5 through 7). Fully aware of how their social performance differs from that of their parents' generation, I was given an insider's perspective of how these island 'princes and princesses' live their lives in this period of tourism. I was also provided with an understanding of how they viewed the development of the tourism industry on the island and, at the same time, how they are preparing themselves for the future tourism development on Koh Samui (see Chapter 7).

While I was with the tourism workers, I used 'informal' interviews or 'semi-structured conversations' rather than direct interviews as a data collection method. Moreover, my data was also collected through an informal grouped interview with those

---

[5] When I started to spend more time with them, a good Canadian friend sarcastically referred to me and the group as the 'princes and princesses' of Koh Samui. In his view, the term refers to my generation, who was educated in Bangkok, came back to Koh Samui with a Bangkok mentality and appreciation of an urban lifestyle and enjoyed the economic benefit from tourism.

local tourism businesses' sons and daughters. Thus, the ethnographic data was mostly gained from my observations and semi-structured conversations rather than direct interviews. To avoid placing my informants in an awkward situation, I did not write down field notes at the point of participations, observations and conversations. Rather, I wrote down field notes and research diaries as a reporting of my everyday life, impressions and interpretations, which I normally did it at the end of the day. This record was used to identify patterns of the land market, the enforcement of the new generation of tourism business owners, economic and social position of Koh Samui society, and sex tourism on Koh Samui. Thus, the data was considered and analyzed in aggregate form. To avoid that 'the detailed information related to an individual may be lost' from an aggregate analysis (Ladkin 2004: p. 248), seven in-depth qualitative interviews were conducted in addition to eleven in-depth life and work stories[6]. In other words, through oral history, I included eighteen individual life and work histories in addition to the aggregate analysis and generalization of Koh Samui society. Particular attention was paid to the historical aspects of the Koh Samui agricultural livelihood and the processes of tourism development, the experiences and behaviors of the new generation of tourism business owners, and the tourism entrepreneurs' experiences. My analysis of the data from in-depth interviews and oral histories engaged with the data from participant observation. Data from notes, daily experiences diaries, and life and work histories were used to provide linkages between them in order to emerge dimensions of an aggregate form and an individual form of the analysis. The resulting insights and stories are presented in the following chapters.

4.3.3 Map survey

After the first twelve months of my field work (March 2005 – March 2006), I returned to Dunedin to carry out more library research and began some analysis of data already collected. Then I returned to Koh Samui for five months (March 2007-July 2007) in order to clarify some points, particularly the issue of Lamai Beach geography, which had been raised during the first stage of writing. During this visit, I decided to map out the processes of tourism development and landscape transformation in the area (Chapter 6). My first priority was to obtain existing maps that represented the area as far back as the beginning of its tourism development period. The most relevant were those with aerial

---

[6] The people that I have interviewed are presented in this thesis as pseudonyms due to privacy reasons.

digital images of Koh Samui from the Royal Thai Survey Department, the Ministry of Defense whom I contacted only to find that there were only two relevant images available. The first, which dated back to the year 1975, showed nothing but a coconut plantation in the area. The second dated back to 1994 and showed some forms of development in the area (see Chapter 6). Lacking an aerial image of the area for the required time period, a sketch map of Lamai Beach tourist area from the late 1970s by Cohen (Cohen 1996: p.185) was used to represent the early stage of touristic transformation. The image of 1994 was then used to illustrate the growth of tourist activities in the area. The image of the aerial survey in 1994 provided a foundation for my own blueprint of tourist activities of Lamai Beach for the year 2007. My draft of tourist activities of the beach was compiled during April 2007 with the help of a research assistant. The survey data was technically mapped and a picture of Lamai Beach was developed for the year. The landscape transformation of Lamai Beach was presented through three images, one in 1970s, one in 1994 and the last one of 2007. The discussion of this survey in accordance with these images is presented in Chapter 6.

4.4 Ethnographic experience: an identity crisis

After extensive reading on fieldwork methodologies and others' experiences, like others who were first-time fieldwork researchers, I had envisioned myself as an ethnographer and was eager to go into the field. After organizing all the necessary things for staying on Koh Samui, I traveled to the island with my parents at the end of February 2005. As mentioned before, I had always continued to go to Koh Samui regularly, like my father who returned regularly to look after our business. Thus, while my father and I had noticed the changes that had occurred on Koh Samui and particularly around our property on Lamai Beach, my mother had not. Driving along the main road my mother could not recognize where to turn into the beach road as so many things had changed. After turning onto Lamai Beach road it was an even greater shock to her to see the 'massive' change in the area surrounding of our business. Then it was my turn to be surprised when I stopped the car and my mother immediately asked 'why did we stop?' I was laughing madly with my father about the fact that she could not recognize our 'home', even though I had stopped right in front of it. The reason for my mother's confusion can be explained by the fact that when we lived on the island we were situated close to the end of the developed part of Beach. But this time, our land was almost in the heart of the beach development area. What I had not anticipated was that my appearance with my parents gave the neighbor the impression that I returned 'home' to run our family business. Almost immediately, after I learned about my neighbor's misperception of the purpose of my trip, I chose not to stay at *Lily House*. After my parents went back to the north, I relocated to my uncle's place – *Galaxy Resort* – on the basis that I did not want to be seen as a businessman and involved with my property. It was nice and comfortable living in *Galaxy Resort*. However, I was completely unaware of similar attitudes regarding the purpose of my visit on the island. My introduction by my uncle to his staff was essential; it had the adverse effect of stimulating my status to that of a dignitary to them. I found that the most uncomforting circumstances I experienced living in the resort were the times when his workers treated me as one of their superiors. I was experiencing the awkward feeling of not knowing whether I was at 'home' or I was in the research's 'field work' and whether or not they were my 'informants' or 'my staff'. By then, I was still physically and mentally at 'home', while I academically had already entered into my 'field'[7]. In the resort, I could move around independently but first experienced a period of 'undergoing a crisis of selfhood' (Killick 1995: 96). Killick (1995: 96) states that this happens 'when suddenly transposed from one cultural context to another – a crisis that [is] particularly acute because of the culture shock'. I did not expect this to happen to me as I was doing a research in a very familiar place. In fact, I was caught in the middle of changing from being people's *boss* to their *friend*. I did not only encounter the difficulty of this transformation, but also encountered the new subculture of a different social group.

My difficulty in conducting research on the island was based on the need to be accepted and welcomed from my informants. For this reason, I also moved out of the resort to a Galaxy workers' dormitory. By doing this, casual conversation emerged between the workers and me and they gained the impression that we could build up a friendship. Thus, my hope of participating in the lifestyle of a small working community group was realized and I was able to spend free time with them. This circumstance was my first lesson on the subject of being in the field in that I learned that equity and friendship would be my main mechanism to become accepted in the field, but also to accept the

---

[7] Useful discussions on 'what is home' and 'what is the field' are in Hume and Mulcock, eds., (2004) *Anthropologists in the Field: cases in participant*; Jackson, ed., (1987) *Anthropology at Home*; Morton (1999); Madden 1999, for example.

'spirit of honest difference' (Strathern 1987: 16) between the informants and myself. In addition, my emotions had gone from not having had a clear sense of whether I was at *home* or at *work* to not having found my actual work site. The boundary of my case study was another challenge since the island had been through a dramatic change by massive tourism development in a very short period of time (see Chapter 5). The situation got worse when I first wanted to start the collection of data without being able to find a place to get started and constantly asking myself 'where to start'. Koh Samui is a big and overcrowded place, with many motorbikes and much traffic. Although I did my research study in the place where I had lived for quite some time, with a sense of place – a 'personal geography' – through a familiar landscape (Sunstein and Chiseri-Strater 2002: 223), the sense of the neighborhood and the place was completely beyond my understanding. Therefore, I was in a stage of 'disorientation' in my fieldwork[8] (Hume and Mulcock 2004a).

In fact, during the first couple of months, I spent most of my time trying to find a new research boundary. In response, I travelled around the island to do a geographic survey and mapping of the place for my thesis. This activity actually turned out to be a powerful method in helping me 'to retrieve and record [my] own internal landscape' (see Sunstein and Chiseri-Strater 2002: 223-224), and to realize as well as to understand the movement of change in landscape and land-use to serve the tourism industry. Thus, I started to have conversations with different agents to complete the picture of encountering and engaging tourism (see Chapters 5, 6, 7 and 8). With more time spent on Koh Samui, my fieldwork fell into a routine. My feeling was very much like Hume and Mulcock's (2004: xiv) experiences in that 'I was moving between the strange and the familiar on a daily basis.' In order to maintain my performance in the field effectively, I sometimes needed to get out and be 'myself'. Furthermore, I started to feel disconnected to my personal academic standpoint. To cope with these issues, I went back to Bangkok from time to time. There, I was in regular contact with the Department of History at Srinakharinwirot University. For me, many aspects of my identity emerged from doing the research study in the field. I developed great relationships with a number of people from different backgrounds. However, as I was part of many subcultures at the same time, I could move among them because of my standard Thai dialect and was thus able to

---

[8] Please refer to Hume and Mulcock 2004a; 2004b; Kulick and Willson 1995 for more details of emotion in the fieldwork.

communicate with my informants easier. I realized that different situations required different personal resources and identities to be accepted by participants. In other words, I understood the ways of behaving and interacting with the different belief systems of each group. However, I had to accept that my own identity was not clear-cut.

4.5 Fieldwork on Koh Samui

Aware that my relationship with the people on Koh Samui with whom I worked could bias the data collected in one way or another, I made sure that my relationships, although casual, remained professional and did not become too personal. To provide a better understanding of this, a brief overview of Thai social structure functions follows. Thais believe that the 'hierarchical structure' of relationships between people and nature result from the interpretation of Buddhist teachings (Jackson 1989). This social system of 'hierarchical order' is reflected in social relationship practices in the form of 'super ordinate-subordinate relationships' (Limanonda 1995). This pattern is predicated on the age, wealth, power, knowledge and religious or political roles of the individuals involved (Limanonda 1995; Mulder 2000). This is reflected in Fordham's (1994: 24) statement:

> Thailand social ideology is [sic] based on the idea that people are fundamentally unequal and all social relations are, of necessity, relations of inequality. Based primarily on religious values and the idea of relative merit, Thais rank everyone as senior and junior, or superior and inferior according to a variety of criteria including age, status, gender and economic position.

During the data collection practice, this norm of 'hierarchical order' was accepted and practiced. Therefore, there were many barriers which prevented me from forming personal relationships with the tourist workers on the island with whom I came into contact during the data collection period. This was particularly true of those who were my uncle's employees as they not only saw me as their boss, which gave me a more powerful economic status, but also I was also older than many of them. The issue of my education further added to the social distance between us. Moreover, studying at a post-graduate level is normally associated with a lecturer occupation and thus receives a 'higher' social status in Thai society[9]. The fact that I was also educated overseas exacerbated the gap making forming friendships between us difficult. Despite the resulting professional and formal relationship, I went out with them occasionally which gave me the impression that they admired my endeavors to get to know them. Fortunately, over time, the issue of an existing social gap between us was less emphasized. With time, I became acquainted with more people in this social group beyond those who worked for the *Galaxy Resort*, including those who were sex workers (further discussed in Chapter 8). Interestingly, one night I agreed to go out to a bar with a group of workers from another hotel. One of them, a bartender, came to pick me up from where I was staying. It was the first time he had entered my room. I had not anticipated that the research documents in my room would raise his curiosity, but they did. Flicking through my books, the young man who has a Thai university qualification, looked at me with great respect which made me feel, both powerful and yet uncomfortable at the same time. He expressed amazement not only at the huge number of articles and books, but more importantly, at the fact that they were all in *English*. 'You read all these?' he asked. I found his surprise simultaneously gratifying and terrifying. It seemed to me that he displayed some of the same respect I had once been given by *Galaxy Resort*'s staff members. My answer, coupled with some more detailed explanations about myself, gave him some appreciation of me being with him without pronouncing my own social background. Indeed, my relationship with him developed into a real friendship because of him perceiving me as a normal person with whom he could relate.

The relationship I had with the group of sons and daughters of the of tourism business owners, on the other hand, was quite different to the ones I had with the other tourism workers. This situation reflected the circumstance that Hume and Mulcock (2004) points out, namely that similar culture, education, and basic understandings of the world are typical catalysts for friendship development. Coupled with my friend's personal introduction into to her social circle, my social rank, which is similar to her friends' in terms of education, financial status and place in society, made it easy to become part of their group. In contrast, even with an effort to bridge the gap of culture and social status with workers at tourism resorts and facilities, my relationship with them remained on an unequal footing. Regardless of whether my relationships in the field were formed as I

---

[9] Fordham (1994) also mentions this issue and points out that he was a student in order to avoid being treated too importantly.

worked towards bridging the social gap between the workers and me, or developed spontaneously based on having a similar social and educational background, my experience on Koh Samui was unique and different to the experiences of other ethnographers. Fordham (1994: 24) states with regard to his ethnographic research that 'I was only there to do research …' In fact, my relationships with others on Koh Samui during my fieldwork were quite different. Regardless of whether the relationships were good, bad, formal, informal, or professional, some of the friendships are permanent and are, in one way or another, attached to my family and the business that my family has on the island.

4.6 Ethical and reflexive remarks

This thesis fieldwork had been granted Category B of the University of Otago's Ethics Guidelines for Conducting Research, but I still had some concerns over the issue of ethics that emerged because of the fieldwork. The thesis required that it did not place any form of physical or psychological stress or present an unsafe situation to any research informants (for more details see   http://www.otago.ac.nz/acadcomm/categoryb.html). However, concerns over the issue of ethics in my fieldwork became particularly obvious when in the middle of a conversation with a sex worker in one of the many 'girlie bars' on Lamai Beach. A Farang (foreigner) came into the bar and sat down next to me. He ordered a beer and began chatting with one of the women. Very quickly, the conversation turned to bargaining on the cost of taking her out. While she could have managed the negotiation by herself, she asked me to help with the 'English' conversation. Thus, I was thrown into the uncomfortable role of translator between this sex worker and the sex tourist. A feeling of guilt overwhelmed as I felt as though I were abetting the sex tourist business. Another time, a tourist took a photo of the area of bar where I was sitting. I convinced myself that the photo would become the subject of discussions or gossip about sex workers, sex tourists and sex tourism in Thailand. I was convinced, it would focus on the girl as the tragic victim, the Farang as the exploiter and I would be labeled accordingly. Given the fact that, in real life I was not the person someone who viewed the picture might perceive me to be, I started to question the pictures of people I had seen in sex tourism literature. Consequently, I have given a lot more thought to the issue of photographic ethics, which resulted in my hesitation to take pictures of others sitting in bars and the use of those images for research.

4.7 My representation and responsibility

Throughout my fieldwork, my personal history as an 'insider' and Thai values provided the key to the understanding the tourism context of Koh Samui. To be of value, the product of my research study had to be the product of my understanding of the world. Significantly, I found myself in a unique position of being an in-group researcher, sharing the same national culture and social conditions as well as identity as those who live on Koh Samui. On the one hand, this identified me to be a *self* to my study subjects. On the other hand, I am originally from the Northern part of Thailand and thus have sub-cultural differences, coupled with my higher education and research training in western countries. Combined, these circumstances have resulted in me living and conducting fieldwork as *other* to study subjects in my own society. Under this circumstance, using Ganguly-Scrase (1994: 44) words, I created 'the situation of simultaneously being an alien and an insider' in the research agenda. The unique positions of being both an insider and outsider of the group, coupled with my experience on the island that covers a period of almost two decades, is important for my ability to understand the overall development of Koh Samui. It also enables me to frame the historical writing, which will benefit me in reflecting on the tourism history of Koh Samui by balancing subjectivity and objectivity within my fieldwork.

The relationships which developed at the site between the informants and me affected the ethnographic data collected. Specifically, the issues of my ethnicity and social class significantly affected the research data collection and ultimately the analysis process. In particular, as my identity was attached to my family's business, the issue of participant observation was challenging. For example, although my relationships with the tourism workers had improved, there were constructed in the context of a 'hierarchy order' and unequal power relations (Limanonda 1995). This was similar to Ganguly-Scrase (1994) experiences in conducting an ethnographic work in her culture. She highlights that higher status was a constraint to the attempt of accessing certain kinds of data, which in turn mostly depended on how the local community allowed her to perform in the field.

Moreover, I found that while my relationship with the tourism workers reduced their fear of spending time with me, it simultaneously increased their awareness of their own personal behavior. For this reason, my appearance, which generally reflected my class, regional, and educational background through dress, manner, speech registers and accent was vital to my cause. Among Thais, particularly in my research experience, Thai cultures and social structure presented a significant boundary and needs to be recognized as a major constraint. Furthermore, regardless of my 'equal-relations' relationships with the local's elites' new generation, my participant observation encountered some difficulty. They knew that I was a Tourism postgraduate student studying Koh Samui's changes and tourism development. Consequently, they expected my strong input into the discussions on tourism development on the island. Once we met over a cup of coffee, when the issue of Koh Samui's tourism future was raised. Ideally, it was a good time for a participant observer to record the issues of tourism activities and competitiveness through an informal focus group. However, in fact, I was not a participant observer, rather one of the participants in the discussion. This was again because my identity was attached to my family's business. The situation did not allow me to be an observer or construct research-related questions. Instead, my role as a participant observer was complicated as I was included in the group of research informants.

Despite this complicated role, I continued to contribute to the discussion so that the data was collected through group discussion and my own story telling. The issue of my relationships in the field needs to be re-emphasized. The group discussion about the future of tourism on Koh Samui with my friends of the new generation of Koh Samui's tourism businesses was of great interest and of great concern to me. This is mainly because I was eligible to take part, in and consequently to add considerable information, to the discussion. Rather than facilitating the discussion, I was merely partaking in the exchange. Undeniably, other ethnographic researchers and research studies of Koh Samui would have produced different narratives. However, my experience on Koh Samui is a contribution to the knowledge of participation observation and ethnographic fieldwork, particularly in the issue of doing ethnographic research at 'home' and as a business-owner's son. Therefore, based on my experiences in my fieldwork, I believe that if I had had a different social status, and had been from a working class family – who in many parts of Thailand struggle to survive (and I would have been lucky to have financial support for my education) – my data collection would have been different. My relationship with the workers would have developed more easily since we would have had some things in common that they could relate to. For those 'socially elite' on Koh Samui, I would have worked my way into their group by their acknowledging my education as a postgraduate student. I believe this would have enabled me to conduct my research study more spontaneously as I would have not had to worry about the consequences of my fieldwork on my family's and business's reputations. Moreover, the social constraints between different groups and me would have been non-existent or minimal if I was a non-Thai researcher. Being in a very different culture or social practices would have allowed me to easier blend in with my informants. For example, Tucker (1999), who, as a foreign researcher in Turkey became, to some degree, 'genderless' in locals' perceptions. Specifically, as an outsider, Tucker was able to move around the village more freely than other women in the village were. Obviously, her position in the field enabled her to participate in both the male and female territories. In my experience, the fieldwork process was not only an important aspect in order to complete my research project, but also to expand my own academic and personal experiences. The unique experience of each researcher is reflected in Fordham's (1994: 10) statement about his own fieldwork experience in Northern Thailand: 'Some do their work, get the data and cannot wait to get home. Others, and this was my [his] own experience, return home only very reluctantly'. To me, regardless of good or bad fieldwork experiences, Koh Samui is part of my home – I might be done with the fieldwork, but I will never be 'done' with the field site. In fact, it was rather the opposite as being Thai and doing research in my neighborhood; my experiences and my relationships with others on Koh Samui during my fieldwork would be permanent and attached to my family and the business in one way or another.

For the issue of research's limitation, it is important to note that language was a relatively minor issue of limitation. As there were the high number of outsiders living on the island (see Chapter 5), local's dialect of different regions is now of only limited use to communicate with each other. To illustrate, when a group consists of people from different regions in Thailand, the Bangkok dialect is spoken. Nevertheless, when locals meet with each other, or among those tourist workers from the same region, they would still communicate in their local dialects. Koh Samui's situation in somewhat reflects Fordham's (1994: 16) argument that the Bangkok and central Thai language and values are the dominant culture, and the symbol of 'modernity and of urban sophistication', thus, language was a relatively minor issue of limitation in my fieldwork.

Another important aspect of representation is that the thesis follows a historical approach, meaning that history as a discipline aims to reconstruct the uniqueness of a certain event rather than developing a general law in social science (Evans 2002; Jordanova 2000; McCullagh 2004). In paraphrasing Towner's (1988) words to fit this context, this study of the tourism history of Koh Samui is undertaken to understand the change of the island during its tourism period. The case study of Koh Samui 'contribute[s] to a dynamic model or concept of the role of tourism in societies in general' rather than 'to develop [a] more general concept of society' (Towner 1988: 51). However, this thesis should not be seen purely as a historical writing as it contains many overlapping points between 'tourism history' and 'tourism anthropology' (Jordanova 2000; Tucker 2003; Walton 2005). In other words, this research should be seen as anthropological tourism history. A thesis of this kind inevitably draws on the language of many different perspectives in social science; ranging from history, anthropology, sociology to geography. Thus no attempt has been made to distinguish between what is tourism history and what is not. Indeed, my account of Koh Samui, like other accounts, is largely based on my own specific background. It is the personal and intellectual product of my time spent in the 'field' and the numerous visits to the island throughout the past two decades. However, the fact that both my informants and I regarded myself as a local led to the difficulty of separating my own emotions and feelings when writing the thesis. Thus, I include myself in this thesis - not only through my interpretation of the observations and interviews, but also as my relationships, experiences and partly my own history-enabled access to the participants.

4.8 Summary

This chapter provided background to my methodological stance and experiences in the field, and any issues and problems that emerged from my fieldwork. I have discussed the data collection process. As the research study was related to the issues of history, cultural characteristic and settlements, tourism businesses, landscape transformation and overall changes on Koh Samui over time, I have discussed the use of different data collection techniques: observation and participation, in-depth interviews, oral history, and map survey to collect information. I also have included the process of forming relationships with participants. At the same time, I have highlighted some ethically significant situations, which affected me and subsequently my data collection and ultimately the writing up of the research study. My research study is built on a strong and intensive ethnographic approach and different life history narratives, which are largely based on my choice of information. The analysis and the writing of the thesis is widely based on oral history and participant observation and is limited only by my experience through a sense of place, personal geography, imagination and identity on Koh Samui. In the fieldwork, I gathered real-life stories about past and present experiences of the people who were relevant for my thesis. I then recorded spoken recollections; personal reflections from people about their narratives of lives on the island; and how this created the tourism history. Overall, this thesis presents an account of the contemporary tourism history of Koh Samui becoming a tourist destination - a historical snapshot as perceived by me - rather than the entire complexity of Koh Samui's tourism history. The following chapters present the finding of the thesis – constructing and representing the tourism history of Koh Samui society during its tourism period.

CHAPTER 5

LOCATING KOH SAMUI: UNDERSTANDING THE ISLAND IN THE CONTEXT OF THAILAND

5.1 Introduction

This chapter presents the geography and political situation of Koh Samui as well as the Koh Samui historical background. Using the case study of Koh Samui to demonstrate the tourism history theory is appropriate due to the island's history of having a distinctive period between the 'pre-tourism period' and the 'tourism period'. Although the two periods are separate when examined in terms of development, they have been built upon each other over time and were influenced by national history (see Chapter 2, section 2.2). Reviews of the Thailand modernization processes, Thai socialization issues, the general Thailand tourism development strategies, and their implications on Koh Samui are also important areas of discussion in this chapter. Thailand modernization and Thai socialization are framed within a 'larger historical processes' position (Duval 2004). This is due to the importance of considering what has 'shaped the very performance [and] culture' (Duval 2004: 58) of Koh Samui society over time.

Whilst the main objective of this thesis is to set out to examining the theoretical conception of tourism history – the extent to which tourism affects on Koh Samui society in particular, it is important to include the discussion on how general Thai tourism affects the development process of tourism on Koh Samui. Therefore, this chapter observes Koh Samui society as a dynamic and ongoing product of structural change and broad tourism processes interacting with its national strategies and its historical and cultural legacies (both, the Thailand modernization processes and Thailand tourism strategies). As discussed in Chapter 2, the focus of this chapter is to present the consequences of the development and implementation of Thai modernity on the processes of changes in lifestyles and mindset of people on the island. This helps in understanding of how people on Koh Samui will react to the development of tourism in the future.

Figure 5.1: Map of Thailand

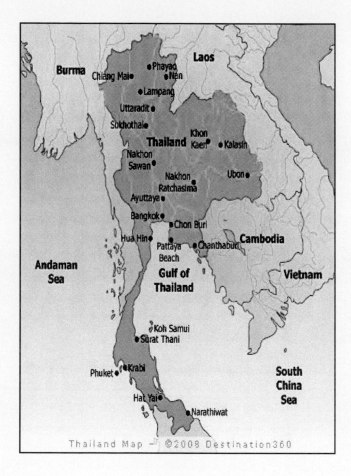

Thailand Map – ©2008 Destination360

Figure 5.2: Map of Koh Samui

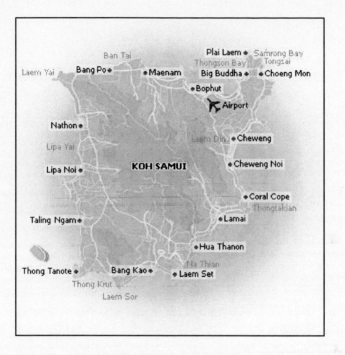

5.2 Historical background of Koh Samui

Koh Samui consists of a group of fifty islands in the Gulf of Thailand, 20 km from the nearest mainland and about 80 km from the coast of its provincial capital, Surat Thani. It is located about 560 km south of Bangkok. For this research, the name Koh Samui refers only to the largest main island that has an area of approximately 231.36 sq. Koh Samui is a tropical island which consists of the plateau area (33%), mountainous area (54%), alluvial fan area (8%) and flood plain area (5%) (Tambon Municipality of Koh Samui 2003). It belongs to Surat Thani Province in the southern part of Thailand. Although Koh Samui has been part of Siam's feudal system since the thirteenth century (Bunnag 1977; Rouhomaki 1999), it was not until the nineteenth century that it was opened to important currents of change. There are no historical documents that have paid full attention to Koh Samui's

78

own merits. The island is presented as just a small part of the national history of Siam or Thailand (Baker and Phongpaichit 2005; Bunnag 1977). Being peripheral to the political arena of Thai history, Koh Samui has been an insignificant place for Thai history in terms of having both historical and political autonomy.

The local folklore of Koh Samui suggests that the first settlement of the island was possibly by Malay fishermen about 1500 years ago (cited in Rangsiwararuk 2003). The island was also frequently visited by passing Chinese traders. In addition, some local historians claim that the island was used as a safe place during the storm season (Rangsiwararuk 2003). During the thirteenth century, the island held a crucial international trading position as it was the primary commercial intermediary between China and India (Clifford 1990; O'Connor 1986). Partially as a result of this international trade, Koh Samui became connected to the outside world and began receiving visitors and immigrants from different ethnic groups and religions (Petkaew 2003). Although the early history of Koh Samui is not well-documented, the controversy of the very meaning of the name 'Koh Samui' confirms and illustrates the island's interconnectivity to the world. There are two main theories on the origin of the name of Koh Samui. According to the Southern Thailand Cultural Encyclopedia, (Volume I 1986: 255-256), there are different origins of the island's name. One explanation is that the Chinese who came to trade in the area and who stayed on the island called it 'Sow-Bouy', meaning the first gate. Later, the Thai pronunciation changed the word to Samui. Another explanation is that Koh Samui is named after a native plant in the southern Thai language, 'Mui' (Rangsiwararuk 2003).

Koh Samui first officially surfaced in Siam history in about the thirteenth century when it was part of Siam's feudal system (Bunnag 1977; Rouhomaki 1999). The traditional Siamese state was essentially a confederation of *muang* (polities) centered on cities. Its territorial organization was based on a hierarchical ranking of these centers (*hua-muang*) and their subordinate settlements (*muang khun*). Rulers of these cities were technically appointed by the King of Siam and enjoyed wide prerogatives regarding manpower control and taxation within those centers and subordinate settlements. Beyond these groups of *muang* were the vassal states (*muang pratetsarat*), that were ruled by their own monarchs (Baker and Phongpaichit 2005; Bunnag 1997; Wyatt 1994). Thus, Koh Samui in the thirteenth century, political, social, territorial, economic and demographic development took place through the management of the *muang* system, which was connected to the centre by transferring manpower. Tribally it was connected through Nakorn Si Thammarat (the southern center of the Siam feudal system). The Thai ethnic majority took on roles in agriculture or various other forms of service to the state. According to some of the elderly folks of the island along with the work of Rangsiwararuk (2003), the Thais who were part of the southern center of the Siam feudal system on Koh Samui became early agrarians on the island. They preferred to live further inland up into the mountainous highlands as they felt that living further inland was cooler, safer and better for agriculture than living close to the sea.

During the colonial period of the nineteenth century, many Chinese moved to Southeast Asia to begin new lives (Skinner 1957). Significant numbers of Chinese also migrated to Thailand and, significantly, to Koh Samui. According to displays of 'Samui Hainan Museum' at the Chinese temple located in Ban Hua Thanon, Tambon Maret, all Chinese on Koh Samui originally came from the island of Hainan. Williamson and Hirsch (1996) also conceded that the ancestors of Hainanese on Koh Samui were Chinese traders from Hainan Island, in the south of China. This new Chinese community built many traditional temples for their religious ceremonies, which were important in terms of preserving the Hainanese culture for future generations. However, through the process of Thailand modernization and mixed marriages with Thais on the island, the Chinese were slowly integrated into Thai society. Consequently, their descendants have adopted Thai practices, which in turn have resulted in a significant loss of Chinese culture and identity. These Chinese settlers started cotton and coconut plantations on the island. In order to transport their coconut products to the mainland, they built boats called 'Panuk Kang Si' (Williamson and Hirsch 1996). As access to the water was necessary for loading and unloading the agricultural products transported between Koh Samui and the mainland, they preferred to stay near the beachfront. Armed with their exceptional trading skills, the Chinese owned and controlled most of the local businesses along the coast line (Samui Hainan Museum). It is important to note that those Thai-Chinese who owned local businesses and land and controlled tourism activities played an important role in the Koh Samui economy and eventually became Koh Samui 'locals'. As a result of their acclimation to being 'Thai' during Thailand's modernization process, the feeling of being Chinese began to fade and is now not as strong as it is to those Chinese who live in Malaysia (Fadzillah 2004). Therefore, as the discussion about Koh Samui in this thesis is in a more recent timeframe – the tourism period, *Chinese* was not emphasized but rather fell into disuse.

Due to the isolation and the abundant natural resources of the island, people on Koh Samui were self-sufficient. Although the residents of Koh Samui had geographically diverse backgrounds, ethnically dissimilar traditions and came from culturally different places (some were Thais serving Siam feudal system, some Chinese traders, and some Muslim fishermen), they enjoyed a good relationship with one another, often made possible through family ties[10]. The Muslim community was and still is located on the corner of the village of Ban Hua Thanon, Tambon Maret. Similar to other Muslim communities in the southern part of Thailand (Rouhomaki 1999) Muslims on Koh Samui are fishermen and trade their marine products in the fresh market. Although they are a Koh Samui minority, about 1500 inhabitants (Tambon Municipality of Koh Samui 2008), they live alongside other ethnic communities (Petkaew 2003).

As the thesis is a tourism history approach, which is a local historical perspective, it is important to link it back to a wider historical perspective (Dymond 1982; Evans 2001; 2002). Therefore, in order to understand social, cultural and physical landscape relationships on Koh Samui during its tourism period, it is important to discuss broader historical and conceptual frameworks as well as relevant social developments that influence Koh Samui society over time. Thus, the following sections discuss the Thailand modernization process and Thai socialization in order to provide a way of understanding the dynamic changes, which in turn shape the process of development on Koh Samui.

5.3 Thailand modernization process

If we are to understand how Koh Samui society, culture and environment has been affected by its tourism development, it is important to emphasize the process of Koh Samui's development before it encountered international tourism (prior 1970s). Therefore, the purpose of this section is to reflect on major social structural features of modernized Thailand and their influence on Koh Samui society at pre-tourism period (prior 1970s). It is important to highlight that throughout Thailand's history there have been many stages of

---

[10] This point was not only confirmed through the oral history and interview with locals but also both Cohen (1996) and Westerhausen (2002) notes that people on the island have been related through marriage.

historical and cultural legacies. Those legacies varied throughout time, place and social level, such as Thailand's old historic period, the period of colonialism and Thailand's modernity. These different stages of national legacies have built upon each other, developed from each other and resulted in a Thai identity. This section therefore describes the Thailand modernization process in order to provide a basic understanding of the influence of Thai modernity to Koh Samui society.

Modern Thai history needs to look far back beyond the time before the name Thailand was formally employed in 1939. Thailand has engaged in international trade since the Sukothai Kingdom, the first kingdom of Thailand (1249-1438), trading largely with China. During the Ayudhtaya Kingdom (1350-1767), Thailand's expanded its trading beyond China including Indonesia, Japan, India, Persia, and European countries such as Portugal, Spain, Holland, England and France. Thailand began to trade with the United States around the early period of the Ratanakosin Kingdom (1782-present) (Baker and Phongpaichit 2005; Wyatt 1994). However, an important modernization of Thailand took place during the reign of King Rama V (1868-1910). During that time, the country encountered Western imperialism. To sustain the country's independence and sovereignty, King Rama V implemented social infrastructure investment, government reform, high-level diplomatic relations and trade agreements. King Rama V himself undertook these trade and diplomatic overseas trips (once in 1897 and again in 1906-1907) whilst he also sent his princes to study in various European countries. Upon the return of these princes, reforms and modernization were high on the government agenda. Reforms took place in many areas such as education, health care, military, public administration, transportation and communication (Bunnag 1977; Krongkaew 1995; Phongpaichit and Baker 1996).

Through the Western colonization of neighbouring countries in the nineteenth century, Thailand experienced its own significant period of modern transformation. As outlined in Tanabe and Keyes (2002a), the processes of modernization that Thailand has undergone is based on the following. The first, Buddhism reform, the goal of which was to have a more scientific understanding of the world (Baker and Phongpaichit 2005; Stephen 1977; Zack 1977). The second, the global economic integration and the capitalization of its own economy (Krongkaew 1995; Panya 1995; Phongpaichit and Baker 1996). The third process was the political transformation from absolute monarchy to democracy – based on a constitution (Bunnag 1977; Burn 1968; Vickery 1970; Wyatt 1969; 1982; 1994). The last process of modernization was the re-identification of 'Thainess' parallel to the process of globalization (Brown 1985; Girling 1981; Reynolds 1991(b); Tanabe and Keyes 2002a; Tantiwiramanond and Pandey 1987; Van Esterik 2000). However, rather than the concept of modernization being superimposed directly upon Thailand's traditional bureaucratic social system of absolute monarchy, it was instead processed by a series of gradual changes which laid the foundation for the country's modern development (Burn 1968; Reynolds 1991). In addition, the constructions of Thai modernity were based widely on 'the broader population through various urban- and elite-controlled means of cultural production: commodity markets, mass media, government bureaucracy, standardized school curricula' (Mills 1999: 16). As the Western colonization of neighbouring countries in the nineteenth century reinforced the political reforms and Buddhist educational reforms Siam successfully achieved the goal of building one nation (Bunnag 1977; Wyatt 1984; Zack 1977; Reynolds 1991b). Since that time, Bangkok became the center for political administration and the education system. The Bangkok dialect became the standard for the Thai language. The Chatkri Dynasty and Theravada Buddhism guide Thai society (Bunnag 1977; Wyatt 1984; Zack 1977).

These reforms reorganized the nation's administrative system. *Mahat Thai* (Ministry of The North) assigned control of all affairs in the north of Bangkok; *Kalahom* (Ministry of the South) commanded all provinces on the peninsula south of Phetburi; and, *Khlang* (Ministry of Finance) was responsible for foreign affairs. Outside the capital, the Siam feudal and social structure were organized into *hua-muang* (principle provincial towns) and *monthon* (group of circles small provinces). The system was linked to Siam's *sakdina* (feudal), and was commanded by Bangkok-appointed governors (Vickery 1970; Bunnag 1977; Phongpaichit and Baker 1996). Western colonial threats resulted in the country's redefinition of its internal political power. In other words, this internal colonialism institutionalized the political, social and economic system, which supported the centralization of social status and the accumulation of Bangkok as the centre of the Siamese political system (Winichakul 1994).

As the process of Thai modernization is a nineteenth century phenomenon (e.g. Krongkaew 1995; Panya 1995; Phongpaichit and Baker 1996), the stage of Thai modernity has largely taken place in the era of globalization (1950s). The nation's industrialization, militarization, and global capital resulted in high performance of the agricultural industry, cheap labour, and an abundance of raw goods. Furthermore, Thailand's industrial growth in the 1960s, coupled with the International Bank of Rural Development (IBRD) guidelines for national development, industry quickly supplanted agriculture as the basis for economic expansion. The country began to export secondary products such as textiles, garments and processed foods (Phongpaichit and Baker 1996). A clear scenario of the country's transition into modernity can be seen in the case of Bangkok's transformation (Askew 2002). The modernity process is reflected in massive construction and real estate projects that have changed the city landscape of Bangkok and led to massive migration from rural areas to cities in search of work (Asker 2002). Moreover, Askew (2002) points out that along with the transformation process 'krungthep[11]' was socially organized around kinship and was politically managed by feudal and monarchical rule. Nowadays, Bangkok is modern, cosmopolitan and open to the forces of globalization. Therefore, the change in Bangkok is more than a change in landscape; it is also the change in social relationships, culture and economic life.

As the issues of modernization in the Thai context have been widely associated with the process of *siwilai* [a transliteration of the English words – civilized or civilization or *thansamai*] (Van Esterik 2000), Bangkok became the destination of great opportunities, a newly liberalized economy and *thansamai* life style (Askew 2002; Van Esterik 2000). Thus, Bangkok developed as a site of new modes of living and values (Askew 2002). This urban-based, cash-oriented economic development of Bangkok placed the city to become the urban center of the country (Phongpaichit and Baker 1996; Warr 1993), which led to huge numbers of villagers migrating to Thailand's urban centers, primarily Bangkok (Phongpaichit and Baker 1996; Phongpaichit and Chiasakul 1993; Phongphit and Hewison 2001). In essence, the urbanized Bangkok and its economic activities resulted in a migration of labour across the country, particularly from the north and northeast of Thailand to the capital. Isvilanonda and Hossain (2003: 109) conceded that 'a wage differential between rural areas and cities encouraged farm labour out-migration.' This is also the case for Koh Samui (Cohen 1996). The effects of the Thai modernization processes became more visible demographically as they grew into recurrent crises of overpopulation and overdevelopment of Bangkok's urbanity (Mills 1999; Tantiwiramanond and Pandey 1987; Van Esterik 2000; Yasmeen 2002).

---

[11] The name of Bangkok in Thai

In addition, modernized Thailand moved traditional education out of Buddhist monasteries and, with its modern educational system allowed women to access higher education. Although in the early 1900s there was only a small number of women who continued their education (Kabilsingh 1991), they did have the opportunity for higher education (Tantiwiramanond and Pandey 1997). Therefore, one side effect of these processes was an increased female role in the national economy (Van Esterik 2000). It offered employment to a well-trained and skillful labor force, which resulted in sex discrimination being less prevalent. It also opened up new opportunities for women, which allowed them to compete with men in the workplace (Tantiwiramanond and Pandey 1987). Furthermore, Thai women increasingly socialized with men. In fact, the image of Thai women is they are strong, independent and highly mobile and that they have played an important part in Thai economic development throughout history (Baker and Phongpaichit 2005; Lyttleton 2000; Whyte and Whyte 1982; Yasmeen 2002). This attitude is also reflected in women developing more mobility, open personalities and freedom from discrimination (Yasmeen 2002; see Chapters 7 and 8). For example, Potter in 1976 conceded from his observation in Chiangmai:

> Chiangmai women are impressive. They have the strength of character, independence, and self-assurance of women who live in a society where they are in a strong position. ... the women share equally with the men; daughters inherit the parental home and matrilineal ancestors... Women work in the fields, rear the children, keep house; they are also the merchants who earn money for the family selling in the markets...' (Potter 1976: 24 cited in Yasmeen 2002)

More than twenty years later, Lyttleton (2000: 129) similarly observed that:

> Throughout the planting and harvesting season, men and women work alongside each other in the fields, and likewise it is common to see men and women working together in factories and on construction sites in the cities.

Thailand's modernization also affected the physical integration of rural areas by upgrading infrastructure, communication, and transportation such as a modern postal system, telegraph services and railway lines (Wyatt 1994; Phongpaichit and Baker 2005).

As Thailand opened up to the world economy, Bangkok entered the international trade network. Bureaucratic reforms, coupled with the development of modern transportation, led to the inner colonialism power – the expansion of the centralization of social statue and the accumulation of Bangkok as the centre of the country's economic system (Winichakul 1994). The development of communication and transportation networks made the hinterlands more accessible to trade, which in turn led to a gradual change from subsistence production to production for the international market (Baker and Phongpaichit 2005; Wyatt 1982; 1994). On Koh Samui the market-oriented farming resulted in the rise of the commercial coconut plantations (Cohen 1996; Wisansing 2004). These factors were significant in the development of a modern economy for the Thai nation.

5.4 Thai socialization: concepts and issues

Tourism has created a modern society on Koh Samui, which has affected the island's social composition, cultural practice, geographical landscape and the production of new identities. Specifically one of the characters of contemporary Koh Samui society is the production of new gender issues through the representations of girlie-bars; women working in sex tourism (further discussed in Chapter 8). As sex tourism through girlie-bars represents a significant tourism aspect of contemporary Koh Samui society, it is important to understand the issue of women and sex tourism. Furthermore, in order to understand the issue of women and sex tourism on the island, it is important to understand the issue of tourism and Thai gender within the national context. Along the lines of tourism history conception and within broader historical and cultural perspectives (Duval 2004; Walton 2005), it is important to discuss the issue of Thai gender and prostitution and sex tourism. As discussed previously, the Thailand modernization processes resulted in Buddhism forming the country's norms and values; it also opened up new opportunities for Thai women to compete with men economically. To understand Thai socialization, it is important to consider the role of Thai gender within the Buddhist framework (Jackson 1989; Van Estaerik 2000). Therefore, this section includes the discussion of Buddhism and Thai gender, prostitution, sex tourism and the Thai social identity as a general background on what and why people on Koh Samui, women in particular, participate in commercial sex. This then helps contextualize Koh Samui's transformed gender landscape.

5.4.1 Buddhism and Thai gender

The issue of tourism and Thai gender is interrelated: Thailand tourism is a field overwhelmingly dominated by women. Therefore, this section sets out to understand Thai socialization through discussion of Buddhism and Thai gender.

Throughout Thai history, Buddhism has been utilized by both the monarchy and government as a tool to modernize and unify the country (Kabilsingh 1991; Reynolds 1991; Tanabe and Keyes 2002; Winichakul 1994; Bunnag 1977). The influence of Buddhism and Buddhist Order, coupled with the monarchy has become 'an important social institution … regarded as essential to the security and survival of the Thai nation as an independent political entity' (Jackson 1989: 1-2). Under a Thai 'geo-body' (Winichakul 1994), Buddhism and the monarchy have been politically reinforced in reconstructing the representation of the country as a Buddhist constitutional monarchy. Furthermore, of all the sources and foundations of Thai culture, Theravada Buddhism is the most fundamental feature for understanding Thai society in terms of 'viewing the world, a sense of reality, moral standards, and shared language and metaphors for analyzing their existing life situation' (Van Esterik 2000: 66). Thus, Buddhism and Thailand are strongly interconnected. Somboon Suksamran (cited in Jackson 1989: 1) stated the following:

> Buddhism is a social institution which is important in giving meaning to and being a symbol of national unity. It is a source and medium of the culture and traditions of the Thai nation. Speaking generally, Buddhism is like a root of our national existence and of the original social, cultural, and political identity of the Thai nation.

The fact that 95% of Thailand's population are Buddhists (Tourism Authority of Thailand, 2007), coupled with Buddhism as the state foundation shows that it is a fundamental element that runs through the entire Thai system, from the family to society. It is important to note that Thailand, unlike neighbouring countries, does not have a strong ethnic, religious and linguistic diversity. Therefore, religious differentiations in Thailand are 'principally a social categorization, not an ethnic classification' (Schliesinger 2001: 104). Particularly through formal education norms and the political-administrative structures created by the central-government, it is generally difficult to distinguish one from another by the fundamental feature of Thai values. This norm also becomes a model to understand many Thai social functions. With Buddhism and Thailand being strongly interconnected, it becomes a basic interpretation in most research studies on Thailand (Jackson 1989; Van Esterik 2000). The exploration of this interconnectedness can serve as an essential tool in an understanding of Thais' culture and traditions. Consequently, the issue of Thai gender should be discussed within a Buddhism context. Buddhism structures Thai genders in a way that 'differences in gender reflect the inequalities of accumulated merit, and Buddhism, by explaining those differences ratified them as inequalities' (Reynolds 2006: 186) [12].

Buddhism is one of the most important makers of Thai social and cultural identity, including defining the roles of Thai gender. However, it would be a distorted interpretation to look at Thai gender representation only in relation to the issue of Buddhism and ignore the other surrounding subjects such as the influence of Indian social values or Chinese gender practices (Kabilsingh 1991). Moreover, while both Thai Buddhism and Thai gender identities are subtle and complex issues that present two sets of shifting phenomena, the studies of Thai gender are mainly based on the grounds of Buddhist activities in Thai society. For example, as in most Buddhist ceremonies in Thailand, women are placed in peripheral locations, which in turn promote the oppression of Thai women (Ngaosyvathn 1995). Ngaosyvathn (1995) notes that in most of Buddhist activities women act as supporters while men are in leading positions. This is also the case for Koh Samui that men appear to be controllers and leaders of Buddhist activities while women seem to be helpers and stay in the backsground (fieldwork 2005). In fact, Buddhism in Thailand varies in interpretation and practices. Gender studies in Thailand mainly emphasize Buddhist's ritual activities rather than its philosophy. Van Esterik (2000) argued that gender studies should operate beyond the periphery of Buddhism and move to discussing the core meaning of philosophy, rather than merely focusing on traditionalist rituals. The pattern of hierarchical structure in Thai society, regardless of different groups, is the result of an interpretation from Buddhist teachings about the place of human beings in both nature and social spaces. This social system of 'hierarchical order' is reflected through social relationship practices in the form of 'super ordinate-subordinate relationship' (Limanonda 1995: na). This pattern acknowledges the respect for individuality regarding the issues of 'age, wealth, power, knowledge, and religious or governments role ... [which means] ... the young are subordinate to the old, women are

---

[12] Also see Van Esterik (2000) for more details on the issue of Buddhism and Thai genders.

subordinate to the headman' (cited in Limanonda 1995: na). Because of the acceptance of this 'hierarchical order', Thai women, including those on Koh Samui, have been placed into the periphery in Buddhist beliefs and Thai practices in both the family unit and society system.

Given the acceptance that children are subordinate to the parents, it is the role of children to pay honorable merit to their parents. However, a proper repay is required differently of daughters and sons as their roles are linked to Thai Buddhist ideology and are thus practiced differently. The repay of sons being ordained into monkshood, is more respected than that of the daughters' repay which is their obligation to care for the parents (Ngaosyvathn 1995). Ngaosynathn (1995: 148) further notes that 'a son can help his mother[13] achieve nirvana ... [while] ... a daughter can only pray for her parents to enjoy a good after-life. ... [and] ... caring for her parents when they are old and sick'. In this cultural practice, they are 'dutiful daughters' (Ekachai 1990; Phongpaichit 1982). These social attitudes in Buddhism portray gender performances in different roles and landscapes. A man was expected to be out in the world, while a woman was trained to be a master of the domestic domain. In other words, the Thai gender-based expectation places women in charge of care-giving, household related work and service positions. Consequently, women were not encouraged to gain worldly knowledge, predicated on the fact that the previous educational ideology in Thailand was linked to temples and Buddhist doctrines, which were strictly male territory. In this context the social structure and educational attitude in Thai society were by no means exclusively reserved for males leaving women behind (Tantiwiramanond and Pandey 1987). It was during the modernization process of Thailand (the beginning on the nineteenth century) that Thai women began to have greater opportunities in education. However, the educational preference of women was traditionally in areas of home economics and commerce – typing, foreign languages and secretarial training (Barme 2002; Tantiwiramanond and Pandey 1997). Therefore, regardless of women having new opportunities to compete with men (Lyttleton 2000) they have traditionally been the disadvantaged subjects in politics as well as economic activities (Tantiwiramanond and Pandey 1987).

In this regard, gender roles in Thailand are neither equal nor fixed. Therefore, the issue of gender development should highlight how women are different from men, rather

---

[13] The text mentioned only 'mother', assumable because a mother has limited access to Nirvana in comparison to the father who himself as a man can ordain into monkhood.

than subordinate to them (Reynolds 2006). Although morals and attitudes are constantly changing because of modernization, Thailand is still a male dominated society in 'the religious sphere and bureaucratic policy' while women remain 'a significant sector of the business workforce, the academy and civil service, they also have most of the control over the household budget' (Yasmeen 2002: 154). Consequently, studies of Thai gender have been relatively contradictory. Men specialize in Buddhist monastic roles and political-bureaucratic occupations while women specialize in economic-entrepreneurial activities. In other words, whilst the roles of Thai women are largely that of housekeeper, child caregiver and producer of food as well as paid employment for household income (Yasmeen 2002) Thai men are installed in higher social positions. However, within this essence, it does not mean women's roles are limited. In fact, Thai women's roles have been underrepresented as Reynolds (2006: 186) notes:

> In most respects, women in traditional Siamese society were subordinate to men. "Traditional" in reference to Siamese society generally means before the middle of the nineteenth century. There must have been changes in the legal and social position of women through the centuries, but the documentary sources on this subject are too meager to perceive much of this change, and historians tend to fall back on the expedient of considering pre-modern society as a static society.

The shift of Thai society towards industrialization (since 1960s) resulted in women participating more fully in economic activities (Kabilsingh 1991). Arguably, Buddhism does not oppress women but, rather, Thai traditional Buddhist ceremonies subordinate them. Thai Buddhist norms which make Thailand an extremely tolerant society produces the acceptance of the norms of women subordination, whilst, ironically, and at the same time, empowering them (see Chapter 8, section 8.4 as an example of this point). It has been mentioned earlier in this section that sex tourism through girlie-bars represents a significant new production of the gender landscape on Koh Samui. To understand tourism on Koh Samui, there is not only the need to understand Thai socialization through a consideration of Buddhism and Thai gender issues, but there is also the need to understand the issue of Thai prostitution and sex tourism in the Thai context. Therefore, the next section provides a discussion on Thai prostitution and sex tourism within the national context as an overview of sex tourism in order to provide a deeper understanding of the thesis findings, Chapter 8 in particular.

5.4.2 Thai prostitution and sex tourism

This section is to address the issue that sex tourism has overwhelmingly developed on Koh Samui. Specifically, in order to understand the present situation on the island, it is important to understand the influence of the national history and legacy of the sex business in a Thai context. Therefore, this section discusses the issue of Thai prostitution and sex tourism including the general development of sex business in Thailand.

During the Ayuthayan period (1432-1767) prostitution was permitted under Siam law and was a source of state income. The practice was carried on throughout the nineteenth century, when prostitution was the subject of female slaves in brothels, owned by bond masters who paid taxes to the state (Mettarikanon 1983). At the same time, the brothel owners gained profits from clients, who were mostly young, single Chinese male immigrants who entered the country because of the growing demand for labor (Mettarikanon 1983). Their customers also included Europeans in the port cities, but 'not high-ranking [Thai] men who had their own concubines and harems' (Van Esterik 2000: 173). The Chinese immigrants resided around the *Sampheng* area in Bangkok, which directly encouraged the growth of brothels around their residences (Skinner 1957). However, at this time the involvement of Thai women in the sex business was small. Rather, larger numbers of prostitutes were Chinese and Japanese women trafficked into the country (Skinner 1957). This phenomenon affected the term used for prostitutes as prostitutes were called *ying sampheng* or *Sampheng* women (Mettarikanon 1983). As part of the country's reformation towards the turn of the twentieth century, the abolition of slavery, which affected the Thai elites' harems, the formation of a male salaried bureaucracy and the boom in Chinese immigration contributed to the expansion of commercial sex in Bangkok and other provincial towns (Barme 2002). In 1909, a royal tour by Prince Vajiravudh to *Ranong* (a province located in the southern part of Bangkok) remarked on the situation of prostitution as:

> Ranong (on the west coast of peninsular Siam) has become quite civilized, as witnessed by various things. For example, in the market they have

beautiful ladies on sale. Doesn't this indicate that Ranong is civilized? Maybe it is not as civilized as Bangkok since the mansions of paradise [wiman sawan] down there are still not adorned by [green] lanterns hanging out the front. But then again, is this an indication that they are more civilized than in Bangkok?　(cited in Barme 2002: 93)

The reason for this comparison between prostitution and civilization is unclear. However, commercial sex expanded in the provincial town, and prostitution composed the landscape of Ranong. Through the above statement, prostitution was ideally reflected in the development of the town. Moreover, the inner colonialising power (section 5.3), 'with the growing monetarization of the economy, served to enlarge the domain of commercial sexual activity, stimulating local male demand for sexual services' (Barme 2002: 77). Accordingly, by 1928 there were 203 licensed brothels with 974 prostitutes and an estimation of another 2000 non-registered prostitutes working in Bangkok (Meyer 1988). In addition to the proliferation of prostitution as state income, the government introduced the legislation titled 'Law for the Prevention of Venereal Disease' (*Phrarachabanyat p' ongkan samch' onrok*) in 1908. This was drafted from the 'Municipal Law on Prostitution' (*Phrarachabanyat Khanikaphiban*) and was originally based on the Singaporean practice to control the rampant spread of venereal disease in the colony. The key concepts of the law were to license the brothels and to collect the payment of taxes from the owners and from prostitutes. The law required prostitutes to be above fifteen years of age and undergo regular health checks (Mettarikanon 1983: 84). The act intended 'to keep them [prostitutes] in good order, to control sexually transmitted diseases, and to collect taxes' (Boonchalaksia and Guest 1994: 4 cited in Van Esterik 2000: 174). Later, with the concern of the coercion of young Chinese females into the transnational prostitution network through male emigration, the promulgation of the Trafficking of Women and Children Act was launched in 1928 (Hantrakul 1983).

The period of industrialization (1950s), brought increased economic opportunities to Bangkok enabling both rural Thai men and women to become part of the formal and informal urban labor market. The annexation of subsistent land and/or promotion of cash-crop farming often had a devastating impact on rural economies and created powerful pressures on young people, especially young women, to migrate to urban areas or tourist resorts in search of work (see, for example, Ekachai 1990). The commercial sex industry in

Thailand experienced a large increase in Thai women in the late 1950s (Hantrakul 1983). Reynolds (2006: 132) summarizes the social historical circumstance that reinforced Thai women into prostitution as:

> There is also deep historical dimension to prostitution. The Thai state licensed prostitution in pre-modern times (Reid 1988s: 633) and continued to earn revenue from it through the Fifth Reign. The political economy of prostitution in Thailand historically helps to explain some of the problems today. The practice of bonding women for sexual services, which is the gateway through which many rural women enter prostitution in Thailand, is a direct descendant of debt bondage for sexual services, which persisted even after the laws on slavery were rescinded at the end of the nineteenth century (Reynolds 1979b).

Prostitution was included as one of the submarkets of the industrialization process (Phongpaichit and Baker 1995). Askew (2002: 258) explains that '[a]lthough prostitution was declared illegal in 1960, it flourished in a disguised form (in hairdressing salons, for example), or through a simple payment to police'. Hotels were a common venue for small massage parlours or brothels. Due to this circumstance, the growing supply and demand for sex services reinforced the commercialized domestic sex businesses, which promoted the growth of brothels, massage parlors, hotels and entertainment venues (Hantrakul 1983; Phongpaichit 1982; Phongpaichit and Baker 1995). However, the structure of the Thai commercial sex industry changed dramatically in association with the influx of the American soldiers' Rest and Recreation (R&R) program during the Vietnam War in 1962-1975 (Li and Zhang 1997). The Rest and Recreation program resulted in massive development of a 'commercial foreign-oriented sex service infrastructure', particularly in Bangkok areas, as Askew (2002: 258) summarizes:

> The R & R program quickly stimulated the development of a commercial foreign-orientated sex service infrastructure. The entertainment demands of US servicemen helped transform Bangkok's premier middle-class district of Sukhumvit (and nearby Phetchaburi Road) into an entertainment strip, comprising bars and hotels. ... By the late 1970s Bangkok's red-light district of Patpong was already famous, and the Sukhumvit area was also well-known.

93

It was the American military program of R&R in Thailand that encouraged the addition of the commercial foreign-oriented sex businesses to the existing Thai prostitution practices. Following the expansion of the tourism industry in the mid 1970s the commercial foreign-oriented sex businesses became sex tourism (Cohen 1996; Hall 1994; Phongpaichit and Baker 1995). Since then, Thailand has attracted single male tourists mostly from Europe and Japan to come for sex tours (Cohen 1996; Hall 1994; Phongpaichit and Baker 1995). Consequently, commercial sex businesses for sex tourism have been constructed in most of the country's tourist destinations such as in Chiang Mai, Phuket, Pattaya, Haad Yai and Koh Samui (Cohen 1996; Hall 1994; Phongpaichit and Baker 1995). Koh Samui's commercial sex businesses have growth significantly and have become one of major attractions of the island in forms of girlie-bars (see Chapter 8, section 8.2). In other words, the structure of Thailand's sex industry changed significantly in the era of the tourist-orientated sex tourism industry of the 1980s. In this respect, the expansion in the tourism sector gave indirect permission for the growth of foreign-orientated sex tourism which was a significant foreign exchange earner for the Thai economy.

5.4.3 Thai prostitutes and social identity

This section discusses the position of Thai prostitutes within Thai social identity. It introduces the campaign for the promotion of the rights and opportunities of sex workers by the Chiang Mai Empower Group (see Appendix I for the detail of the campaign) to explain where those sex workers in Chiang Mai positioned themselves within Thai society. Particularly, the discourse represents the perception of sex workers and illustrates the general attitude towards them in Thai society. This section offers a more negative identity, as it focuses on Thai female sex workers in Chiang Mai[14] only. This section sets out to compare with stories of sex workers on Koh Samui in Chapter 8, section 8.3, all of which showed positive experiences in relation to sex tourism.

In addition to the voice of the empowerment group (Appendix I), there was a seminar on the legislation of prostitution on the 27th November 2004. During the event, the

---

[14] Chiangmai was chosen due to its observable local-oriented sex commercial characteristic compared to other destinations such as Phuket and Pattaya.

Chiangmai News (27th November 2004) interviewed the prostitutes who attended the seminar;

> Most of you will have seen us working in bars, karaoke bars, massage parlours or brothels. We sell drinks, sing [and] entertain clients while they drink, play snooker, dance and some of us sell sex. It seems everybody has an opinion on who we are, why we work and what we want. [...]
>
> However, it was clear to us that many academics and non-sex worker groups are continuing to quote old and often inaccurate information about us. Most of us are women. Most of us are single mothers and [we are] the main supporters of our extended families. We are blood donors and voters. We are good Buddhists and take our religious responsibilities seriously. We worry about social issues like youth violence, drug use and the environment. We are active in our communities caring for others. We contribute to the economy via sales tax and tourism promotion. We participate in social and medical research. We eat, we sleep, we do housework, we dream. We are Thai, hill tribe, and we are from other countries in the region. Like all workers, we work to provide a good life for our families and ourselves. Most of us have had many other jobs like cooking, waitressing [sic], laundry, sewing or running small businesses. Sex work is not the last resort but rather that job that we have chosen because it offers us the best opportunities.

In most literature about Thai sex workers' social life, either directly or indirectly, the traditional appearance of doing something bad, being a victim or helpless (not necessarily to be emphasized) is certainly acknowledged (Askew 2002; Barme 2002; Cohen 1996; Ekachai 1990; Hall 1994; Hantrakul 1983; Mettarikanon 1983; Meyer 1988; Phongpaichit 1982; Phongpaichit and Baker 1995: Van Esterik 2000). The sex workers themselves, and those in the local-oriented commercial sex trade in particular, are aware of how society perceives them. How the sex workers see their place in society is reflected through the *negative* words of Chiang Mai Empower Group's campaign (see Appendix I). The group emphasizes the place of sex workers in Thai society negatively, by offering a description that is 'embedded in other people's views of Thai prostitution [of them]' (Van Esterik 2000: 166). Through their common voice, we immediately observe the negative connotation that society has put on their identity. Their perception gives give us a detailed glimpse of the depth of their lives in Thailand's society. It shows the complexity of life in which they struggle to reconstruct their identity. For many people, therefore, the image and perception of Thailand's sex tourism industry is problematic and ambiguous rather than optimistic. In this respect, the positive self-dignity of sex work that drives women to work in the industry is often excluded in traditional research studies, which reject such optimistic aspect. Instead, the victimization is as a model for studying Thai sex tourism. Indeed, the overwhelming perception is based on an image of sex tourism being a multilayered exploitative phenomenon (Ekachai 1990; Hantrakul 1983; Phongpaichit 1982).

Simultaneously, the intertwined ideologies of sex, gender, and Thai societal roles indicate that a female's identity in society is tainted if a woman has been involved in different sexual relationships with men or women. The instituted social and sexual norms are modelled on responsibility and 'dutiful daughter morality' (Ekachai 1990; Phongpaichit 1982) which mark the boundaries of womanhood (as previously discussed in Section 5.4.1). Subsequently, these norms are reflected in the eyes of sex workers, who are tied to the transactions of the sex tourism industry, because of its very intense economic strength (Cohen 1996; Hall 1994; Phongpaichit 1982). In other words, regardless of their positive participation in society as 'blood donors', 'voters', 'good Buddhists', in their care for 'social issues ... youth violence, drug use and the environment', their involvement 'in [the] communities', contribution 'to the economy via sales tax and tourism promotion' and participation 'in social and medical research' (Chiang Mai News 27th November 2004), they are obviously still perceived as living in an intolerable situation while struggling with social stigma. This situation, however, is different to those sex workers on Koh Samui. Where they have become economically active, they have begun to learn the language of freedom, sexuality, new identity and life (Askew 2002; Cohen 1996). Moreover, the view of women in sex tourism on Koh Samui has reflected the growing space for women. This has affected the shifting of Koh Samui's gender landscape on the island's public area (see Chapter 8).

5.5 Center and periphery: reflections of Thai modernization process on Koh Samui

This section discusses the rapidly changing society of Koh Samui, a place that is peripheral to Thailand's modernization process. Major social structural features of modernized Thailand and their influences on Koh Samui society are reflected upon in this section. As it has been mentioned throughout, Thailand's history encompasses many stages of historical and cultural legacies. Those legacies varied throughout time, place and social level, which have built upon each other, developed from each other and resulted in a Thai identity. Therefore, this section explicitly expresses reflections on how those Thai legacies influence Koh Samui's norms and values. It provides a basic fundamental discussion of Koh Samui to reflect back on the representation of tourism on the island and to provide a better understanding of the reactions of Koh Samui to the process of touristization of society throughout this thesis (see Chapter 2; section 2.1).

During the country's modernization period between the late nineteenth century and the time of Thailand became an industrialized country in the middle of the twentieth century, Koh Samui society had shown almost no physical change, at least in comparison with other areas in Thailand (Baker and Phongpaichit 2005; Mill 1999; Molle and Srijantr 2003a). There was no ring road around Koh Samui (Koh Samui Community Magazine 2004). In fact, a concrete 52 km ring road around the island was not constructed until the early 1970s. Traveling around the island to pick up coconuts or passengers could take as much as three days by boat. Small boats were rowed out to sea where the coconuts and passengers would be transferred to larger boats for their trip to Bangkok. There was no electricity in most of the villages. Only Nathon community had an electricity generator that worked only during certain hours of the day. Even in the late seventies when tourism started, there were only two generators that provided electricity to the entire island, one in Nathon and another on Chaweng Beach. Water was taken from small local wells. Although Koh Samui was a part of Surat Thani province, it had only few government officers housed in Nathon. Tambon headman with the district system ran the administration from the central government. The units smaller than Tambon were controlled by village headman. Buffalo and cock fighting were the main forms of entertainments on the island (Koh Samui Community Magazine 2004). With regard to the Thai modernization process, Koh Samui benefited mostly through modern education and administration reforms. The island was unified with the country's social and cultural identity. Buddhism, royal family and the central Thai language became the norm on the island. Koh Samui experienced a change of organizational and social behavior based on norms and values of the nation and the unified feelings of Thainess; influenced by hierarchy, status, personal loyalty, tolerant social etiquette and social stratification in terms of gender, age, education and family prestige. Indeed, this process evoked a meaningful feeling of nationalism, capitalism and collective cultural identity.

5.6 Thailand tourism development: center strategies

This section discusses Thailand's tourism development and particularly emphasizes Thailand tourism development strategies and the country's tourism promotional plans. It does so in order to provide a basic understanding of the influences of Thai tourism to the development of tourism on Koh Samui before it moves to the implications of tourism development on Koh Samui society in the following chapters.

Thailand has been acknowledged as the fastest growing tourist destination since the 1960s (Elliott 1997). The diversity of cultural and environmental resources, coupled with the phenomenon of R&R trips (rest and recreation) for American soldiers' to Thailand during the Vietnam War (1962-1975) resulted in a booming of Thailand's tourism development (Li and Zhang 1997; Higham 2000). Interestingly, tourism development in Thailand started almost at the same time that the country entered into the industrialization process (the late 1950s). To respond to the country's expanding capitalist economy, the central Thai government launched 'The National Economic and Social Development Plan'. It provided the guidelines and directions for the country's development. The main objective of the First, Second, and Third Development Plans (1961-1976) was to construct and improve the country's physical infrastructure in order to cope with the modernizing centralist state. In 1960, the Thai government established the first national body to promote tourism in Thailand – the Tourist Organization of Thailand (TOT). In 1979 TOT was renamed 'Tourism Authority of Thailand' (TAT). The Fourth Development Plan (1977-1981) emphasized economic recovery after the world energy crisis. During this period, tourism was primarily considered as a major means of earning foreign income. As tourism is an important economic activity that plays a vital role in Thailand's socio-economic development, the Tourism Authority of Thailand (TAT), a government body, received an increasingly important role in tourism development.

Through the support of the TAT, the tourism industry in Thailand became internationally competitive (Tourism Authority of Thailand 1998). The government sought to provide an extensive development process at national, provincial and local levels in response to the growth of tourism. Coupled with the economic importance of tourism, tourism development was recognized and the first national tourism policy was integrated into the Fourth National Economic and Social Development Plan (NESDP) 1977-1981 (Phongpaichit and Chiasakul 1993). Since then, the tourism policy has followed the National Economic and Social Development Plan (Tourism Authority of Thailand 1997). At the beginning of the National Tourism Plan, it highlighted the development of tourist attractions, infrastructure and facilities for the main tourist destinations around the country. Consequently, the TAT (1998) has marked places such as Pattaya, Phuket, and Koh Samui as the main tourist areas of the country. According to Meyer (1988), tourism businesses and development in Pattaya took place when the city became a place for R&R visit, which shifting the town from the small fishing village into one of the Thailand principal tourist destinations. Due to easy accessibility and its close proximity to Bangkok, tourism development in Pattaya has grown steadily and become one of the most popular Southeast Asian seaside resorts. Tourism Authority of Thailand statistics (1980) showed that 405,888 foreign tourists visited Pattaya in 1980. The numbers of visitors to Pattaya has grown significantly since then. Tourism Authority of Thailand statistics (2001) notes that on average one-third of all foreign tourists in Thailand visit Pattaya (Refer to Table 5.1 for the estimate numbers of tourists' arrival to Pattaya).

Table 5.1 Tourist arrivals in Thailand 1998-2007

Year	Numbers (million)	Revenue (million Baht)
1998	7.76	242,177
1999	8.58	253,018
2000	9.51	285,272
2001	10.06	299,047
2002	10.80	323,484
2003	10.00	309,269
2004	11.65	384,360
2005	11.52	367,380
2006	13.82	482,319
2007	14.46	547,782

Source: Tourism Authority of Thailand 2010

Smith (1992) notes that the growth of tourism in Pattaya resulted in urbanizing the area that is associated with changing the physical landscape and the configuration of tourist accommodation. To accommodate the growth, the numbers of tourism infrastructures including tourist accommodations and entertainment businesses in forms of beer bars have grown significantly over the years (Smith 1992). Furthermore, the tourism urbanization development in Pattaya caused a rapid deterioration of its natural resources. Besides natural environment degradation, the unplanned growth of tourism development has created the typical image of sea, sun, sand and the sex in Pattaya, revolving around a cluster of discos and outdoor bars (Cohen 1996). Although Pattaya increasingly received family group tours from Europe, Russia and the Middle East (Tourism Authority of Thailand 2001), the 'erotic' image remains (Cohen 1996). Similar entertainment patterns such as in Pattaya have evolved in Thailand: similar nightlife entertainment is prevalent in many places such as Phuket, Had Yai and Koh Samui (the Venereal Disease Control survey reported in Bangkok Post 3 August 1999).

The development of tourism in Phuket, however, came late compared to Pattaya. Phuket's economy was originally based on the exports of tin, rubber, coconuts and fish. However, as the price of agricultural products dropped massively, tourism development was then perceived as an alternative economic development to replace agricultural and mining activities (Phuket Tourism Master Plan 1976). Although tourism development in Phuket started in the early 1970s, the island did not become an international tourist destination until the opening of the Phuket airport in 1979. Coupled with a bridge connecting Phuket to the mainland, the island became easily accessible for both domestic and international tourists. Since then tourism development has grown significantly with tourist arrivals increasing from 752,000 in 1990 to 1.6 million in 1996, 2.7 million in 2001 and 4.5 million in 2006 (Tourism Authority of Thailand 2007). Moreover, as tourists continue to arrive at the island, massive infrastructure in form of international hotel chains and entertainment businesses such as discotheques and bars were built (Kontogeorgopoulos 1998). In addition, the TAT was also responsible for international marketing and the promotion of new tourism sites. The TAT promoted better understanding of tourism issues and assumed a leadership role in developing a clear statement of vision and mission for the Thai tourism industry (Tourism Authority of Thailand 1985). In the 1980s, a significant tourism boom was witnessed with an increase in the number of tourist arrivals from 1.8 million in 1980 to almost 5.3 million in 1990, and an increase in revenue from 17,765 million *baht* in 1980 to 110,572 million *baht* in 1990 (Li and Zhang 1997). The reason for this impressive growth was the success of the Thai governments' intensive marketing and promotional campaigns (Elliott 1997; Hall 1997; Higham 2000; Richter 1993). A series of tourism promotions, in particular 'Visit Thailand Year 1987' and 'Thailand Arts and Crafts Year 1988-1989' made Thailand one of the world's favorite tourist destinations (Li and Zhang 1997). With the recognition of the important role of tourism to the country's economy, many projects were designed to attract more tourists. "Visit Thailand Year 1987" was one of the early promotional campaigns that played an important role in the development of the country's tourism industry (Qu and Zhang 1997).

However, tourism development in Thailand came at a price. The social impacts of tourism were first recognized because of American soldiers visiting during the Vietnam War. The image of Thailand as a sex paradise and Bangkok as the sex capital has been a permanent label since then (Li and Zhang 1997) (further discussed in Chapter 8). With the growth of massage parlours and nightclubs with sex workers, the sex industry in general, the AIDS epidemic and environmental degradation, the negative impacts of tourism gained greater attention (Chon and Singh 1994). In response to the negative consequences of tourism development, the Fifth and the Sixth Development Plans (1982-1991) recognized the impact of tourism on the environment. The Development Plans introduced land use and building controls as well as the concept of sustainability. Moreover, the Seventh and the Eighth Development Plans (1992-2001) emphasized stabilizing economic growth at an appropriate and secure level. The notion of 'people-centered development' was also discussed. The main strategy was to increase the potential of economic and social development and to practice sustainable management of natural resources. In addition, different plans and regulations for appropriate tourism development were introduced, including Thailand's Environmental Protection Act in 1989 (Li and Zhang 1997). Furthermore, the 'Women's Visit Thailand Year 1992' campaign was also projected to encourage female tourists and at the same time to promote a new, more wholesome image which down-played the country's sex tourism image (Chon and Singh 1994; Hall 1997; Li and Zhang 1997).

During 1982-1997, tourism was the largest foreign earner in Thailand's economy (Tourism Authority of Thailand 2002). Tourism was the means of economic growth at all levels as well as a tool for the country's economic recovery after the Asian Economic Crisis of 1997-1998 (Higham 2000). Regardless of the suffering from the economic crisis, Thailand was synthesized for tourism growth due to reasons such the quality and diversity of tourism products and services and the favorable exchange rate for shopping tourism (Wisansing 2004). In addition, the 'Amazing Thailand 1998-1999' promotion was introduced after the devaluation of the Thai *baht* in 1997 in the hopes of attracting and encouraging visitors to spend more money in the country. Coupled with the location of Thailand and easy access to Bangkok International Airport (Chon and Singh 1994), the Amazing Thailand campaign was highly successful and became the country's image to the world (Intarakomalyasut 2001). Consequently, the on-going 'Amazing Thailand' campaign during 2000-2003 was further expanded, resulting in a dramatic increase of tourist arrivals: from 5.3 million in 1990 arrivals rose to 10.79 million in 2002, with a revenue of 360 billion *baht* in 2002 (Tourism Authority of Thailand 2004). To respond to the economic downturn in 1997, the Thai government adopted the philosophy of 'sufficiency economics' bestowed by the King of Thailand into the Ninth Development

Plan (2002-2006). The philosophy was to overcome the long-term economic crisis and achieve sustainable development. The Ninth Development Plan desired to improve the quality of Thai people's lives, the local economy as well as the preservation of tourist attractions, local arts, and archeological sites. The TAT adopted the Ninth Development Plan's policy through the tourism promotion and development policies from 2002 – 2006. Within this concern, tourism development was discussed as the need to create employment and improve income distribution at a local level. The tourism plan was to build on the success of the 'Amazing Thailand' marketing and promotional campaigns. The plan was also to develop new marketing strategies. The TAT intended to encourage the diversification of the country's tourism products and to identify opportunities for future investments. The plan also included the issues of the creation of tourism employment and the enhancement of the industry standards (Tourism Authority of Thailand 2002). Although the protection of local culture and environment was included in the national tourism policies, in practice these plans and regulations have not been fully implemented (Elliott 1997). Environmental destruction in Thailand still occurs given a lack of environmental awareness on the part of the general population and the short-term goal for profit of businesses (Baecharoen 2000; Hall 1997; Pongponrat 2007; Sirisaard 2001). The Thai government must take part of the blame for not being more vigilant in terms of enforcement and for not leading the way regarding sustainable development awareness and education, locally and nationally, more strongly. Indeed, tourism development in Thailand comes with costs. Environmental problems such as water shortage, waste management and destruction of national forests are currently prevalent. Pattaya and Phuket were one of the very first places of a rapid deteriorating environment, becoming prime examples of the rapid deteriorating conditions of once-booming destinations (Chatrudee 2002). This directly reflects the Butler life cycle discussed in Section 3.3: these destinations evolved into the *consolidation stage* by the end of 1990s. Clearly, the accelerated development of tourism in Pattaya and Phuket without the appropriate infrastructure, policy and control mechanisms being put in place can provide negative outcomes for other destinations to learn.

5.7 Koh Samui and tourism development

Tourism development on Koh Samui started in the latter part of the 1970s when western backpackers came to the island (Cohen 1996). There were only a small number of tourists who came to the island then. Local people also had little awareness about the benefits of tourism. They offered simple accommodation and services to cater to basic backpacker needs. However, in the eighties, when tourism development started to emerge beyond Bangkok, Pattaya, and Phuket, Koh Samui became one a major tourist destinations (Tourism Authority of Thailand 1998). The island started to attract large numbers of foreign visitors and external investment. The very first development projects were initiated in Chaweng Beach (Cohen 1996). After that, steady growth followed and larger resorts gradually began to appear. At that time, tourism contributed around 30% of the total island income (Koh Samui Community Magazine 2004). The potential of the tourism economy from Koh Samui resulted in Thailand's Fifth National Economic and Social Development Plan (1982-1986) which designated Surat Thani as a principal town for tourism development. To follow up with the Fifth Development Plan, the TAT launched the Master Plan for Tourism Development of Ko (sic) Samui/ Surat Thani (1985), one of the very first tourism plans on Koh Samui. It was to utilize natural resources and improve the structure of industrial production. The Master Plan recognized the lack of tourism infrastructure and public utilities such as roads, transportation, water and electric supply. In order to improve those tourist facilities which would serve the potential tourism growth on Koh Samui, the Master Plan suggested to 'slow down the growth of accommodation service but emphasized the upgrading of its standard' (Tourism Authority of Thailand 1985: (4)25). The Master Plan aimed to allow Koh Samui to respond to the economic and social development of the country because of tourism development. The Plan targeted 'the foreign tourists, especially the high class tourists, by improving the quantity and quality of services and amenities' (Tourism Authority of Thailand 1985: (5)2).

With the traditional image of Koh Samui as a tropical island paradise offering sea, sun and sand, the tourism industry on the island continuously developed. Along with its beautiful beaches and neighbouring islands, Koh Samui developed various opportunities beyond its natural environments for special interest tourism. Thus, the island provides a wide range of sports and other activities such as Thai massage, herbal spa facilities and other amenities. The island also offers a variety of entertainment such as pubs, bars and other nightlife activities. Besides these entertainment options, historical and religious attractions are available throughout the island. Table 5.2 illustrates some main tourism attractions on the island.

Table 5.2: Main Tourism Attractions on Koh Samui

Hinta Hinyai (Grandfather and Grandmother Rocks)	One of the most visited places on Koh Samui. The rock formations represent male and female genital organs.
Buffalo Fighting	One of the most popular sports on Koh Samui. Buffalo fighting occurs at irregular times, signaled by signposts on the edge of roads announcing a show. Fights end when one of the two buffaloes turns over, generally well before harm occurs. The main purpose of his kind of event is for local entertainment and gambling.
Wat Phra Yai (Big Buddha)	This is the best known temple on Koh Samui due to the 12 metre high Buddha statue. It is situated on a peninsula, surrounded by small shops, local craft workshops and restaurants.
Waterfalls	Koh Samui has two easily accessible waterfalls with good facilities. They are Hin Lad and Na Muang.
Chaweng Beach	This beach is located on the eastern part of the island. It is the most popular beach on Koh Samui. Chaweng is popular for its nightlife entertainment. The beach is 6 km long with many international hotels, bars, restaurants, and other international businesses.
Lamai Beach	This beach is the second largest on Koh Samui. Lamai Beach is quieter compared to Chawang Beach. It is famous for its nightlife entertainment and girlie bars.
Bo Put Beach	The beach was once a little fishing village located on the north of the island. The beach is one of the island's older settlements.

Sources: Comprised from Koh Samui tourist brochures

The issue of accessibility was once an obstacle to tourism development on Koh Samui. The problems of infrastructure and facilities were great. However, there were insufficient roads to support an increasing number of vehicles. This included the poor condition of roads connecting communities and tourism spots. With increasing tourism growth in Thailand, which extended to Koh Samui, an airport was constructed on the island in 1989. Because of operating the airport on the island, a significant tourism growth began and tourist arrivals increased dramatically (Bangkok Airway 2002). Moreover, with continued tourism growth, rail and bus services particular from Bangkok were linked with ferry lines for the convenience of tourists to Koh Samui. Table 5.3 present numbers of tourists to Koh Samui by mode of transport.

Table 5.3: Numbers of tourists to Koh Samui by mode of transport in 2007

Thai tourists	Types of transportations	Foreign tourists	Total
24,135	Airplane	323,914	348,049
21,599	Train at Surat Thani station	154,005	175,604
44,440	Bus	177,363	221,803
38,273	Private cars	68,424	106,697
712	Others (cruise)	18,834	19,546

Source: Tourism Authority of Thailand 2007

In the 1990s there was an increased amount of large-scale investment and tourism on the island grew significantly resulting in the island changing rapidly into a tourism-oriented modernization. The emergence of international chain hotels put a further demand for the upgrade of the island's infrastructure in order to keep up with the rapid growth. In other words, the period of the 1990s was a decade of mass tourism on Koh Samui, which was characterized by 'an unprecedented building boom' (Westerhausen 2002: 201). Like other Third World destinations that are within the reach of airplanes, the connectivity to the outside world represents the beginning of the era of mass tourism (Gmelch 2003). Thus, toward the end of the nineties, Koh Samui developed significantly (see Chapter 6). The central government in Bangkok started to reorganize the island's local government administrative procedures and the Tambon Municipality started to manage and oversee what was becoming a substantial influx of capital (Tambon Municipality of Koh Samui 2003). Tambon Municipality consists of seven Tambon (sub-districts): Ang Tong, Lipa Noi, Taling Ngam, Na Maung, Maret, Bo Phut and Mea Nam. The Tambon Municipality

Council, which serves as the local government body on Koh Samui, has twelve civil servants who are elected by the local people and who serve 4-year terms. Figure 5.3 illustrates the structure of Tambon Municipality of Koh Samui. The Mayor, who heads the council, takes responsibility for the administration of Tambon Municipality in terms of formulating plans and policies for public services and development. The council's responsibilities also cover allocating budget for development tasks and monitoring the works of the City Council according to the laws and regulations (Tambon Municipality of Koh Samui 2003). The council is therefore the main stakeholder of tourism development on the island.

Figure 5.3: Structure of Tambon Municipality of Koh Samui

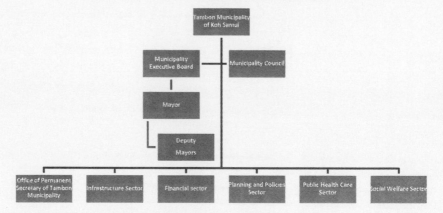

Source: Tambon Municipality of Koh Samui 2003

During the 1990s, the island witnessed substantial modernization and infrastructural improvements. Koh Samui had a strong international tourism growth. As tourist arrivals increased by air and by ferry, it became obvious to the locals that the tourism industry offered substantial incomes. Local landowners, in particular, realized the huge potential of tourism. Leases and joint ventures replaced direct land sales (Koh Samui Community Magazine 2004; also see Chapter 6, section 6.6.4). In addition, the devaluation of the Thai *baht* and political instability in Indonesia in the late 1990s benefitted Koh Samui, as it was positioned as – relatively speaking – a safe and inexpensive place to visit (Jariyasombat 1998). Experiencing the island's unspoiled natural environment coupled with its recreational activities, placed Koh Samui on the list of world-class tourist destinations (Jariyasombat 1998). After the year 2000, tourism's significant growth was accompanied by an increased number of flights to Koh Samui. There were numerous flights from both domestic and international destinations to the island. Regular ferry services fed by bus and rail services from Surat Thani on the mainland brought significant numbers of tourists to the island as well. Table 5.4 presents tourist arrivals to Koh Samui.

Table 5.4: Tourists Statistics of Koh Samui 1990-2007

Year	Thai	Foreigner	Total
1990	355,623	319,970	675,413
1991	400,646	270,997	671,643
1992	553,357	252,031	805,388
1993	197,916	260,699	458,615
1994	208,578	292,153	500,731
1995	186,197	511,260	697,457
1996	101,052	567,839	668,891
1997	102,891	569,949	672,840
1998	95,451	637,759	733,210
1999	87,106	634,750	721,856
2000	-	-	823,122
2001	-	-	837,533
2002	-	-	857,335
2003	-	-	846,281
2004	-	-	937,763
2005	-	-	1,014,909
2006	-	-	1,030,623
2007	-	-	1,059,642

Sources: Tambon Municipality of Koh Samui 2003; Tourism Authority of Thailand 2007[15]

---

[15] From the year 2000 onward, there were only total numbers of tourist arrivals available.

The increase in tourist arrivals reinforced the need to construct and redevelop tourism and accommodation facilities (Jariyasombat 1998). In other words, the transformation of the island from the 1970s up until recently has occurred rapidly due to the boom of tourism on the island with accommodations having been constructed to respond to the growth of tourist arrivals. Table 5.5 shows the growth of the numbers of tourism rooms during the 2000s as well as the occupancy rate of those rooms.

Table 5.5: Numbers of rooms and its occupancy rate on Koh Samui in the 2000s

Year	Numbers of rooms	Occupancy rate
2001	9,256	56.78
2002	9,870	60.51
2003	10,913	55.01
2004	12,315	62.04
2005	12,769	66.42
2006	13,290	68.29
2007	14,405	64.23

Source: Tourism Authority of Thailand 2007

During the decades of tourism development on Koh Samui, the demographic profile of tourists has increased in European middle-class families in the form of mass tourism (Westerhausen 2002). Therefore, it was a growing occupancy rate of more luxury type of accommodation on Koh Samui. Table 5.6 represents occupancy rate of different type of accommodation on Koh Samui.

Table 5.6: Occupancy rate of accommodation establishments in Koh Samui 2007 (%)

Month	Hotel Group 1[16]	Hotel Group 2	Hotel Group 3	Hotel Group 4	Hotel Group 5	Total
January	76.76	76.42	67.93	62.28	60.21	70.84
February	88.60	89.27	73.40	67.45	62.30	79.55
March	81.95	78.71	72.80	65.63	64.90	75.15
April	74.91	74.21	72.03	68.64	66.48	70.91
May	70.50	65.90	63.06	62.08	60.08	64.40
June	69.93	61.41	56.91	54.37	52.47	59.46
July	68.02	60.83	65.34	65.25	59.41	63.82
August	75.13	71.75	69.36	63.33	54.50	65.91
September	72.32	77.18	53.90	53.73	50.47	60.94
October	67.96	56.56	54.51	52.15	52.18	57.54
November	48.68	45.56	49.04	51.60	45.83	48.02
December	57.20	64.95	68.43	55.36	56.39	59.00
Total	68.63	65.72	62.63	58.96	57.61	64.23

Source: Tourism Authority of Thailand 2007

As there was the growing demand for the more luxury hotels, this type of accommodation was further encouraged. International hotel chains, along with regional hotel chains, also made large-scale investments to respond to this demand. The number of accommodation establishments and rooms on Koh Samui increased dramatically. Specifically, by the next decade (2010s) international hotels such as Banyan Tree and Sheraton on Lamai Beach, Conrad and Element on Panga Beach (the west side of the island) and Dusit Thani on Charngmon Beach are expected to be in operation. This led to a tourism development on Koh Samui representing the 'development stage' in Butler's lifecycle (see Chapter 3, section 3.3).

---

[16] These groups of hotels are categorized by the room price. Group 1= 2,500 *baht* up; Group 1 = 1,500-2499 *baht*; Group 3 = 1,000-1,499 *baht*; Group 4 = 500-999 *baht*; Group 5 = below 500 *baht*

5.8 Tourism and Koh Samui society's transformation

As it becomes clear from the above, tourism on Koh Samui has become an almost overwhelming success internationally, particularly because of the island's natural environment. Given the natural beauty of the island's physical and marine environment, Koh Samui reflects the image of a tropical paradise island. The visitor is able to experience the natural wonder of what was, and relatively speaking still is, an unspoiled tropical island. Combined, these attractions have placed Koh Samui as one of the 'must visit' destinations in Thailand. Consequently, since the 1990s, Koh Samui has switched from an economy dependent on agriculture to one that exploits the opportunities of tourism. Table 5.7[17] shows the number of locals whose names are registered with the Koh Samui Municipality, the number of local people who work in agriculture and the number of immigrants on the island.

Table 5.7: The population size and distribution in agriculture/tourism employment

Years	Local population	Locals working in agriculture	Immigrants working in the tourism industry
2004	42,990	4,839	40,000
2006	49,131	4,839	100,000
2007	49,871	7,875	100,000
2008	5,1600	7,875	103,000

Sources: Tambon Municipality of Koh Samui 2008

With the accessibility to Koh Samui by air, the island has become, using Picard's (1996) words, of 'touristic interest'. With regard to the economic aspect of tourism development, dramatic transformations have occurred due to significant investments. Similar to other such destinations, tourism attracts people from different cultures from

---

[17] There is the lack of precise number of local population. The Koh Samui Tambon Municipality only provided the record of population size and distribution in agriculture and tourism employment on the island from 2004 to 2008.

around the world to the island and thus brings them into contact with the locals. In this sense, tourism contributes to the globalization process by drawing upon the interconnectivity of diverse cultures (Picard 1996; Tucker 2003). Accordingly, 'a certain degree of commonality evolves and echoes of different cultures will be found' (Sofield 2001: 105) on the island. Specifically, the rapid growth of tourism activities attracts many people to Koh Samui who come in search of work and new opportunities. Tourism brings diverse cultures from within Thailand together through an influx of local immigrants from other provinces[18]. This results in a high rate of migration of workers to Koh Samui leading to a large number of unregistered residents and some overcrowding (Tambon Municipality of Koh Samui, 2003; see Table 5.7). Undoubtedly, the rapid growth of tourism has transformed this natural paradise with its coconut plantations and fishing village into a growing international tourist destination.

There are research studies which suggest, either directly or indirectly, that tourism 'impacts' negatively upon the island's infrastructures and its population (e.g. Boonsirichai 2002; Chon and Singh 1994; Green 2005). Boonsirichai (2002) points out that Koh Samui needs to improve the quality of its infrastructure services and environment in order to create good tourism conditions on the island. In addition, according to the Action Plan Formulation for Rehabilitation of Tourism Attractions Final Report 1998 (Tourism Authority of Thailand 1998), the growth of tourism on Koh Samui has negatively affected its natural environment. There is evidence that validates the claims of these studies. For example, tourism related activities have caused the degradation of the water system, which includes a shortage of potable water, lack of proper drainage, and wastewater management. Furthermore, the tourism phenomenon has negatively impacted the fragile environment of the island with its increased water demand, resulting in water shortages during the high season. This critical shortage was brought to light when 39 villages and local communities were unable to access tap water during the summer of 2002 (Antaseeda 2002). The Tambon Municipality office claimed that this was because the need for water exceeded the supply. The island's water supply authority holds that the number of visitors to the island should be limited to 12,000 per day in order to stay within the daily quota of 300,000 liters. In fact, during the peak season, there are 10,500 arrivals daily resulting in over 100,000 people making demands on water supply (Antaseeda 2002). This problem is similar to what Cohen's study (1996) demonstrates: the impact of the excessive water

---

[18] See Hall and Williams (2002) on the issue of tourism and migration

demand on Koh Samui created by tourism forces the local people to compete for the available water supply. Moreover, there are many other tourism impacts on the island as well, such as traffic congestion, air and noise pollution, and flooding after rains because of inadequate sewers (Swarbrooke 1999). Tourism has caused the conversion of land use on the island from agricultural to commercial in order to accommodate hotels, resorts, pubs, bars and other tourist facilities. Along with its positive economic impact, mass tourism has also caused some major environmental problems such as over use of natural resources like the forests and the problems of what to do with the excess waste created by the boom of tourists. For example, the Koh Samui Community Newspaper (2007: 20) reported:

> Passing through the supposedly protected natural forests on Samui is not always a pleasurable tour. In the mountainous areas of the island you can't fail but notice large areas where trees have been cut down or are dying, various types of waste is also regularly dumped in the forests away from visitors' eyes.

Because Koh Samui lacks effective measures to preserve and protect tourism resources and the environment leading to the destruction of natural resources, the rapid development of mass tourism on Koh Samui has had a detrimental effect on the island's natural and social environments. A study on Koh Samui conducted by Mahidol University (1997) shows that this was partly due to a lack of awareness and knowledge in conservation management by investors, as well as by tourists. Parnwell (1993) concedes that environmental destruction is a result of a lack of coordination between government departments and agencies. This suggests that the powers that are on Koh Samui are unaware of the long-term effects of rapid tourism development on the natural environment. It could also indicate that tourism developers are rather focused on short-term business income instead of considering long-term environmental effects. Ownership of the tourist infrastructure on Koh Samui, coupled with their often pure business interests, clearly impacts on the protection of the island's environment. A chairman of the Tourism Business Association of Koh Samui commented in a newspaper (The Nation, 9.5.89 cited in Parnwell 1993: 295):

> [M]ost tourism business owners are outsiders who immigrated to the island after tourism boomed. Some local residents even pessimistically commented that business owners do not realize the importance of

113

environment conservation because they just came to make profit. When the island is totally destroyed and cannot give benefits to them anymore, they will leave.

Clearly, the issue of non-local ownership and ensuing lack care about long-term environmental degradation is important one in the context of studying the tourism period in Koh Samui. While the local community is facing serious environmental problems and agricultural land scarcity, there are positive aspects as well to this transition – people on the island are gaining economic benefits from tourism-related endeavors such as working in restaurants, hotels and resorts and selling products. Jarujittiphan (1993) notes that the consequences of tourism as an opportunity of people on Koh Samui to access a quality education. However, the enhancement of the quality of education does not only come from the improved financial situation, but also from the improved infrastructure of education at local schools. For instance, there is more emphasis on English language and tourism studies in an effort to prepare the students to enter the tourism industry upon completion of their education (Jarujittiphan 1993). Rapid tourism development is likely to be responsible for the livelihood change on the island (Jarujittiphan 1993; Kontogeorgopoulos 1998).

On a more optimistic note, the development of tourism has by no means been all-bad for Koh Samui. For example, the infrastructure that provides support to the tourist industry is also available for the use of local people. An example is the 50-kilometer ring road system connecting all the major beaches to the airport and the main harbour that was developed to support the island's tourism (Bangkok Airway 2002). In addition, on Lamai Beach, Chawang Beach and other major beach areas the beach roads have been expanded and upgraded and new roads built (Tourism Authority of Thailand 1985). Other advantages are the increased electrical capacity made possible by the undersea cable from the hydro-electric plant on the mainland, the introduction of more sophisticated communication and postal facilities and increased protective in both police and medical, cultural and educational services. Although the initial plan of increasing the volume of electricity was to cover the area of major tourist attractions on the island, it later covered the island; undoubtedly, local people are to benefit from the service (Tourism Authority of Thailand 1985). Discussion about tourism on Koh Samui comes at a time of strong interest in the concept of sustainability and its application in many sectors (Pongponrat 2007; The Tourism Authority of Thailand 1998). In the development of a strategy for sustainable tourism, there is a need to pay close attention to the relative roles and responsibilities of the government agencies, tourism businesses, and local communities, and the relationships between them (Apostolopoulos and Gayle 2002; Richards and Hall 2000; Vivian 1992). However, the Koh Samui Tambon Municipality Five Year Plan (2002-2006) claims that there is a lack of community participation in the tourism planning process, particularly limited cooperation among the various sectors when it comes to the achievement of local development goals. Furthermore, the study by Pongponrat (2007) shows that the barriers to participation of local people come from a low level of local education, a lack of knowledge and skill and also locals' lack of interest in participation (Pongponrat 2007).

In addition, the concern that Koh Samui would become a duplicate of other destinations such as Pattaya and Phuket in terms of unchecked development in the absence of long-term planning did not go totally unnoticed. Because of the awareness of the potentially negative impacts of tourism, regulations to control land use and building heights have been introduced through Thailand's Environmental Protection Act in 1989. Land use has been capped at 50% of the total area and building heights limited to three-storey or 12 meters (Jariyasombat 1998). In an effort to complement these formal regulations, there are groups of local tourism businesses owners and locals who have implemented some environmental activities such as the 'Beach Cleaning Project'. The main objective of these activities is to promote environmentally related activities that are geared to raising awareness and responsibility for keeping Koh Samui clean. The project also enhances the beach cleaning system provided by the local government. Equally, there is a group called the 'Samui Power Community' established in 2003 that aims to promote local tourism development in a cultural and environmentally sustainable manner. To address the issue of sustainable management, the 'Samui Eco-Tourism Club' was established in the year 2002. The club is a local organization that plans to protect and preserve the delicate marine environment. Their target is to help monitor and minimize the negative impact on the island's natural resources. Furthermore, in 2006 a group called 'Spirit of Samui' was set up by a committee consisting of various social groups including business professionals, resort owners, education specialists, and senior government officials. They place high hopes on the ability of people on Koh Samui to respond to local community development issues. The aim of the group is to support Koh Samui through finding alternative solutions to some of the problems facing the island. In addition, an environmental conference on Koh Samui in January 2007 gave some hope of protecting the island's environment (Samui Community Newspaper 2007). The Island's local government considered the water shortage problem with the outcome being that Koh Samui was able to increase its water supply to 1,257,572 million cubic meters yearly (Koh Samui local government plan 2008). As tourism continues to expand unabated, the future of the island is unclear – it can go either ways rejuvenation and restoration or further decline (Butler 1980). While Conlin and Baum (1995) claim that the small scale of an island's physical resources puts it in a defenseless position against the negative effects of mass development, Maiava (2001) argues that locals are not always passive victims to development projects. With reference to both Conlin and Baum (1995) and Maiava (2001), Koh Samui itself might be incapable of controlling the increased impact but people on Koh Samui are becoming increasingly critically aware of their situation and have begun defining their problems and needs. Therefore, the question arises whether it is appropriate to focus on the consequences of tourism on the island as *only* 'impact of tourism'. The wider issues surrounding the consequences of tourism development on Koh Samui as discussed throughout this thesis are here noted as locals having abilities to *change* and *adapt* their needs towards tourism development, if they wish so.

5.9 Conclusion: Thailand modernization, tourism development and Koh Samui's modernity

This chapter began with a discussion on the background history of Koh Samui before moved to discuss the Thailand modernization process; Thai socialization; Thai gender, Buddhism and prostitution; Koh Samui in Thailand modernization process; Thailand tourism development; and Koh Samui and tourism development in order to place Koh Samui within Thailand's history. In turn, this provided the connection of Koh Samui society to Thailand modernity during its 'tourism period'. Within a large historical process (Duval 2004), Koh Samui has been significantly integrated into the country in two major stages mainly: during the country's modernization process and during the boom of the Thai tourism industry. The chapter has explained the influences of the two stages on Koh Samui society - the Thailand modernization process to Koh Samui pre-tourism period prior 1970s and Thailand tourism development of the Koh Samui tourism period (from the 1970s until the recently). While the Thailand modernization period has inserted the identity of Thainess in people on Koh Samui, tourism development represents the process

116

of transformation of Koh Samui towards modernity. In turn, this has shaped the character of Koh Samui society largely as espoused in this chapter.

The Thailand modernization process led to the state-authorization of Thai language, Buddhist-based cultures, Chakri dynasty and Bangkok as a center of administration. In this respect, inner colonialism reflects the country's 'internal spatial and social peripheries ... that are dominated by a metropolitan core [Bangkok]' (Hall and Tucker 2004: 2). Accordingly, Thailand defines the dominant national culture and inserts the *Thai identity* into every location in the country including Koh Samui. In essence, the process of the modernization of Thailand has formed the lifestyle and mindset of people on Koh Samui during the island pre-tourism period (prior 1970s). Furthermore, from the mid 1980s to the early 1990s, a series of investments, primarily in the tourism related industries, set in motion a process that rapidly changed the character of Koh Samui society. Because of these developments, Koh Samui became one of the major tourist destinations in Thailand, along with Bangkok, Pattaya, Phuket and other places. Tourism development spread rapidly across the island and today there is scarcely an area that is not influenced by tourism. Thus, the tourism industry on Koh Samui can be described as the instrument that transformed the whole island.

The discussion of the emergence of Koh Samui's modernized society has focused upon the development of the tourism industry on the island. The reason for this is that large-scale tourism development has shaped the character of the island's society to a greater extent than any other single aspect of its economy. Major developments in transportation, communication, recreation, accommodation and many service industries developed for the most part in response to the needs of tourism. The tourist growth, improvements in the infrastructure and the demand for more tourist facilities contributed to the promising growth of the island and thus presented the set of conditions for the island's development. Thus, tourism is the most aggressive and pervasive mechanism of change in the modern history of Koh Samui. It has reached all levels of locals, educational, cultural, and religious life of people on the island. In fact, tourism affects negatively on Koh Samui's environment as Conlin and Baum (1995) point out small islands are incapable of controlling the increased impact that the growth of tourism has on them. However, Maiava (2001) argues that locals are becoming increasingly critically aware of their situation and have begun to define their own problems and needs. Therefore, the following chapters examine the implications of tourism development, including sex tourism, on Koh Samui that has created a modern island economic framework and accelerated the structural changes which have affected the island's social composition, cultural practices and geographical landscapes, including the production of new identities.

CHAPTER 6

TOURISTIZATION OF KOH SAMUI: GEOGRAPHY IN TRANSITION

6.1 Introduction

As discussed in the previous chapter, more than three decades of tourism development on Koh Samui have remodelled the physical and social landscape of Koh Samui into thriving tourist destination linking the touristization of the island to its modernization process. Integrated with massive tourism development, Koh Samui today is not an isolated island what Cohen (1996) described as a backward and stagnant society. Because of the emergence of tourism as a driving force of the island's economy, Koh Samui no longer functions merely as an isolated-traditional periphery of its country (see Chapter 5). Instead the well-developed infrastructure on the island has facilitated the development of modernization, urbanization, touristization and commercialization. The new trend of urban growth on Koh Samui, however, has raised questions concerning the changing essence of the island as seen through its tourism modernization. This tremendous modern transition, namely the experience of the island's political and economic processes illustrates some unique characteristics of Koh Samui.

This chapter analyses the notes and daily experience diaries – the recording of my everyday life and interpretations of those experiences as well as the records of locals' life and work histories (see Chapter 4). As discussed in Chapter 3, Young (1983) presents touristization as being largely monitored through the changes of spatial representation to achieve tourist activities. Thus, one of the important facets of this deconstruction involves analyzing the mapping survey (Chapter 4), to reveal the spatial consequences of the accelerated growth of Koh Samui's touristization. This process involved a repositioning of the perception of the island in relation to its 'centre' and its increased economic competitiveness. Such perception resulted from the expansion of the island's infrastructure, which stems from opening formerly low-fertilized agricultural areas and encouraging an influx of international and Thai capitalists. This in turn has resulted in a dramatic transformation of both social and geographical landscapes. Therefore, this chapter discusses the complexities of the production of tourism space on Koh Samui and in a broad conceptual sense. It also explores the drivers of the island's touristization process. This involves a discussion of the cultural and traditional practices, which offers the most valuable theoretical insights. Furthermore, the assumption that Thailand's development practice offers an opportunity for tourism development is significant in the understanding of the touristization process on Koh Samui. It then leads to a discussion of the spatial pattern of the island's touristization and the changing form of modernity, with particular attention given to the emergence of touristic regions and spatial differentiation to the traditional system. The chapter begins with the examination of the shaping of a tourist landscape and continues to explain the general findings of the chapter. It then moves to a discussion of how traditional Thai space practices benefited the inevitable growth of the island's tourism industry. The chapter then discusses the basis of Koh Samui's transition into a modern island and how this has been an important influence on the growth of tourist activities on the island's space. The chapter also discusses the development of a land market with some inside perspectives of how locals perceive their land and how that encouraged tourism growth in the area. It also presents the life stories of some new local tourism entrepreneurs in order to exemplify how the new generation, educated in Bangkok, increased the capacity for local competitiveness and added a new layer of touristization to Koh Samui.

6.2 Koh Samui: the shaping of a tourist landscape?

The situation on Koh Samui can be broadly summarized as the growth of an effective space that is reflected in the increased control and integration of the tourist landscape. The chapter reflects on the increasing control and integration of tourism development through elements of tourist destination change. In terms of the economy, the tourism period witnessed a massive transition towards a tourism-dependent industrial economy and the commercialization of lands and properties on Koh Samui. This was heavily driven by national and international capitalists, was facilitated by a development-oriented private sectors and the Tourism Authority of Thailand and was supported by urban-thinking local businesses. The massive influx of tourism capital, which began after the building of the airport in the 1998, decisively changed the nature of land development and tourism on Koh Samui. This marked the beginning of Koh Samui's transformation from its agricultural period to one of tourism boom. This phenomenon changed the patterns of the island's landscape and improved its economic value. Previously agriculture-unsuitable land was developed to support tourism-related industries. In the process, Koh Samui underwent substantial transformation, which resulted in a change to the way people lived and the basic organization of its society. Tourism development on Koh Samui involves the natural environment and elements and its spatial systems. The effective arrangement and integration of traditional land use within the political as well as physical boundaries of Koh Samui has played a significant role in the growth of a 'tourist landscape'. Tourism settlement not only implies the breakdown of traditional patterns of settlement, but also the creation of new forms of settlement to suit the attainment of new goals – tourist landscapes.

The tourism development integration processes encompasses four areas - social, political, economic and geographic issues. The approach can be described as a study of developing tourist destinations based upon growth alone. A well-developed tourist landscape represents the ultimate means of organizing a geographic area into social, political administrative and economic space components in favor of tourism development (Young 1983). In the case of Koh Samui, the island's development has been significant to the transformation of the tourism industry. This has come about through both external and internal influences such as the influences of Thailand itself on tourism development, regional political instability (e.g. the island of Bali in Cole 2008) and the urban mentality of the new generation of the local tourism business owners (see Chapter 7, section 7.3). The central growth of services provided on Koh Samui, and the livelihood provided by the tourism industry helped the place to grow out of a rural phenomenon. This tourism urbanization ran parallel to the development of improved transportation and marketing systems. The questions of Koh Samui's modernization and urbanization, or more specifically 'touristization', and its population growth again emphasize the incorporation of the island into a tourist destination - the geographical spread of change from agrarian land-use to tourist landscape. It is important to note that this approach is a process and as such affects both the tourism expansion in the area and its population. It also results in changes in land use, landscapes and affects people and their economic activities. In other words, the identification of local traditions, the embodiment of the culture and society, and the change in physical landscape is reflected through tourism development on the island.

The unprecedented scale and speed of the touristization of Koh Samui resulted in the majority of locals now living in and amongst these new tourist landscapes. This is also mentioned in Macleod's (2004: 7) study of the Canary Islands, Spain, where a 'locally run small-scale tourist economy' was replaced by 'a capital-intensive tourist industry'. In the case of Koh Samui, however, it was not only outsiders who developed the island, but also local businessmen who upgraded their tourism businesses to cope with the global tourism competition (also see Chapter 7). Wisansing (2004) concedes that although tourism businesses on Koh Samui were under local management they became more internationalized standard. Thus, much of tourism expenditure does not necessarily remain on the hands of outsiders.

6.3 Cultural practice and the emergence of touristization on Koh Samui

This section discusses Koh Samui's traditional settlement and how it significantly affected the transformation of the island's touristic space. The section follows the tourism landscape perspective, which Ayala (1991: 572) summarizes as tourism developments and tourist activities *epitomizing*[19] the experience of 'the ecology of the natural environment, landscape ecology, and human ecology'. In this respect, it is a way in which the touristization process can be investigated by reflecting on the traditional settlements on the island that are described through models of local settlement patterns. The traditional spatial organization in both geographical landscape and social organization in Thailand is constructed on the interrelation of environment conceptualized under the concept of *mu'ang* or *muang* (city) and *pa* (forest) (Stott 1991). These patterns provide analytical insights into the initial growth of tourism development at various scales and provides an understanding of uniquely emerging tourist activities that are spread all over the island. Therefore, the growth of tourism urbanization on Koh Samui reflects the traditional settlement pattern that administers the touristic areas in various capacities. Stott (1991: 145) explains the concepts of the two words as;

> [M]u'ang has remained essentially constant, a brilliant linking of religion and geography ... in the centre of mu'ang and usually aligned with the main river of the basin, ... is the princely capital, containing the most important

---

[19] The emphasizing is mine.

Buddhist temple and palladium, the city pillar (lak mu'ang), and the royal palace. This is the 'merit-heart' of the mu'ang, from which the 'umbrella' of merit will spread to the very edge of the intermontane basin, the foothills of which rise dark on the horizon.

Pa (forest) in contrast as;

> [A]t the edge of the [intermountain] basin, there rise the mountains that hem in the mental map of the mu'ang, for here is a forested land, ... which is filled with spirits, wild animals, ... such regions lie outside the essential social organization of the mu'ang, outside the 'umbrella' of merit emanating from the king, and outside controlled and benign nature (ibid: 146).

Accordingly, great spatial division of the self and the environment was characterized on early Koh Samui. There are two common ways of talking about Koh Samui's geography. When thinking of the east and the west, it can be divided by the mountains in the middle of the island and sketching towards the northwest and southwest of the island. This is similar to the way the local people traditionally divide the island: mu'ang (the west side of the island) and hlung-kou or pa (behind the mountain) which refers to the east side of the island[20]. Significantly, this geographical division not only affected Koh Samui's historic settlement, but it also replaces the old structures with the diverse and complex landscape of Koh Samui's agricultural livelihood and tourism landscape in recent decades.

In general, the physical environment they inhabit influences people. This is also true of Koh Samui that has two major seasons – rainy and summer. Due to the location of the island, the seasons of Koh Samui are based on the relationship of the rain to annual cycles of temperature. The island receives winds from all directions, particular from the south, creating significant rainfall from May to October (Tambon Municipality of Koh Samui 2006). From November through January, winds from a northerly direction bring a cooling breeze resulting in less than sufficient rainfall. This period represents the start of the dry season that lasts from February through April when the island experiences the

---

[20] According to one of my informants, she points out that once people who lived on Chaweng Beach called Kon Hlung-Kou, literally means people who live behind the mountain.

highest temperature of the year. It should be noted that, starting in October, the winds reverse, and there is an outflow of dry, cool air going towards the south from the north. This climatic period is called the monsoon season (Tambon Municipality of Koh Samui, 2006). These natural conditions result in the east side of the island, facing the Sea of China, being most affected by natural hazards in forms of heavy rainfall, monsoonal storms and floods during the monsoon season (Jarujitiphan 1993; Petkaew 2003). Moreover, as Koh Samui is traditionally a coconut orchard island, the settlements were built in suitable ecological systems and farming areas. Given that the east side of the island experiences the most direct impact of natural hazards, these fertile lands are mainly found on the west side. The west side of the island has two major streams created from Namaung waterfall and Hin-Lad waterfall. Although the streams are small and too narrow for transportation purposes, they were significant for supplying water as well as for agricultural purposes (Southern Thailand Cultural Encyclopedia 1986).

Traditionally, villages were located along river or canal routes (Phongphit and Hewison 2001); accordingly, Koh Samui's patterns of settlement were associated with and concentrated on the west side where ecological and historical factors resulted in very significant regional differences between the two sides of the island. Furthermore, on the west side of Koh Samui, the result of trade expenditures, coupled with the abundance of natural resources, had consequences for the people, religion, agriculture and the political power. It became clear that geographical dimensions, natural conditions and the early economic formation of the island are crucial to understanding Koh Samui in terms of its settlement and livelihood. The point to be emphasized here is that traditional Koh Samui primarily focuses on the western side of the island, particularly Tambon Na Muang, Hau Thanon, Tambon Ang Tong (Nathon area) and Tambon Marat (Lamai Beach). In this part of Koh Samui, life was easier and more secure. In addition, natural hazards in the form of monsoonal storms and floods, which mainly occur in eastern Koh Samui, were always considerably more moderate in the west. Consequently, western areas were more open, well-organized and reflected cultural heterodoxy[21]. By the late 1970s when one of the earliest tourism researches was carried out, Lamai Beach was as the subject of the research study (see Cohen 1982; 1996 for example).

---

[21] My family's resettlement to the western side of the island – the Lamai Beach area – reflected the traditional ideologies of settlement and conditions on Koh Samui.

Koh Samui has an extensive record of tourism development and urbanism that originated in the west (Cohen 1996; Jarujitiphan 1993; Petkaew 2003; Westerhausen 2002). Historically, the early settlers established themselves near Ban Don Tang, in the area of Wat Pra-deum (Pra-deum Temple), and Tambon Namuang in the south-west of the island (Petkaew 2003). At the beginning of 1900s, as commercial activities began to flourish and the island became connected to capitalism, a large number of small commercial towns developed all over the island (Rangsiwararuk 2003) particularly in the area called Hau Thanon which was used as the port for travelers and transport of agricultural products and thus became the place for the interchange between Koh Samui and the center (see Chapter 5, section 5.3). The area, as a part of a growing commercial center, was a favored site for markets and businesses that served the locals. Chinese as traders and Muslims as fishermen settled in this area (see Plate 6.1-6.3).

Plate 6.1: The Chinese settlement at Hau Thanon

Plate 6.2: The mosque on Koh Samui, located in the Hau Thanon area

Plate 6.3: The Hau Thanon fresh market

After the national political reform (see Chapter 5, section 5.3) and the continued growth of the island's urban center, the town shifted from Tambon Namuang to Tambon Ang Tong in 1906 (Rangsiwararuk 2003) (located on the west side of the island, as Nathon (the center of Tambon Ang Tong) which is geographically closer to the mainland (see Plate 6.4).

126

Plate 6.4: The Nathon pier, where the ferry connects to the mainland

Although the town of Koh Samui was still on the west side of the island, Koh Samui retained its livelihood with its main commercial area and its urbanity on this side only until the beginning of its tourism development periods. In other words, by the middle of the island tourism period (the middle of 1990s), tourism activities had shifted the island's commercial area toward Chawang Beach, east side of Koh Samui.

6.4 Development of land market: agriculture turns to tourism

The area where the main cluster of tourism development took place was once an abandoned landscape with no commercial value. Lined with palm trees and giving the impression of a tropical paradise, most of the empty land along beachfronts was not suitable for agriculture due to the poor quality of soil and salt-water contamination of underground water that made the area basically useless. Consequently, these lands were let out or given to unfavorable children (Petkeaw 2003: fieldwork 2005). When outsiders saw the potential of developing these areas for tourism, they approached the landowners and most of it was sold to them. As discussed in Chapter 5, like many other places in Thailand, Koh Samui was once an agriculturally dependent society. At a time when the land was not productive, it was plagued by ownership insecurity. Thus, driven by poverty, many locals sold their un-productive properties to land developers, one after another (see Plate 6.5-6.7).

Plate 6.5: Old houses and land being advertised for sale or lease

Plate 6.6: Land on the hills on Chaweng Beach area has been cleared for development projects.

Plate 6.7: The Koh Samui golf course

Plate 6.5 to Plate 6.7 show that as development increased, Koh Samui's coconut orchards were retired in order to be developed or replaced to address the growth. Moreover, tourism development did not affect only agricultural areas. Along with coconut orchards, local housing had also been eliminated. Chaweng Beach on the east side of Koh Samui, in particular, was not only unsuitable for agriculture due to the poor quality of its soil, but also because the area was most strongly affected by natural conditions and hazards (see Section 6.3). Therefore, most of the area was sold to outside businessmen. Kan, a seventy-eight year old man from Chaweng Beach, who once owned a large section of land, recalled: 'that was the reason I started selling my land: to trade off the unproductive land for, at that time, good money and keep only inner lands that were good for coconut growing'. The unforeseen future development of tourism, at the beginning at least, did not totally benefiting the locals, but created the tourist landscape. This point is further reflected in stories of local people in Lamai Beach area.

6.4.1 Local perspectives

Noy was born on Koh Samui. Her house was located on the main road close to the temple and a local market on Tambon Marat (where Lamai Beach is located, further explain in this chapter). The location was very much a residential area rather than the tourist cluster that the beach area was. She lived with her husband who would spend most of his early time in the field where they planted coconut and durian trees. She stayed home to look after their four children. Her role was similar to other women on Koh Samui in terms of looking after household, children and husband. If her help was required, she would go to help in the field, but mostly she would help when it was time to sell their products on the market. Her children had gone to Bangkok for further education and all decided to stay there permanently. About two decades ago she turned her house into a souvenir shop to accommodate the tourist scene in the area. With tourists exploring the area and not much competition, her shop was doing well. Then, about fifteen years ago, the area started getting more tourists both Thai and international. The road was paved for the expansion of tourism. There were bars, restaurants, a wide range of accommodation facilities and souvenir shops clustered together in the beach area. This began to affect her business as most tourists stayed, shopped and ate near the beach area and thus only sometimes passed by, rarely stopping to shop. She was later approached by a businessman from Bangkok who wanted to purchase her land, but not the place where she stayed. The offer price was far more than she and her husband could imagine getting for a coconut orchard. Coupled with the fact that none of her children were willing to return home, she sold a three *rai* section of her land for about 300,000 *baht*. Nowadays, there is a spa resort on her former land and, even though the land is not directly on the beach, it is already worth millions of *baht* per *rai*.

The story of Noy shows that although she did not receive much benefit from her land from the tourism boom, the land market influenced the growth of tourism activities. Moreover, as a result of the rapid increase in land demand, it is not only land at the beachfront that has long been absorbed by outsiders, but also land further inland as well. Ben, a forty-five year old man, who now runs a small business along the main road in Tambon Marat, shares his story: 'I sold my land of 5 *rai* in the year 2000. I thought only the beachfront area was good for tourism. So when I was approached by someone who wanted to buy my land with that amount, I immediately sold it'. Although some land is still owned by the locals, a lack of capital, irregular crop yields and a slump in crop prices, have resulted in locals felling their plants in preparation of renting the land out to tourism businessmen. This situation is reflected in Don's statement:

In order to develop the land into a competitive tourism business, I would have had to invest a lot of money. For some businessmen, the amount of money might not seem much, but for me it would have been impossible. And most important, I had no one to help since all my kids were studying in Bangkok.

Don is a sixty-two year old landowner on Lamai Beach, who has rented out his land to a businessman from the mainland who runs a resort. He indicated that even though he knew the potential of his land for the tourism industry, lack of access to capital, lack of management skills and manpower were his main obstacles. In other words, the increase in land demand, the uncertainty of the coconut crop, crop price and massive capital investment requirements forced many locals to sell or to rent out their orchards to outside land developers. Cohen (1982; 1996) and Westerhausen (2002) also state that these were the important factors that drove the issue of shifting or sharing landownership among locals and outsiders. Consequently, large numbers of beach front areas and inland lands are managed by outside tourism investors.

The introduction of the land market started as early as in the 1980s when Koh Samui moved from the 'involvement stage' into the 'development stage' of Butler's evolutionary model during the 1990s. The land marketization was one of major features of Koh Samui's touristization process. The island's land ownership transferred to developers or different users by sale or lease. Thus, while the ownership of land remains in locals' hands, it has become a major source of capital generation. The transfer of land-use rights and the infusion of outside capital has become the main impetus for tourism development on the island, both through the conversion of agriculture to tourism land and through the raising of revenue to update tourist facilities.

6.5 Renewed touristization: the enforcement of princes and princesses of Koh Samui

As discussed in Chapter 5, section 5.3, Buddhist educational reforms that inspired the locals to seek higher education in Bangkok, had a strong influence on Koh Samui society. If the older generation on the island did not have the chance to continue their education, they would encourage their children to do so (fieldwork 2005). Every successful Bangkok graduate was the pride of the family and represented elevation to what was traditionally the most highly respected state of being to the people on Koh Samui (Petkaew 2003)[22]. This is particularly true for those who were in the social group of the islands' landowners. The landowners in this discussion were divided into groups according to their economic and social roles. Most of them owned and managed small businesses while others owned slightly larger estates that they would rent out either in part or in their entirety. These landowner/entrepreneurs can be categorized by the size of their businesses – small-scale entrepreneurs who owned shops providing goods and services such as souvenir shops and travel agencies; medium-sized entrepreneurs who owned restaurants, bungalows; and large-scale entrepreneurs who owned resorts. The return of the Bangkok-educated generation to the island affected the face of tourism development. Starting in the early 2000s, many areas of land that had been rented out were reclaimed by this new generation of entrepreneurs. The following presents two new-generation life stories, *Nee* and *Sak*, in order to illustrate how this group of local influenced the touristization process on Koh Samui.

Nee's Story

Nee was born in a relatively wealthy family on Koh Samui. At the age of twenty-seven, upon her return from Bangkok, she took over most of her mother's role in the family business. Her grandparents owned a large amount of land on Koh Samui. While some of the land had been given to other relatives, her parents still owned a significant amount of beachfront property and inland coconut orchards. For her primary schooling, Nee had been educated at the Catholic school on Koh Samui which was mainly attended by the wealthy children of the island. Back then, her family ran a resort on Lamai Beach. In addition to the accommodation facilities of about forty bungalows and a beachfront restaurant, the business included a wide range of tourism-related facilities, such as a laundry service, motorbike rentals, a shuttle service, a tour excursion desk and a foreign exchange service. With not much competition, the family's business was progressing quickly and earning a lot of revenue. Upon finishing primary school, Nee attended a boarding school in Bangkok and later entered a university there. After getting her degree, Nee returned to Koh Samui to work in her family business (see Plate 6.8). Soon after

---

[22] Most houses on Koh Samui, or Thailand generally have pictures of family members in graduation grown hanging on the wall as a source of family pride.

returning, she took over responsibility for most of the business including managing the bungalows and restaurant and dealing with government officials and bank business, all under her parents' supervision.

Plate 6.8: Nee's bungalows – the traditional resort style in the late 1980s and the early 1990s

Nee's childhood friends with whom she socialized had also returned home after completing their education in Bangkok or overseas. They shared a very similar life-style as children and young adults and a similar family background in terms of social stature and financial ability. Interestingly, Nee and her friends enjoyed the urban development of Koh Samui that provided them with a similar standard of facilities as they had been accustomed to in Bangkok. Moreover, Nee and her friends, who had also taken over responsibility for their family businesses, appreciated the economic benefits afforded them by tourism on the island. Their social conversations would generally include a discussion on the direction of tourism development on Koh Samui which helped them to decide what and how their new tourism projects on the island would develop. Specifically, during my stay on the island (2005-2006), Nee was considering replacing her 'traditional tourist style' bungalows (see Plate 6.8) with a modern resort that would cost millions of *baht* (similar to Sak's resort) (see Plate 6.10) to fit into the overall picture of the tourism boom on Koh Samui.

Sak's story

A similar story is that of a thirty-one year old man, Sak, the son of one of Koh Samui's biggest landowners. Sak's family owned a small resort on a big beachfront section in a famous area on the island. After university, Sak returned to Koh Samui and helped in the family business. Recognizing the potential profit from tourism Sak built many small shops for rent on part of his family's beach property. The monthly rental payment he receives from his development project has paid off very well. In addition to the land development, Sak decided to upgrade his family's resort from what his parents' defined as a 'resort'[23] (see Plate 6.9) to one that fits in with modern Koh Samui – a modern and luxurious resort (hotel building, a group of villas, swimming pool and spa service). The redeveloped 'resort' opened for business at the beginning of 2005 (see Plate 6.10).

Plate 6.9: Sak's business, which is a resort in his parents' idea

---

[23] Some accommodations on the island although they are just a simple bungalows with no swimming pool, they still use the word 'resort' as for their names.

Plate 6.10: Sak's resort – recent trends for resorts and spas in the 2000s

At the beginning of 2000s, a spa facility was necessary for a resort or a hotel on Koh Samui to be recognized as a luxury accommodation. Sak, understanding this, added a spa section to the resort renovation plan. Consequently, he invited his friend who was a spa manager of a five star hotel in Bangkok to come to the island and run his spa. His friend accepted the offer and moved to the island. As a result of Sak's commitment of capital investment and quality employees, his spa resort is now ranked as one of the top spa treatment centers on Koh Samui. Indeed, the 'new blood' of local tourism development or the 'princes and princesses' of the local elite (see Chapter 7, section 7.2 on the issue of local elites), who have been mostly educated in Bangkok or overseas, have had a significant influence on the recent renewal of Koh Samui's touristization. Their familiarity with the urbanity, education and capitalism has directly influenced the island's space in various capacities in which tourism activities occur. As this group has a varied entrepreneurial background, they influence a diversity of tourism spaces. In fact, the new generation of island entrepreneurs was heavily involved in the economic development process and played an important role in bringing up local businesses to international standards. In this respect, the group of educated young Thais served as one of the major players in the island's tourism growth, its landscape development and renewal of the island's touristization.

6.6 Touristization on Koh Samui – Lamai Beach case study

One of the most immediately recognizable images of Koh Samui's physical landscape is that of a coconut island. Coconuts were once exported to the mainland as the driving force of the economy on the island (Chapter 5). In the mid-1970s the first Westerners began to come to Koh Samui, hearing about the island paradise mainly through word of mouth. At that time the island had the reputation as being a place away from mainstream tourism where one could live close to nature on a minimal budget (Westerhausen 2002: 189). Since then, Koh Samui has become an established stop on the tourist trail through Asia. The growth of budget tourism on Koh Samui developed along the two most important beachfront areas – Chaweng Beach and Lamai Beach (which located next to Baan Lamai). While Chaweng Beach was developed, mainly by outside investors for up-market tourists, Lamai Beach was developed by locals and lower capital investment which targeted budget travelers. Before the beginning of the tourism era on Lamai Beach, the area was an alien space to locals. The beachfront was mostly used by the fishing community as a way to access the sea to earn a living. Ann, an elderly lady from Baan Lamai remembered that Lamai Beach was quiet back then. She further explained that although the soil was poor, not as good as further inland, it was still covered by coconut palms. This was how she remembers the early stages of tourism development in Lamai Beach. Before the dawn of tourism there was nothing much to do and not many things going on on Lamai Beach. The common scene was fishing boats where the canal reaches the beach. She commented that later on many *farang* spent their days lying on the beach and doing nothing but reading and swimming in the sea.

The increasing number of tourists coming to Koh Samui, including *farang*, was an impetus for the realization of the hidden value of the beachfront area. Tourism statistics show that from 1990 to 1995 the tourist numbers went from 675,413 to 697,457 per year and in 2005 to 823,122 (Tambon Municipality of Koh Samui 2003; Tourism Authority of Thailand 2007). Thus, the beginning of tourist activities on Lamai Beach provided some material rewards from an area which initially only provided limited spatial utilization of agriculture. In that way, it was the new social and spatial relationships that represented the area. Because of the profound land usage changes and an improving value of once valueless land, locals were ready for further tourism development. However, at that time, tourism and the modern tourism style did not impact much on the locals' perceptions of the benefits of tourism development and the spatial usage of landscape. This would appear soon after. When the tourism industry started at Lamai Beach, it was small and only offered a few simple tourist facilities. Characteristically, businesses on Lamai Beach were bungalows which consisted of a row of cabins, each divided into single rooms: "simple huts, built of plaid bamboo walls on a wooden frame and covered by a triangular thatched roof...'(Cohen 1996: 184). The tourism establishments on the beach were owned and operated by locals. There were no more than a few small beach bungalows and restaurants serving backpackers as a means of providing additional income to agriculture (Cohen 1996; Williamson and Hirsch 1996). Lamai Beach was then a relaxed place for budget travelers (see Plate 6.11). Tourism was small and with growth potential.

Plate 6.11: Some of the very first bungalows on Lamai Beach

The infrastructure of services and publication of travel and accommodation guides (such as the Lonely Planet) reinforced the reputation of Koh Samui, focusing on Lamai Beach, as a paradise for young and budget tourists, which saw a highly commercialized form of budgeted tourism activities. The budget tourists' facilities, infrastructure and services developed so much that they stood apart from the neighboring areas. Indeed, the initial differentiation of the perceived value of landscape between leisure (outsiders) and livelihood (locals) increased the value of the agriculturally poor quality landscape.

6.6.1 The characteristics of Lamai Beach

Lamai Beach is part of the sub-district of Tambon Marat and has two main boundaries – Baan Lamai and Lamai Beach. The first boundary, Baan Lamai, is the ring road (*thanon rob koh*) which runs along the old settlement area (see Plate 6.12), Lamai Temple (*Wat* Lamai), Lamai Market (*talad* Lamai), and Lamai School (*rong rean baan* Lamai), whereas the other boundary, called Haad Lamai, stretches along the beach road (*thanon rim haad*).

Plate 6.12: The road in front of the Lamai Temple in Baan Lamai area

The ring road is part of the main road connection that runs around the whole island. The section in Lamai Beach that runs through the old local settlement area is called Baan Lamai. The houses in Baan Lamai are wooden structures built in the style of the traditional local architecture and are neatly situated in rows on either side of the ring road. Increasingly, however, the houses are built using a modern design. The traditional buildings that narrow this section of the road have become an increasing traffic hazard. Baan Lamai used to be a heterogeneous area for everyday business – shops, market, petrol and other facilities, which served as a local hub for meeting and exchange for local consumables. Nowadays, the township increasingly serves tourists. It is important to note that this research focuses on Haad Lamai boundary (the beach road area). In other words, Lamai Beach in this research refers to the beach road area, an area about two kilometers long, can be easily explored by foot.

6.6.2 Lamai Beach touristization process

The strong pull of Koh Samui's natural beachfront drew more tourists into the area and ensured that side incomes through tourism became the primary income for many people. The favorable conjunction of circumstances in Lamai Beach (Haad Lamai area) at that time led to the multiplication of tourism activities and growth of tourism investments that caused competition among tourism businesses, leading to increasing conflict and a demand for continued improvement and extension of existing activities.

The 1980s

In the 1980s, because of the continued effect of touristic values and the increasing number of tourists and their demand for better services and facilities, many business owners obliged and improved their existing bungalows. The necessity of having accommodation in resort-type designs initiated an appreciation of a more private, comfortable way of living that reflected the urban life of the period and was a step towards 'modernity'. The common products that were offered to tourists required new forms of businesses including bars, discotheques, daily shops, travel services, tailor shops, souvenir shops, currency exchanges, and restaurants. To add more of a competitive edge among businesses, evening entertainment in the form of videos was arranged in some restaurants. The challenge became more and more intense as the beach area opened to wider competition. For most of the local tourism businesses on Lamai Beach, it was the first time that they had business competition (at the 'involvement stage' of the Butler's evolutionary model). The opportunities for relatively unskilled business operators to rise higher within the tourism environment in comparison to the traditional agricultural circumstances were beyond comprehension for many. This unyielding escalator of material prosperity was not achieved without considerable adjustments to working attitudes amongst local landowners. It was one thing to adapt to a structure of land ownership and another to deal with a situation where rewards could be easily achieved. In this respect and to comprehend the massive self-transformation from being an agrarian to being a businessman, an increasing number of beachfront areas were leased out or sold partly to outsiders. Consequently, at this time, beside national and local governments' investments on infrastructure such as improved transportation, and basic infrastructure to create the potential of tourism growth (Tourism Authority of Thailand 1985; see Chapter 5, section 5.7), there were some additional private investments from both Koh Samui and off-island to address the growth of tourism. Indeed, fighting the tourism battle resulted in land marketization (see Section 6.4), along with absentee landowners along Lamai Beach and ultimately to the expansion of the Lamai Beach tourist landscape. However, it is important to note that, as the pattern of Koh Samui's settlement, Baan Lamai was different to the Chaweng Beach area. The leased out or sold land sections were too small for multinational tourism projects. Although the land was developed extensively, it was mostly within local or national standards. Thus, the structural relationships among locals – partly businessmen and agrarians – the beachfront, tourism production, tourists and outside investors were essentially the beginning of the large scale of tourism development. During this development stage unproductive agricultural land was successfully converted into tourist landscapes in every aspect of tourism – both activity and attitude. This characterization of the area was the beginning of modernity, shifting the spirits of Lamai Beach.

The 1990s

The 1990s showed a turnaround in the tourism development of Lamai Beach. It was symbolized by the significance of the tourism economy on the island; the shared and changed attitudes of landowners; the inflowing population in search of tourism employment; the rising of new types of tourist activities under more innovative and commercially minded owners; the improvement of communication and the facilitation of the tourism industry through a new ferry route, sealed roads and the new airport; and the growing connection to the mainland which had previously caused accessibility issues. All of these processes contributed to the general turnaround and spectacular touristization of Lamai Beach (coming in at 'development stage' of Butler's evolutionary model). In the turnaround period, the improved facilities and growth of tourism, coupled with the continued romantic appeal of a 'paradise', attracted an increasingly prosperous clientele to Koh Samui. Following the pattern of touristization of tourist destinations (Young 1983), the development of the beachfront was a product of the acceleration in the tourism industrialization of the landscape and the disappearance of the natural traditional look. This touristic landscape was colonized by up and coming groups of small entrepreneurs who provided 'resort'-style accommodations, travel agencies, souvenir shops, accessories shops and, along with Thai restaurants, a wide variety of international food and bars. The growth of land usage on Lamai Beach resulted in the development of a tourism-urbane townscape, which was centered on tourism service. By then, the island received growing investments from both national and local governments to keep up with tourism competition with other destinations (Tambon Municipality of Koh Samui 2003). Such growing investments, particularly from the local perspective, for expanding the existing businesses were all prevalent. There were also some small scales foreign investments in forms of girlie-bars that resulted in a larger presence of women on the island (further discuss in Chapter 8). Undoubtedly, at this time, tourism businesses were the dominant feature in the area.

The 2000s

The growth of the tourism industry on Lamai Beach in the early 2000s required cultural and economical innovations. The business of tourism was in relatively high demand and the up-market demand required more entrepreneurial spirit (at 'development stage' of Butler's evolutionary model). The stronger need for quality labor and the desire for a higher standard of material comfort for the new tourists were necessary to ensure a competitive advantage, particularly given the international standardization on Chaweng Beach. The decision of the local businesses to reach international standardization competitiveness was made to reposition the tourism space to achieve rapid economic development. Some local businessmen leased out their lands for longer periods to allow developers to invest more capital. However, as discussed earlier in this chapter, when they had urban educated children who returned to the island, some took back the ownership after the end of the leasing contract. Such new management of tourism businesses brought about changes to the tourism space in Lamai Beach. The combination of landownership, parents' commercial credit and a new vision of tourism growth and competitiveness encouraged newly structured tourism facilities in the area (see Plate 6.13). Consequently, there were massive investments in the already existing tourism spaces, which resulted in expanding, upgrading and restructuring as a means for local business owners to reposition and reassert themselves in the competitive environment of the tourism economy. Furthermore, there were also large amounts of foreign investments in luxury type of accommodation such as Marriot, Beach Republic, Banyan Tree, and Sheraton, for example. This addressed the changing demands that came with significant growth of tourism development on Koh Samui. As such, the competition was featured in the development of multi million *baht*-projects and of signature style buildings.

Plate 6.13 – A local tourism business in the face of global competitiveness

6.6.3 Mapping survey on Lamai Beach touristization

The transformation of land use on Lamai Beach over the past thirty years has followed a path that began with land that was valueless to highly commercialized land use for tourism production. The tourist-oriented landscape along the beach was represented as an alien intrusion into the traditional settlement pattern – a lessening of social distinctions between the livelihood setting and touristic area. In other words, as discussed in Section 6.3, the beach area was a cultural product of the Thai settlement pattern, which was encouraged through dynamic and unfettered tourism development. Moreover, in order to understand the development of tourism on Koh Samui, we need to look at the changes to the island in the period since the late 1970s within the wider context of the political landscape of tourism urbanization. To demonstrate the character of Koh Samui's touristic transformation, Lamai Beach is used as a representative model of the island's changing landscape. The process of the beach's transformation into a tourist destination will be analyzed – specifically how the changes in the area and among the population affected the development of new patterns (see Plates 6.14-6.16).

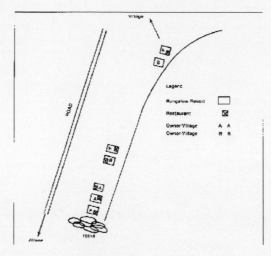

Plate 6.14: Lamai Beach touristic area in the late 1970s (source Cohen 1996)

Plate 6.15: Lamai Beach touristic area in 1994 (the black block is the coconut orchard)

-Blue color represents Accommodation
Pink color represents girlie bars
The black block is coconut orchard
Other color represents small tourism business activities such as
restaurant, touring, bank, souvenir shop, internet cafe, laundry.

Plate 6.16: Lamai Beach touristic area in 2007

Aerial military images of Koh Samui from the Royal Thai Survey Department, the Ministry of Defense coupled with Cohen (1996)'s initial sketch of Lamai Beach (Plates 6.14-6.16) indicate that the prodigious growth of Lamai Beach makes it a unique place. This is reflected in how the once valueless traditional Thai settlement has become a distinctive tourism urbanity space. The settlement process on Lamai Beach encouraged the initial growth of tourism development as the prime catalyst of economic growth. Land marketization sped up the transformation while the new modern educated generation facilitated the upgrading of local businesses to international standards. In essence, the development of the island was derived from an axiomatic relationship between the failure of agricultural quality and the rise of a flourishing tourism imaginary. It is the creation of a purpose-built touristic place for its own initial benefits without the possible clashing of the social and environmental tensions that would affect the industrial touristization of the beach. Therefore, dynamic well-to-do tourism businesses have become the driving force for the alternative proliferation of capital and landscape in the seaside areas.

6.6.4 Renting verses owning

This section will explain the process of changing the ownership on Koh Samui, particularly on Lamai Beach. Initially, data was gathered along with the mapping survey presented in Plate 6.16. However, because I encountered many foreigners who were managing tourism business illegally (based on Thai laws which dictate who can own land and what business foreigners can engage in, in Thailand), there were commercially sensitive and privacy reasons which precluded my asking about the ownership of these tourism businesses. Consequently, rather than presenting an exact number of outsider or foreigner-owned businesses, this section discusses tourism business ownership in an aggregate form.

The transformation of Koh Samui during the second stage of the era of mass tourism, the mid 1990s onwards, was different from the changes observed during the first stage – in the late 1980s to the early 1990s. In the first stage, although the tourism industry was heavily developed, it was developed only in a limited and temporary way. This was mainly because land ownership and business management was still in local hands (Cohen 1996: Willamson and Hirsch 1996). During the first stage of tourism development on the island, proprietors of the local businesses were mostly first-time business owners who had previously worked in agriculture (involvement stage of Butler's lifecycle). Others were business owners who upgraded existing bungalows with the aim of developing them into resorts. Tourism related businesses, beyond restaurants, were mostly restricted to souvenir shops, dive shops, car and motorbike rental shops, travel agencies and grocery stores, all on a relatively small scale. The second stage, from the mid-1990s to the time of my fieldwork during 2005-2007, saw a significant change from an island of resorts and small businesses into a resort, spa and international-standard business island. Many of the locals had given up their land, as they had either been unable to compete with other businesses or had preferred to sell their land for a big sum of money (Westerhausen 2002; Cohen1996; Williamson and Hirsch 1996). However, in some areas, Lamai Beach in particular, local landowners realized the huge potential of tourism. Consequently, instead of direct land sales, local people preferred to either lease their land or enter into joint ventures with outsiders (either Thais or *farangs*). Clearly, judging from the Plates 6.14- 6.16 of Lamai Beach, there has been significant growth in tourism business there. In the late 1970s, tourism facilities in the area were limited to seven bungalow resorts and six restaurants.

Within the last three decades, the number of tourist activities has raised dramatically (compared Plate 6.14 and 6.16). Beyond basic bungalows and simple restaurants, there are far more sophisticated tourist activities, including travel agencies, proper laundry shops, souvenir shops, supermarkets, bars and discotheques, foreign owned restaurants with international foods, along with more varied forms of accommodations.

By 2007, most tourist activities had been upgraded, changed ownership and received additional investment capital. This was particularly true of some types of accommodations that had been upgraded by the local new generation who had returned to the island after being educated in Bangkok or overseas (see Section 6.5). Many local businesses have now spilt their property into small shops that they rented out[24], making it easier for them to manage. As a result, there were more small businessmen launching tourism businesses in the form of travel agencies, laundry shops, souvenir shops and bars. Most of these small tourism businesses either belonged to outsiders or both Thais and foreigners, for example, almost every bar in the area is owned by a Thai lady who has a *farang* boyfriend (see Chapter 8). Koh Samui locals mostly own tour counters and internet cafes while souvenir shops mostly belong to the same owner or their relatives from Northeastern Thailand. Grocery stores, such as 7-11 and Family mart, are franchise branded. Therefore, on Lamai Beach most of the properties are still in the hands of locals, but tourism businesses are operated by outsiders, either Thais or *farangs*. In other words, outsiders own tourism activities, with the local people functioning as landlord.

6.7 Summary

Of the many changes occurring on Koh Samui, the transformation of the low quality beach into a highly touristic space is possibly the most evident sign of Koh Samui's 'urbanization' – a form of the island's modernization process. The beach area, traditionally associated with low-value agricultural production, now evokes the image of a hot bed of tourism activities. Tourism development, which has become a major force of change in the past thirty years, has literally reshaped the landscape of Koh Samui's two distinct geographical regions: the beachfront area and inner agricultural farmland. The beachfront area ensured future security and provided direct and indirect personal income

---

[24] In the beginning of 2009 there were increasing numbers of bungalows turned into small shops for rent.

through tourism business activities. It offered a new type of constructed tourism space and a centre of activity. It also had attracted a flood of investments and businesses along with visitors and a new wave of tourism immigrants. The geographical features of Lamai Beach are illustrated in the different tourism activities, and particularly in the way the growth in and around the beach area have influenced and expanded the local urbanity. These new spaces have given new meaning to the touristic transformation. Indeed, the area is a collection of tourism activities with their own histories and characters. These unique transformations of Lamai Beach directed and increased the desire for growth of tourism development. Local residential land ownership and the changing dynamics of tourism facilities were the key influences on the ensuring tourism patterns and land transformation. Tourism transformed the beach into a place with an international tourist culture and a social life of its own, which was characterized by tourism standardization and commercialization (similar to Pattaya and Phuket). This progress in the region facilitated the development of urbanization, tourism industrialization and service commercialization.

The increasing size and complex organization of the leisure and service industries at expanding tourist areas made it inevitable that there would be a general tendency towards a functional differentiation between residential (Bann Lamai) and tourist areas (Lamai Beach). Since rapid development of Lamai Beach commenced, the area has created its own complex, self-sufficient tourist and tourism-related business district. In beach front areas, the contradiction of local history and ecology of settlement and the modern tourism establishment can clearly be seen. While recognizing the importance of the economic restructuring of tourism in areas that have previously been defined as non-touristic land, this chapter was mainly concerned with emphasizing the repositioning of the landscape of Koh Samui that occurred as a consequence of economic restructuring. The chapter also focused on the creation of a touristic landscape in which territorial place is occurring. The forces that drive this process were analysed and inter-related throughout the chapter, instead of limiting the discussion to the transformation of the touristization process. This chapter discussed the transformation process as one of the most important processes shaping the physical landscape of Koh Samui – if not even the most significant. The manner in which the settlement pattern was involved in the tourist landscape formation, shaping the space of Koh Samui through changes in traditional land use, land stature and land value were all examined. The process of land acquisition is central to the creation of a tourist landscape and is often characterized by conflicting claims on land that are a cause of much competition. Within the broader spaces of a transforming Koh Samui, space and tourist landscape have been reproduced through the continued consumption and production of the tourism industry. As this chapter argues, new generation local entrepreneurs are the major drivers of tourism-urbanism growth and transformation of the tourism facilities. Thus, the next chapter will exemplify the implications of tourism on the social transformation of Koh Samui by discussing the economic changes that have had consequences for both the social and political configurations of the island.

CHAPTER 7

THE TOURISM ECONOMY AND KOH SAMUI'S SOCIAL LANDSCAPE

7.1 Introduction

Chapter 6 observed that in the last thirty years Koh Samui has witnessed profound landscape transformations because of tourism development. The island has shifted from having coconut orchards to hotels, bars, restaurants, shops and a myriad of other tourism services. This new phase is characterized by an ever-extending tourism-urban landscape. Consequently, Koh Samui nowadays enjoys a reputation of fabulous wealth, similar to other international tourist destinations around the world. Before the tourism period (prior 1970s), the region, which was seen as being on the 'periphery' of Thailand's political history, has in recent decades undergone a fundamental transformation. Today it is one of the main 'centers' of the Thailand's national economic income generation (see Chapter 5).

Since the colonialism period of the nineteenth century, and despite its isolated location, the local culture of Koh Samui has traditionally been in harmony with the cultural identity of the nation. With that in mind, the social make-up of Koh Samui can best be understood as being a particular variant of a common Thai phenomenon (see Chapter 5, section 5.3), the move towards modernity. This phenomenon resulted in the island exercising its cultural landscape as what Peleggi (2007: 47-56) categorized as 'peasant culture', which implied that the residents chose to live in rural communities. Although the power of the center grew and resulted in the primary form of identity on the island (Poole 1999 cited in Reynolds 2006: 247), the tourism industry (like globalization in other regions) affected the social and cultural landscapes of Koh Samui significantly.

Other regions of Thailand, particularly in the North and Northeast, have long been prominent research sites for both Thai and foreign scholars of development, the flow of capitalism and the issue of migration (see e.g. Krongkaew 1995; Limanonda 1995; Mills 1995; 1999; Molle and Srijantr 2003a; Morris 2000; Mulder 2000; Panya 1995; Phongphit and Hewison 2001; Somswasdi and Theobald 1997; Tanabe and Keyes 2002b; Van Esterik 2000). Only a few research studies have paid attention to the broader significance of Koh Samui society (notable exemptions are Cohen 1996; Green 2005; Petkaew 2003, amongst others). Many research studies that focus on the people, livelihood and society of tourist destinations suggest that the life of the locals is shaped largely by host-guest relations (Cohen 1996; Macleod 2004; Maitheson and Wall 1982; Stonich 2000; Tucker 2003; Waldren 1996). The focus on everyday life of locals, which is a complex web of associations and meanings, has traditionally been a focal point for analyses in these research studies.

The nature of the economic, political and social relations created by capitalist tourism has been at the center of these analyses. Accordingly, this chapter illustrates how the tourism economy has shaped the social landscape of Koh Samui. In the following sections, a concise outline of that process is presented. It should be noted that while the economic development of tourism is outlined in this chapter, the focus is on the people and their representation on the island during the tourism development period. For the purposes of this thesis, it may be assumed that the economic changes have had consequences for both the social and political configurations of the island. Therefore, some statements that have been made are based on a comparison of a variety of groups, some of whom occupied the island in the past and some who occupy it presently. Thus, the objective of this chapter is to exemplify the social transformation of the island.

7.2 The economy in old times: the creation of local elites

After the country's reformation in the reign of Rama V (King Chulalongkorn (1868-1910), Koh Samui entered the stage of economic and cultural restoration and development. Land reform encouraged a tendency towards agriculture on the island (Chapter 5). Although the land on Koh Samui is not as well suited for agriculture as some other regions of Thailand, (the central plain in particular) it was gradually developed as an agricultural area characterized by self-sufficiency and small agricultural productions run by peasant households (Cohen 1996). Furthermore, Koh Samui was marked by ethnic variety and diverse settlements. The Muslim Thais of the island, descendents from Muslims of Pattani (the most southern province of Thailand) for instance, have lived on the island since the Siam political reformation at the end of the nineteenth century (Southern Thailand Cultural Encyclopedias 1986). The Muslims settled mostly on the corner of Hau Thanon Market, working as fishermen who have supplied products to the island communities for generations. Chinese immigrants, who were free of the Sakdina System (Skinner 1957) and originally came to the island to work in a tin mine, later became traders who operated small shops around the Hau Thanon area. Through expanding trade with the center, the Chinese significantly controlled the island economy and later, through land marketing, owned major sections of land (see Chapter 6; Petkaew 2003). The Chinese on Koh Samui who have assimilated the Thai culture and way of life and who consider themselves more Thai than Chinese differ from the Chinese in Malaysia who put a strong emphasis on being Chinese Malay. In other words, as a result of their assimilation to being 'Thai' during Thailand's modernization process (see Chapter 5, section 5.2), the feeling of being Chinese began to fade and is now not as strong as it is to those Chinese who live in Malaysia (Fadzillah 2004). Consequently, these Chinese are now local Koh Samui residents who still play an important role in the Koh Samui economy in the form of businesses and land ownership and are providers of tourist activities.

Agricultural development contributed to the early political stability of Koh Samui and drove progress in many ways. There were only a small number of educated ethnic Thai involved in the local politics. In those days, it was the custom that land remained in the possession of the person who first cleared it and was thereafter passed to his descendants (see e.g. Ekachai 1990; Molle and Srijantr 2003a; Panya 1995; Parnwell 1996; Phongphit and Hewison 2001). This practice was a huge benefit to a small group of local bureaucrats and ruling families who, because of having free labor at their disposal, were able to take possession of a relatively large amount of land. After the Second World War, Thai peasants were directed by the government's policies through national economic development plans to produce cash crops. Moreover, Thailand's enforcement of many policies, including a guarantee of land ownership for peasants, encouraged the development of agricultural production (Baker and Phongpaichit 2005; Molle and Srijantr 2003a; Panya 1995; Peleggi 2007; Phongpaichit and Baker 1996; Sithiratbut 1983). Consequently, many regions were radically transformed from a self-sufficient subsistence economy to a market-based economy. Under the national economic integration process of the 1950s, the island experienced its first wave of economic capacity. The development of agriculture, the essential element of the local economy of Koh Samui, exerted a strong effect on the scale and speed of the economic development of the island in general: the island became a mass producer of coconuts (Jarujitiphan 1993; Petkaew 2003; Wisansing 2004). After receiving land, the governments' guarantee of land ownership added to the peasants' enthusiasm and created favorable conditions for productivity. However, improvement in agricultural conditions and the implementation of new technology resulted in a more intensive type of agriculture. The method of shifting cultivation originally practiced, required an availability of large areas of cultivable land (Molle and Srijantr 2003a). This resulted in a growing imbalance between the smaller coconut plantation owners and those who owned massive coconut orchards. Those who owned these immense plantations enjoyed relative prosperity because of the national demand for coconut during that time (Wisansing 2004). At the time, hostilities appeared in the agriculture and production development industry as some peasant households faced the need for an increase in capital requirements and more experience in order to cope with the production of the new agricultural commodities. Following land reform, a division and separation appeared between successful households and those households facing financial difficulties. As a result, those with financial problems were obliged to sell their land or be trapped by their debts (Petkaew 2003).

Similar to other regions in Thailand, when family farmland was divided among family members, the sections were too small for agricultural activities in such competitive environment (Ekachai 1990; Molle and Srijantr 2003a; Panya 1995; Parnwell 1996; Phongphit and Hewison 2001). Therefore, many families had little to gain from coconut capitalism, except of being able to work on coconut plantations. Thus, only some locals remained on the island, holding small farmland or on a daily wage basis (fieldwork 2005; Petkaew 2003). Responding to increased economic capitalism and the ever prevalent need for commercial goods, coupled with the difficulty of living in such a remote area, many families abandoned the island and migrated to the mainland. Most went to Chompon province to work on clearing the land where coconut gardens and coffee plantations would be established. Others, who felt negatively about their agricultural past, moved out of the agricultural sector and migrated to other areas, Bangkok in particular, to work in the industrial sector where they expected to get a higher and more stable income from wage-employment. This is similar to what Cohen (1996) observed;

152

The island is much less incorporated into the national society than Phuket. A prevailing conservative attitude, combined with meager natural resources and remoteness from the mainland, limit the possibilities for economic development. Many members of the younger generation migrated to the mainland, especially to Bangkok, in search of employment.

Some locals who continued to live on the island were increasingly hindered by the limited availability of land, uncertainty of coconut prices and limited government positions (Petkaew 2003). Those locals, who owned a lot of land, felt a newfound enthusiasm as they were mainly impacted in positive ways. They were able to provide a higher quality education for their children, who in turn would be in a better position to qualify for those few available government positions. Although a formal school for both male and female students was built on the island around 1910 (Petkaew 2003), local people preferred to send their children to receive a *better* education or training in Bangkok[25]. This preference for a 'Bangkok' education was based on an image of Bangkok as being 'better' in almost every aspect of modern life (Askew 2002). This picture included the sophisticated bureaucratic images of Bangkok presented through the stereotypical educational system by sending local scholars to Bangkok for training at *Makarmakut* Academy at the beginning of Thailand's educational reforms. Such perception was also because the central Thai dialect is the standard for modern education. Thus, Bangkok was perceived as the centre of *thansamai* (civilization), and therefore gave people the perception that Bangkok was a better place for education.

Because parents did not want their children to be farmers or fishermen like their ancestors and because they believed that a Bangkok education would give their children better opportunities in life, the tradition was that every child born there should study in Bangkok. This was especially favored by the local Chinese and those large landowners who valued business and social skills (fieldwork 2005). Over time, the combination of the improving economic situation of the rich landowners on the island and the migration of small landowners to the mainland resulted in a higher rate of land ownership among a few elite locals who were primarily involved in local politics and governmental administration (Rangsiwararuk 2003)[26]. On Koh Samui, the group that received an early education and

---

[25] One of my informants points out that Bangkok is perceived as having a better education system.
[26] Asia Magazine (Vol. 1 no. 23, 1989: 2 cited Westerhausen 2002: 193) notes that 'All the land on the island was owned by only seven family groups'. Although my informants did not confirm with exactly number as

were connected to national politics became the economically and socially privileged. This, along with the successful development of agricultural productions, created a stratum of rich local elites that in turn resulted in a fast change of Koh Samui's political, cultural and social landscapes. In addition, this 'local elite' became increasingly connected to the broader changes that affected the transformation of the island, and particularly its touristization (discussed in Chapter 6). Thus, the elites were the ones responsible – for the most part – for the tourism growth on the island – the ones that owned the very first group of tourism facilities, the ones that promoted the land marketization during the tourism period and the ones with the new generation responsible for renewal of the island's touristization.

7.3 Economics in the tourism era: emergence of a new middle class

Prospects for a better standard of living seemed to improve from the 1980s onwards. The key word for the economic turnover was tourism – which promised higher returns on land use than agriculture. Thus tourism development investors have played a very important part in the transformation of the island landscapes. In this respect, tourism on Koh Samui represents both an important agent of and a response to change on the island. It was a form of adaptive economical activities for people on Koh Samui, for both locals and outsiders. As discussed in Chapter 6, the island's economy improved significantly through land speculation and the construction and development of tourist related buildings and activities. No one could have predicted that the new economic generator would have such consequences, as the composition of landscape and the local attitude suited the international growth of tourism perfectly. This resulted in more than 14,405 rooms for tourists having been built on Koh Samui over its tourism period (Tourism Authority of Thailand 2007). In addition, tourism required massive land sections along beachfront areas to fulfill tourism amenities. These were easily found and absorbed on Koh Samui (see Chapter 6). Consequently, almost everyone on the island engaged in tourism one way or another as part of the new commercial product. Although agriculture has a long history of being the main source of income for people on the island, once tourism was introduced, the idea of a new form of cash flow that required less skill and

seven families, most of them agreed with the fact that only a few family owned most of land on Koh Samui during the beginning of Thailand modernization processes (nineteenth century).

had only a short waiting period before profit realization was readily embraced. In comparison, agricultural producers had to wait for the harvest season to get their income, which resulted in the islanders welcoming the change that tourism brought. To supplement their income, owners of coconut plantations began working in the island's tourism businesses. In time, when their coconut orchards were not productive, this changed and the tourism business became their main source of income. As one local resident highlighted;

> Tourism is easier to start and take care of than plants. It does not need any chemical pesticides and a middleman to control the products. The money is fast, I can collect it immediately from *farangs*. This was unlike coconuts that I had to wait for some time after planting before I could sell them and let alone pray that the harvesting would not go wrong. (Ton)

Another local man who turned his plantation into rooms for tourism workers emphasized how much he enjoys working in the tourism industry;

> I think doing what I am doing now is good. Having rooms for rent for those who are working in hotels is easier for me to look after. As long as those hotels still have workers, I still have people to stay in my places. I do not have to worry much if the rooms are not fully occupied. Unlike those crops that I used to do have, besides relying on so many pesticides, fertilizers and time, they were easily getting spoiled, if I could not sell them on time. (Aem)

In addition, tourism employment is perceived as a job that puts less pressure on life when compared with agricultural work. This is reflected in the statement by Ferm, a man at Chaweng Beach, who commented on his work as a waiter in an international hotel chain;

> I was at the hotel about 9 hours a day, but normally I would not come back immediately after finishing work. I have friends from the work place to hang out with – drinking and playing. I am so free and do not need to worry about anything after finishing the daily work. Unlike my father who had to look after our orchards and kept on worrying about everything until the coconuts were sold. I think my life is much easier than my father's. (Ferm)

A young man with a university degree also concedes how attractive tourism employment is:

> I don't have to worry much about my career. I could get a job easily. There are plenty of jobs on Koh Samui. The job is good and fun. There are so many people around me, both workers and tourists. I also can have a good time with my friends after the work and sometimes with the customers. Although the work is sometimes hard and customers can be problematic, the circumstances are not directly pressuring me. It is different to the work on the farm. I was alone and carried all the pressure myself. (Kak)

Furthermore, the tourism industry provided new job possibilities for the islanders and other immigrants.

> There are lots of things to turn into money here. I have worked as a waiter in restaurants for almost 15 years. So I have known many *farangs* who have come back almost every year. They need my help when it comes to dealing with local businesses. Many of them now have houses on the island. So I get paid to help them to maintain their houses. Now I am matching local landowners and potential land buyers, mostly *farangs*. If the mission is completed, I would get at least 3% of the land price. Nowadays land is worth millions per *rai* on this island. (Bon)

The above is a statement of Bon, a 37-year old man who works in a restaurant in Lamai Beach and at the same time acts as a middleman for real estate sales. Despite his landless state, he considers himself lucky compared to other people on the mainland. He can do many jobs and earns a lot of income without leaving the island, while many people on the mainland have to leave their homes in search of jobs in Bangkok. The island's touristization prompted people's adaptation skills to the changing economic environment. Moreover, the increasing competitiveness forced many owners to become more entrepreneurial and to invest more capital into upgrading facilities. Given the expansion of services because of the rapid growth of tourists on the island, tourism has brought prosperity to Koh Samui. Thus, large-scale investment increased employment opportunities in the area. This circumstance invited people to come to Koh Samui for increasing tourism employment opportunities. It also attracted locals to return home, especially those who originally left the island for educational purposes. The catalyst that brought the urban educated people to Koh Samui was the local prosperity that was a result of the great economic boom on the island (Chapter 6).

The enthusiasm for a specialized Bangkok education had manifold implications for the social life on Koh Samui. Thus, modernized education, capital and vision all influenced the direction of Koh Samui's development. Such urban flavor allowed locals to identify themselves with Bangkok urbanity – the love of *thansamai* (being modern) (see Van Esterik 2000). The result of the differentiation between place of birth and place of education became a symbol of success and intelligence, and as well as a synonym for a modern urban mentality. Therefore, the beginning of the 2000s was arguably the beginning of Koh Samui's social reformation. It was the period of the internationalization of tourism, localism and the creation of a new middle class on the island. The economic boom of Koh Samui throughout its tourism development encouraged the transformation of life and the appearance of the island's new social landscape. Accordingly, the economic boom has become associated with an improved status of people, which has resulted in a new social identification of the island. In this respect, the boom prompted the rise of a new middle class that, following in the footsteps of the country's capital city, encouraged modern lifestyles on Koh Samui by adopting the status symbols of Bangkok's lifestyle. Indeed, the eventual outcome of the financial flourish was the ascendancy of a new kind of middle class in the new generation of both 'local elites' and urban tourism entrepreneurs, the very embodiment of urbanization. In fact, the new middle class, the 'princes and princesses' (Chapter 6) of the island, emerged from the transformation of the 'local elite' of previous generations through the tourism development process.

7.4 Tourism entrepreneurs

This section discusses how tourism has moved people out of the traditional circle of the agriculture-based social class and given them a new social identification. The men and women of Koh Samui who are discussed in this section belong to the Thai ethnic group and come from different regions of Thailand, including those of Koh Samui origin. As such, the following depiction of their personal traits and activities is intended to express the various roles that tourism plays in their respective occupations as well as their social identification.

Jit

Jit, who is thirty-two years old, comes from a typical Northern Thailand agrarian family – in other words, poverty and hardship. She came to Koh Samui with her friends when she was twenty. At first, she worked as a waitress in a small restaurant in a busy spot on Koh Samui. After gaining more confidence in the job, she moved to work in a chain hotel in the same position. Although the new job was much harder with higher expectations, she was happy with her co-workers and the workplace as she worked under the work system hierarchy, which was more comfortable than working under an owner's pressure. Most importantly, the job included free accommodation and meals. With higher pay and tips from up-market customers, at the age of 23, she earned enough to free her family from hardship. Jit met her husband, who came from the same Northern Province, when he was working as a waiter at the same hotel. They traveled back to their hometown for the wedding ceremony. Soon after Jit had her first and only child, she and her husband left their jobs to open their own small food stall. While the location was a bit out of a tourist area, it was in a Thai tourist worker zone so the rent was affordable and the place was big enough for the whole family to stay in. Although the income was not as predictable as working in a hotel, Jit believed that she could earn more than the relatively fixed salary she had received at the hotel, and more importantly, she could look after her child while she worked. Jit would get up around six o'clock in the morning to go to the market. She would prepare the family breakfast around eight o'clock. After breakfast, she washed the family clothes, did the dishes and cleaned up the place. While she was away at the market, preparing food and doing the household jobs, she would put her child in the baby cradle and her husband looked after him.

Her shop mainly served Thai customers, most of whom worked in tourism related businesses. Although the island's low season affected many businesses, it had an insignificant impact on her shop since most of the tourism businesses had to have workers regardless of the occupancy rate. While owning a small food stall was economically significant for her family, it also had its drawbacks. For example, when Jit and her husband worked for the hotel, they received a paid vacation and were able to return home for a holiday. However, now that she owned her own shop, if she closed it for vacation, it would affect her income. Working every day, she sometimes lost track of time. She often forgot special Buddhist days that resulted in her rarely going to the temple even on religious festival days. In addition, Jit regretted that her child was not able to speak the northern dialect. She used her own dialect when speaking with her husband, but spoke the central Thai dialect to her child. At the time of this fieldwork, her child was six years old and going to a local school in the community. The child spoke Thai with a mix of accents, central, north and south dialects. Jit hoped that she and her child could go back to her hometown so that her son could at least attend high school there. She wanted to have the opportunity to reconnect with her roots and to teach her son about her culture. The problem is she did not know what she could do for a living if she went back to her hometown.

Pong

Pong, who was originally from Northeast Thailand, had been on the island for seventeen years and was 43 years old at the time of research. His wife joined him about seven years before. He was a food vendor on the island. When he first came to the island, he worked at a construction site with other people from his village. After he completed his contract, he became a food seller on a beach where he carried his food so he did not have to pay rent. With only a little competition and low investment, his profit was significant. His wife was at home in the northeast bringing up their sons. Although the family's income from their rice farm was not enough to live on, the money he sent home from Koh Samui was more than his wife could imagine. As soon as his youngest son entered primary school, his wife came to Koh Samui to work with him. Koh Samui, to her, appeared to provide better economic opportunities. Pong and his wife rented a small piece of land and built a small shelter with other people, mostly from their home region. Every day, the wife would get up around 6 o'clock in the morning to go to the market with him. They would buy all the ingredients that they needed for the day. The wife then prepared meals for both of them, while Pong prepared the food to sell, which included cut papayas and marinated chicken. Pong and his wife went to trade their products on the beach in the afternoon. They would carry and sell their food, which consisted of a Northeastern cuisine such as *som tum* and *kai yang*[27], by going from tourist to tourist along the beach. Since their customers were visitors who were mainly sunbathing on the beach, their trading activity ended before sunset. After that Pong and his wife would return to their house, bathe and head to their jobs as kitchen assistants in different restaurants. They would work then from six o'clock until eleven o'clock, sometimes until about midnight. The long hours were paid generously and as a result they were able to retain their parents' rice field and buy new land.

Six years later, after their youngest son had finished primary school, they brought all their children to stay with them on Koh Samui. The youngest one started junior high school at a local school on Koh Samui. The older son who had already finished his high school diploma started working in a bar and restaurant as a kitchen hand. Everyone's work progressed. However, in 2005, they all decided to quit their jobs and rent a place where they built a small food shop. Pong started their rice and noodle business with money they had saved from everyone's work. The shop was a little bit far from the tourist area, but well supported by local customers. People would stop for lunch, dinner and late meals after work. It turned out to be a good spot for tourism workers as well as bargirls. The shop was also frequented by budget tourists. Nowadays, Pong's wife gets up around 6 o'clock to prepare breakfast for everyone and help the son to get ready for school. Then she does the housework including cleaning the house and washing everyone's laundry. The eldest son goes to the market by motorbike, while Pong socializes with the neighbors. The oldest son, with the help of Pong, opens the shop and arranges everything for the daily activities. The shop is open from around 11 o'clock in the morning to midnight and the eldest son is the main cook in the shop. Everyone has dinner together at the shop. Pong and his wife normally help their son at the food stall until it closes. Even though their income is less than before, Pong recognizes that his family's life is much better. They are happy with the fact that they have all stayed together, and, because their house is located among houses of people from the same region in Northeast Thailand, their neighborhood carries on their regional culture. In other words, it is like a small northeastern diaspora on Koh Samui.

---

[27] Som tum is a spicy papaya salad and kai yang is barbeque chicken. It is a popular food in Thailand for the idea of Thai's holidays. In other words, most tourist destinations, particularly for Thai tourists, always have shops to sell this kind of salad, including barbeque chicken and spicy meat salad for example.

Joy

Joy, who was twenty-four years old at the time of this research, was a tourism entrepreneur on Koh Samui. She had married her schoolmate and operated a travel agency on the busy beach. She came from a family with a small local coconut plantation. The income from the coconut products supported her family and her education. Joy, like other girls in Thailand (see Chapter 5), in addition to her studies, helped her family with household tasks. She hardly ever got involved in the process of coconut planting or harvesting, only accompanying her mother when it was time to sell their field products to a middleman. Having observed these trading negotiations between her mother and the middlemen, over time she developed a mind for business. Although Joy's family did not have any stake in the tourism industry, she had witnessed the tourism boom and saw its effects on her everyday life. Consequently, after finishing junior high school on Koh Samui, Joy entered a commerce school in Surat Thani where she studied tourism. After receiving her three-year diploma, she came back to the island with her boyfriend. They married soon after and opened a travel agency on a busy beach on Koh Samui. Because her family's orchard was situated further inland, she had to rent a small shop on the beach area to run the business. She and her husband worked together at the agency whenever he was free. Their shop opened at ten o'clock in the morning and closed at eleven o'clock at night. Joy dropped off their laundry at a laundry service on the way to work. They bought all of the meals and thus did not cook for themselves. It was easier and cheaper for her to buy already cooked food and to let other people do the laundry. In other words, homemaker duties were not a task that she dealt with. Since Joy did not carry out the traditional homemaker duties, she considered herself as working less than women of her mother's generation. Her mother, for example, would get up in the morning to prepare food, do the household chores, help in the field and manage the family's income and expenditures, which would take her the whole day to complete. The family's well-being was her mother's responsibility. In addition, her mother regularly took part in Koh Samui's festive life.

In contrast, because Joy had been working in one of the most touristic areas of Koh Samui everyday for more than six years, she associated herself mostly with tourists and other tourism workers; some of whom were also born on the island and came from similar circumstances. Without intending to, this situation placed her into the tourist culture and at the same time separated her from the local culture. Joy attended some special traditional Buddhist days if she could remember when the day was. However, she hardly attended any local activities, such as weddings, ordinations or housewarming ceremonies. The reason for this was a considerable one: she was no longer familiar with the people of Koh Samui.

Som

Som, who was sixty-nine years old when I talked to her, married into a well-respected family on Koh Samui when she was eighteen. Soon after her wedding, she and her husband moved from her husband's family home to start their own family. Her husband had inherited two pieces of land along Lamai Beach and another big section with a coconut orchard further inland. Her husband, who had one sister and one brother, was the eldest son. The sister was an elementary school teacher on Koh Samui but retired and lived on the island. The brother was a policeman, who served his duty on the mainland and had retired to the island. Som did not complete primary school, but could read and write. She had two children, a son and a daughter who soon after they entered primary school, had been sent to Bangkok for their education. They stayed with their uncle, who was a policeman in Bangkok. During that time Som, with her good cooking skills, opened a Thai restaurant that served traditional Southern Thai food. Later, they extended their business to include the operation of bungalows for low-budget tourists which became their major source of income. Since her family was relatively wealthy, she could afford to have staff for her business to help her in the kitchen, serve in the restaurant and clean the bungalows. Som's restaurant and bungalows were one of the earliest tourism businesses on Koh Samui and were always busy. She would get up in the morning for the market and prepare food for the monks, her husband and herself. Then she would get the kitchen ready for her customers. She would stay in the restaurant accompanied by her workers for most of the day. Since she was the major work force in the business, her husband was free to go to the field, to visit friends or to participate in village activities. However, her husband would help her in the restaurant when it was busy, particularly during the evening. She could also leave the shop in her husband's hands to go out and socialize with other women at the temple. She would help with cooking when her neighbors had ceremonies. Som did not have to spend much time on housekeeping work as her children were in Bangkok. She passed all her household jobs, including cleaning and doing laundry, to her workers.

Moreover, she and her husband would eat their meals in the restaurant. Even though she had cooked the meal, it did not have the sense of eating at home. She did not think of herself as a traditional homemaker and mother, as her main task was running and managing the restaurant. The family business was her domain.

As her family was financially wealthy, after the uncle was transferred out of Bangkok, her husband, with her blessing, decided to buy a house in Bangkok for their children. Som claimed that having a house in Bangkok for the children was the first step for them to settle in Bangkok. Since they have all been educated in Bangkok, all of her children now live in Bangkok and have no plans of returning to live on Koh Samui. Som has four grandchildren who were all born in Bangkok and do not speak a southern dialect. All of the children and grandchildren come to the island to visit her and her husband from time to time, and vice versa. Therefore, Som stayed on the island with only her husband to run their business. Her bungalows were the same as when she first built them, as she only performed maintenance on them. She had been charging tourists almost the same price for forty years - about five US dollars a night at the time of our conversation. About five years ago, she and her husband proposed to her children that they come back to take over the family business. Her husband complained that he could not sleep with the noise of bars and motorbikes at night and Som had leg problems as a result of standing for long hours all her life. The children were reticent to return after spending their whole life in Bangkok. However, after the tsunami hit Phuket on 26th December 2004, tourism on Koh Samui unexpectedly boomed. Many tourism developers from the west coast of Thailand, the areas that were affected by the disaster, proposed to buy Som's property that was an underdeveloped space in one of the most developed areas on the island. In 2005, at her children's suggestion, she converted her business to shops that she could rent out. She found that in this way she could keep her land, earn money and not have to work. In addition, most importantly, she and her husband could move further inland and stay on their farmland, a win-win situation for entire family.

7.5 Old and new: economic and social position

When looking at Koh Samui's local history from an economic conditions perspective, it can be divided into two periods. Before tourism was introduced, Koh Samui was a poor region except for a few people who were involved in the national administration and the traditional educational system. Educated locals who were linked to politics and who owned huge sections of land had risen to an elite social status. In the agricultural principal period the wealth of these people, who retained political power and remained installed as the local elite, was principally based on and expressed in the ownership of coconut plantations making coconut orchards the standard measure of wealth. The old elites were characterized by their involvement in the political history of the island, as well as being a reasonably well educated. In addition, they possessed a forceful attitude. These characteristics were important to their garnering economic power from their coconut orchards that provided them with financial security and placed them in a strong position to take advantage of early tourism opportunities. This in turn reinforced their economic and social status adding to their power. For example, Som, who was in her late sixties, was among the economically successful elite of the island. She had a traditional, prosperous family that was associated with the history of the island, she was recognized as a successful entrepreneur in her role as a tourism pioneer and she had a progressive attitude towards providing education for the next generation. Nee and Sak (discussed in Chapter 6) were also members of traditional elite families. They were highly respected locally, partially because of their continued economic strength, their urban education, landowner status and, of course, being members of local elite families. Their tourism businesses, which they themselves managed, were successful due to the help of their powerful, long existing network that comprised of their kin and local politicians. Although Nee and Sak had maintained their positions as members of the local elite, something was changing – tourism was beginning to transform the current generation of elite families into a new form of middle to upper middle class.

Koh Samui's era of socio-economic development began relatively late in comparison to other regions in Thailand – around the 1950s (see Krongkaew 1995; Limanonda 1995; Mills 1995; 1999; Morris 2000; Mulder 2000; Panya 1995; Phongphit and Hewison 2001; Tanabe and Keyes 2002b; Van Esterik 2000). Even though tourism first appeared on the island in the late 1970s, it is only a decade ago that the island embarked on a modernization process. Yet the standard of living as an indicator of the health of the tourism industry has already improved. Although not everyone shared the fabulous wealth that tourism brought to the island in the tourism-dominant period equally, most people, including the landless and even tourism migrants, benefited economically at least in part. The nature of the expanding tourism industry meant that in comparison to the agriculture industry, even those who had only little land, were landless or had only a small amount of capital could start small holding activities on Koh Samui (similar to Yasmeen (2002) studies on small holding activities in Bangkok; see Plate 7.1).

Plate 7.1: Food venders on Koh Samui, who traditionally served mostly local clients, are now serving growing numbers of budget and long-stay tourists.

Undoubtedly, tourism enabled the formation of social classes and supported a new social class – the middle class (*chon chan klang*) – that was formed from the lower-income local families and tourism migrants. The urbanization process of the island is reflected in the term *chon chan klang* (middle class) which refers to the socio-economic formation of people (Phiriyarangsan and Phongpaichit 1992). Askew (2002: 172) explains that *chon chan klang* refers to the 'economic condition' where people do not suffer from extreme hardship, but neither do they enjoy the discretionary income of the rich. Jit, Pong and Joy were from financially insecure agricultural families that due to the external market and uncertain climatic conditions lived in social and economic 'poverty' (*kon chon*). The growth of tourism attracted them and turned them into entrepreneurs on the island where they played an active part in the growth of tourism and in the diversification of tourism activities. Their situation changed dramatically during the tourism period when they managed to escape from the agricultural hardship of older generations. The new opportunities presented by tourism armed Jit, Pong and Joy along with others on the island with more negotiating power than they had had in their previous agricultural work. This

165

was especially true with economic improvement and social class. In essence, the dramatic rise in tourism development and the consequent prospect of economic opportunities opened a new phase of Koh Samui's social landscape that cut across traditional social boundaries.

7.6 Conclusion: tourism and social configuration

The Thai modernization process during the nineteen century emphasized the change of economic transformation of the island from the status-ridden *feudal* past to the creation of an open *capitalist* society. Throughout the country's modernization and industrialization process during the first part of 1990s, the island engaged in market-oriented farming systems that mainly focused on coconut products as a major export to the mainland and other countries. However, with the limitations on land available for agricultural economic activities, along with a decline in coconut prices and the quest for more diverse economic opportunities, the agrarian lifestyle began to be less attractive to the locals and they began migrating to the mainland (Cohen 1996; Petkaew 2003).

Although Thailand's modernity process did not directly cause physical changes on Koh Samui in terms of new buildings, roads, or transportations systems for example, it did insert some basic foundations of Thai values and norms into the island residents (Chapter 5). In this respect, the key factors of Thai modernization and modernity provided the understanding of Koh Samui's Thai identity. Moreover, this identification with Thainess and the nature of Thai urbanism linked Koh Samui to the process of accumulating a central focus on Bangkok. Such critical reflection of this identity assists in understanding Koh Samui's identity change during its tourism period. Therefore, it is important to recognize the emergence of Koh Samui society and the origin of its norms and values, which has been greatly impacted upon by Thailand's historical and cultural legacies. In other words, to understand Koh Samui society is to acknowledge the significance of the 'larger historical process' (Duval 2004: 58) particularly the process of Thailand modernization. This provides perspectives on how the island's society and geography reacted to and developed in response to tourism shaping Koh Samui society's modern history. Indeed, while tourism development played a critical structural role in transforming the physical landscape (Chapter 6), discussed in this chapter, tourism also restructured the social positions of Koh Samui society with a generally positive outcome. The expansion of the tourism-urban region on the island, the process of change, particularly towards the island's population, was part of the strong influence of tourism development. Furthermore, while the coconut orchards used to be synonymous with the old elite class, the creation of tourism related business ownership contributed to the formation of a new middle class. However, while the tourism business has rapidly brought spectacular (and uncertain) wealth to the island, it is *landownership*, which has always been and for the most part still is the symbol for local wealth.

Even though the process of social change was initiated by tourism development, it would be too simplistic to focus on the external influences while disregarding existing internal social dynamics. These internal dynamics formed the basis of an already existing social inequality, the upper class of the indigenous society, which are now the middle and upper-middle classes. Moreover, the greater opportunities that have emerged with the booming of regional economic and social functions, now associated with the island's modernity and the increased emphasis upon capitalism, has created multiple social identities. In addition, the identities of *old version* local elites were based on such aspects as money, land holdings and politics. However, economy is a major area of transformation with the rise of a new social identity – the upper middle class of the island and the recognition of a variety of economical orientations and lifestyles. Therefore, the reorientation of the identity of this group resulted in a loss of local agricultural livelihoods to tourism capitalism and urban lifestyles. These many facets of identity affect how individuals interrelate with each other, family, friends, partners, neighbors and co-workers. It also provides a basis for new forms of Koh Samui's identity construction. Thus, the modernist preoccupation with class politics, trade activities and urban attitudes through the development of the tourism-urbanization process has increasingly given ways to more fluid social movements and opportunities, which emerged out of, are based on the struggles over personal and collective identities and thus provide a more varied and fragmented political, economic and social landscape.

For some, tourism economic development leads to more empowerment as these economic social movements present positive opportunities (also see Chapter 8). This development acts as a release from the stultifying politics of class and the implications of the traditional feudal system. Thus, it is potentially liberating, holding the promise of new forms of social organization and practice. However, the improvement of social class comes at a price, particularly to those tourism workers from off the island. Having moved away from their region of origin, they often struggle with how to maintain their cultural identity, especially when they have children to whom they would like to pass their part of heritage, as in the case of Jit. In other words, at the same time that these island immigrants are working to improve their social condition and resolve the problems that poverty presents, they are being distanced from their roots. Indeed, changes in the form of economic practice have accompanied the varied social changes on Koh Samui society. Economic space continues to be a significant part of how people on Koh Samui organize and give meaning to their lives and create a sense of new identity. They extend from integrative trends demanding 'modernity' in existing society to reformulate social groups. In the next chapter, the 'adaptability' of a specific social group to tourism values is discussed as the integration of tourism values in the island's gender landscape permits a constructive way of dealing with social change.

CHAPTER 8

TOURISM IMPLICATIONS AND KOH SAMUI'S GENDER LANDSCAPE

8.1 Introduction

In the previous chapters, I explored the development of the tourism industry and the ensuring changes in Koh Samui's physical and social landscapes. Both are characterized by an increasing 'modernity' and a new 'identification' of Koh Samui society. Thus, tourism has been a dynamic force on the shifting cultural boundaries and the shaping of the local social and cultural arrangements. This chapter focuses more on the social consequences of such changes. In the main part of this chapter, I explore the processes of Koh Samui's gender landscape in association with tourism development and examine the nature of the Thai gender practices as they relate to the tourism and service industries. In line with the thesis approach of using a tourism history concept, this chapter presents how tourism and Thailand cultural legacy of values and practices of Thai genders has influenced the changing roles and representatives of Thai women. Such analysis then leads to specific discussion of women working in the sex industry on Koh Samui. Women working in the sex industry are a well-known feature of Thailand. The aspects of women's space and mobility in the Thai culture, especially with their nature as 'caregiver' (Yasmeen 2002), have drawn them into certain occupations, especially in the tourism service industry. Thus, women have a prominent place in the tourism industry. A prime example of this would be the images of beautiful Thai women shown on a variety of tourism marketing campaigns throughout the country. However, the key of the gendered geography of Thai tourism is the expanding number of sex workers. In essence, the main factor that shapes the gender landscape in Thai tourism is the constant growth of both demand and supply of the sex tourism industry.

Tourism development and the service industry are the main economic drivers on Koh Samui, which has resulted in women (both locals and immigrants) being engaged in

169

the industry. Due to this, women have become economically active and have begun to learn the language of freedom, sexuality, new identity and life (Askew 2002; Cohen 1996). Moreover, the roles of women in the various social statuses on Koh Samui including the old elite women (e.g. Som) and the island princesses (e.g. Nee), as discussed in the previous chapters, have reflected the growing space for women on the island. Even though the role of women in the economic development of Koh Samui had become greater and more various as seen through the life stories of Nee, for Noy (discussed in Chapter 6), Jit, Joy and Som (discussed in Chapter 7), the expansion of the infrastructure of commercial sex on the island resulted in Koh Samui visibly becoming a gendered geography. Thus, women have become important agents of the island's tourism landscape, particularly as the development of commercial sex shaped the island's gender landscape profoundly.

This chapter discusses sex tourism development as a major influence on gender issues on Koh Samui that has slowly arisen over time. This discussion on sex tourism includes an explanation of the context in terms of the cultural, political and social circumstances in which it was created. The historical development of sex tourism on Koh Samui is discussed with special reference to the construction of the commercial sex landscape on Lamai Beach. Based on my observations during collection of my fieldwork data in 'girlie bars' and the life story memory conversations with 'sex workers', the chapter presents life stories of sex workers in order to highlight some important aspects of the status change of women that has taken place through sex tourism. In revealing my sensitivity to commercial sex, I suggest that sex tourism provides spaces for women (sex workers) to renegotiate or rebuild their identity. It is important to note that there might be male sex workers on Lamai Beach; however, I focused only on bars where obvious sex business takes place: open bars, all of which are girlie bars on Lamai Beach. For this reason, I focus only on and discuss only female sex workers throughout the chapter. It is important to note that while sex workers' backgrounds are marked by problems in their family, work and marriage, these aspects will not be discussed in my analysis. Moreover, literature on sex tourism tends to emphasize the 'negative' elements of prostitutes' lives. However, in this chapter I highlight mainly 'positive' aspects of working in the sex industry. This includes, for instance, pride *beyond* the political struggle of sex tourism, thus altering the understanding of sex work in a Koh Samui context. The discussion is not intended to support the sex industry or to suggest other females should look for opportunities through sex tourism. However, since they are already working in the sex industry, this thesis examines what keeps them in this work.

8.2 Sex tourism: constructing a women's landscape on Koh Samui

Nowhere in the literature on early tourism development on Koh Samui in the late 1970s did there exist documentation about the nightlife entertainment, let alone the sex tourism scene. Cohen (1996: 153) noted that Koh Samui, at that time, offered '[q]uiet relaxation, rather than strenuous activity, [which] characterized the ambiance of those beaches'. In fact, bar and nightlife entertainment was not added to the island tourism facilities until the late 1980s onwards. Originally, there were nightclubs and discotheques offering music, cocktails and beer. Their purpose was not to offer sex services; however, over time these places become sites for women in search of customers. The places unintentionally served as meeting places for independent prostitutes and (usually) intoxicated, lonely male tourists[28]. Towards the end of the 1980s, the immense growth of tourism in Thailand coupled with the growth of the sex trade, led to the development of the commercial foreign-oriented sex infrastructure. Specifically, in the words of the landowners where commercial sex is located, 'girlie bars', which were characterized by small, round and open-air bars with thatched roofs, were built during this boom period. They came to symbolize sex tourism in Thailand. Based on my fieldwork, most of Koh Samui's 'girlie bars' had at the centre an area where customers sat around a pole, where scantily clad women danced. The shape of the bar was generally similar to the shape of a mushroom called *bar dok hed* in Thai (literally meaning mushroom bar). This bar development on Koh Samui led to the following scene: a dozen or so bars grouped together in one area, with many bar girls dancing and drinking with foreign tourists, particularly males.

In the early stages of bar development, bar owners, who normally were sex workers, rented land with financial support from their *farang* 'boyfriends' (see Cohen 1996 for the concept of *farang* boyfriend). This land was generally located away from the beach. These bars established the new commercial sex infrastructure in the area. The girls

---

[28] My field notes illustrate similar circumstances to what Askew (2002) and Cohen (1996) point out about sex activities in Bangkok.

consisted of both sex workers from the area or from places like Pattaya, Phuket or Bangkok. Such development also drew 'newcomers' to the sex industry from rural areas. Because sex workers become sex business entrepreneurs after finding *farang* boyfriends, the sex industry continued to expand. It is important to emphasize that this kind of 'girlie bar' was easily set up and opened, and also as easily shut down and reopened again. This easy and informal development was due the fact that it required little space, capital and business planning. As mentioned in previous chapters (particularly in Chapter 6), in comparison to Chaweng Beach, Lamai Beach was initially developed on a smaller scale, and mostly by locals. Therefore, the nature of the beach development was compatible with the characteristics of girlie-bars. Consequently, many local Koh Samui landowners turned the land that was unsuitable for bungalows or resorts into plots for girlie-bars. They built their own bars with strong material, keeping the traditional shape. With already built bars ready to rent, it became even easier for sex workers to open their own businesses. Therefore, the combination of landowners and sex workers reinforced and accelerated the already booming sex tourism trade on Lamai Beach.

Nowadays, such nightlife activity (and related sex businesses) is one of the main reasons why tourists are attracted to the beach. Sex businesses have therefore become one of the particular tourism characteristics of the place (Samui Explorer 2006). This image, which is important to the overall tourism industry of Lamai Beach, has highlighted the various tourist establishments in the form of sex workers and sex related tourism. The beach has been transformed from a pristine natural environment to a nightlife entertainment area that offers increasingly diverse commercial sex activities. At the time of my fieldwork there were 'girlie-bars' along the beach road where sex tourism took place (see Plate 8.1). Because each bar hosts dozens of women, bar girls have become an obvious part of Koh Samui's social landscape. However, the infrastructure of the commercial sex industry on Koh Samui is different to other tourist destinations, particularly when compared with Pattaya. This is due to the sex trade on Koh Samui being mostly developed in form of beer-bar complexes with a more personal approach compared with the big brothels in Pattaya or in Bangkok and their 'hard selling techniques'.

Plate 8.1: 'Girlie-bars' and nightlife entertainment on Lamai Beach in 2007 (the pink area shows the commercial sex businesses).

As seen in Plate 8.1, Koh Samui's sex tourism industry has developed in the form of 'girlie-beer-bars' that are grouped together away from the beach. The common scene is large numbers of friendly women standing in scanty outfits and heavy makeup in front of the bars. Their job is to get male tourists who pass by to come in and buy drinks. Ironically the selling of beer, not the offering of sex services is still the main purpose of the bar business. The bar girls earn a small commission on the drinks they talk their bar guests into buying and in the process get a drink for themselves. This reflects the result of other studies about Thailand's sex industries (see, for instance, Askew 2002; Cohen 1996; Hantrakul 1983; Phongpaichit 1982; Phongpaichit and Baker 1995), where it is noted that the bar girls would get a commission on the drinks a customer orders for them. While the girls are at work, their job is to be cheerful and to sell drinks to the bar's customers. In order to encourage customers to buy more drinks the bargirls usually need to drink more. Generally, the bar workers get about 1500 *baht* a month from the bar owner to ensure they belong to a specific bar. They have to turn up at the bar every night in order to get the commission. They use their attractiveness, innocence and friendliness to 'turn a trick' for the night. Then the bar owners would get a fee from the customers who took the girl out during her work shift. It is important to note that the fee is not paid to buy a girl from the bar, but it is a compensation for the bar's loss in manpower. Each time a worker went off with a customer, the bar would get 200 *baht*. The negotiations for sex are in the hands of the bargirls alone. Thus, theoretically, prostitution is not the business of the bar and thus is not against the law. Therefore, if a girl wanted to go out with a customer, the customer

173

would pay the negotiated amount of money to the girl directly. In the short term, the girl's goal is to stay with one *farang* throughout his holiday. This case is common in Koh Samui: the bar girl becomes a *Mia Chow* (literally means 'hired wife' or 'rented wife'). In fact, many male tourists come to the island and spend their holiday with one girl. As the relationship develops, the 'boyfriend' ends up buying presents for his *Mia Chow* as well as giving her a lump sum payment at the end of his holiday. Ultimately, the long-term goal of the girl is to have a more permanent relationship with the boyfriend, which brings security through constant financial support. Using their charm, grace, fun, care and sweetness, a girl aims to have long-term relationships with her boyfriend, hoping that he might return to her for his next holiday or even come to live on Koh Samui. In such case, the boyfriend offers monthly payments to support the 'girlfriend' and her family until his return. Notably, many couples' relationships have become deeper with some girls marrying a *farang* and withdrawing from the sex industry. Many migrate overseas with their new 'husbands', while others bring their 'husbands' to live in their home towns.

8.3 The life of sex workers

In this section, I introduce the life narratives of women who work or used to work as sex workers on Koh Samui. The following discussion of sex workers' life shows the specific 'adaptability' of women and the opportunities that emerge from sex tourism. The personal qualities of Thai women, particularly the image of a 'dutiful daughter' (Ekachai 1990; Phongpaichit 1982), begins to explain the rapid development of Thai women involved in sex tourism.

Pen

Pen was forty-five years old when I spoke with her. She was married to a German man and lived in Germany permanently with a son and a daughter from the German husband and a daughter from her previous marriage. I saw Pen many times over the years when she was spending her holiday on Koh Samui. When she learned I was doing fieldwork for my research, our conversation became more than just saying 'hi'. After a while, I started talking to her about sharing her life story, particularly how she had come to move to Germany. Pen, who was originally from the Udonthani Province in the Northeast of Thailand, was nineteen years old when she married a man in her hometown. In the beginning, her married life was great. His family gave her husband a small piece of land. Although small, the land was enough to start a family. Pen opened a small shop selling daily products and her husband worked on his own baby corn plantation. With her business doing well and the support from the harvest, the family was financially well off. However, after a while, her husband ended up losing the plantation due to a gambling problem. After losing the land, he worked on a daily wage basis, the income from which was not enough to keep the family. The whole family was then reliant solely on the income from her shop. In addition to his gambling problem, her husband had developed a drinking problem and eventually became domestically abusive.

Pen technically raised her daughter alone. She would get up around five o'clock in the morning and prepare food for everyone. After her child had gone to school she would wash the family clothes and sweep the house, and then operate the shop. The socializing scene for the neighborhood was mainly at her home. Although Pen looked after the family income, the property was under her husband's name. As a result, he was able to gamble away the business without her being aware. This, in the end, left them homeless. Consequently, they moved into a small hut that belonged to Pen's mother. It was difficult for her to bring up her child with no reliable income as the family had to rely on Pen's and her husband's daily wage. Pen, who had only completed primary school and thus could only read and write, wanted her only daughter to continue studying up to tertiary level. Unfortunately, soon after losing the shop, her husband died in a motorbike-accident and left her nothing except the sole responsibility of the child. Pen, then in her early twenties, took a housemaid's job in a nearby town. She stayed at her boss' house and left her three-year-old daughter with her mother. Although the town was only 65 kilometers away from her mother's house, she was only allowed to go home once a month. Once, during Pen's home visit, she met her friend who had been working in Pattaya, but was planning to go to Koh Samui to work. Her friend's lifestyle and income caught Pen's attention, so when her friend mentioned the plan of going to Koh Samui to work, Pen decided to join her. Pen ended up working in a bar on Lamai Beach. She thought that because she was twenty-five years old, she had nothing to lose by working as a bargirl and could make a significant income. Although she was scared to talk to *farang* because she was unable to speak English, she quickly learned that English was not totally necessary.

For the first two years working in a bar, Pen was easily able to support her mother to raise her child. Then she met John who was on his first trip to Koh Samui - Pen became his first *Mia Chow*. After two weeks on Koh Samui, John returned home, but left her with a sum of money for her to send home. Pen still worked in the bar, but all the while kept in contact with John with the help of a translator. John returned to the island on his vacation in the following year, this time taking Pen to Phuket, Bangkok, and Pattaya and back to her hometown. The relationship developed with John sending her money every monthly. Later when he returned to Koh Samui, Pen agreed to quit working in a bar. John took Pen back to her hometown where he opened a small convenience shop for her. Thus, the relationship became more serious. Pen operated her shop for three years while John traveled back and forth between Udonthani and Frankfurt. Then he asked her to marry him and join him in Germany. Pen passed her shop to her mother and moved overseas. A couple of years later Pen and John had a son and a daughter together. Pen built a new house for her mother and took her first child from the Thai husband to Germany. Her husband's income was good enough for them to have a holiday in Thailand from time to time. More importantly, she was able to support her mother financially, making her feel proud when she returned home to visit.

Yaa

At the time of our conversation, Yaa was thirty-eight years old woman who lived with her husband[29], a retired English man. Yaa was originally from Nakhon Ratchasima, in the Northeast of Thailand, but she had moved to Koh Samui from Bangkok approximately four years before. Yaa had one daughter from her first boyfriend, a man from the same village who had abandoned her and the child and moved to Bangkok to work on a construction site. She had stayed with her parents who were agrarians until she was 23. When her daughter's father stopped sending money, she left her three-year-old daughter with her parents and moved to Bangkok too. In Bangkok, with her high school diploma, Yaa worked as a waitress in a restaurant which offered entertainment in order to support her parents and her daughter. She had a relationship with a co-worker, which did not last

---

[29] It is important to note that when a man and woman move in together in Thailand, particularly in rural society, they are widely recognized as husband and wife, even though they are not married or officially registered to each other.

long enough for her to inform her family. As the financial pressure on her increased when her daughter needed to begin school and the family crops failed, her waitress job was no longer enough. Consequently, she took on a new position as a hostess at one of the hundreds of nightclubs in Bangkok, which offered her a much higher income. Through that, she became involved in the prostitution scene. One of the reasons Yaa stated for taking this new position, beside the pressure from poverty, was that after having had two failed relationships with men, she had lost her self-esteem and had concluded that no man wanted to build a 'normal[30]' family life with her. Unable to see herself in a 'proper' family setting, she focused on her new job and kept her mind on supporting her family. She kept her life in Bangkok a secret from the family at home, not letting any of them know how she earned her living and how she was able to support them.

Yaa went back to visit her family at least once a year, particularly on Thai New Year, the *Songkran* Festival on the 13th of April. While there, she saw nothing but the poverty of the area, which in turn only strengthened her belief that she was doing the best thing that, could improve her daughter's future. When she decided that her daughter should come to Bangkok for her secondary education, her parents disagreed. It took Yaa a very long time to convince them that her daughter's life would be better if she got an education in Bangkok. Eventually, they agreed to the idea and Yaa's daughter moved to Bangkok where she stayed with her aunt who had a food stall in an area away from Yaa. In that same year, Yaa left for Koh Samui. There were two reasons why Yaa left the city. First, to avoid questions from her family about what she did for a living that prevented her daughter from staying with her. Second, at the age of thirty-three she was becoming too old to work in Bangkok's nightlife entertainment, and was unable to make enough money to support her family and her pay for her daughter's education by working in any other field. She was convinced she would remain in her field of work but in a new location.

A friend, one of Yaa's coworkers at the nightclub where she worked, suggested she should go to Koh Samui where the customers were mostly foreigners who did not care as much about the age and the looks of the women the way that Thai customers do in Bangkok. Yaa understood what her friend meant when she saw the nightlife scene on the island for the first time. She remembered seeing women of all ages, many of whom were and looked older than her. They were mostly wearing poor, cheap, sexy outfits and thick,

---

[30] The words 'proper' family and 'normal' were her own, but I have emphasized them to reflect the tone of her voice and the body language when she stressed the terms.

unprofessional makeup. She was surprised about the relative 'unprofessional' scene, compared with Bangkok, stating that she could not imaging that what she saw there would ever exist in Bangkok clubs. As her first job she took a cashier position in a 'girlie-bar' on Lamai Beach where she met foreigners (by that time, her English had improved significantly). The work offered a place to stay, which she shared with other women who worked as bargirls. She would get up around noon, have lunch with her housemates before heading to the bar. Generally, the afternoon was a time for the suppliers to deliver beers, soft drinks, ice and other goods. Yaa's duty was receiving, checking, shelving, and getting ready for the big night. Normally, the bargirls would arrive at the bar in the late afternoon, no later than six o'clock. Then they all would have something to eat before the evening began. Because Yaa's job was cashiering and not entertaining customers, the owner would not allow her to drink while she was working. Moreover, she was not permitted to leave until after the bar closed, which was sometimes as late as dawn. The money she made from her job and customer tips was enough for her to support her family as well as paying for her daughter's education without doing what she had initially come to Koh Samui for. She did, however go out with foreigners a couple times during the year she worked at the bar. Although these foreigners paid Yaa, she was with them because she *wanted* to be with them, not because she *needed* to. She was happy to find that for the first time in her life, she had a choice.

In her second year on Koh Samui, she met Mark, her husband. When she moved in with him she quit the bar job and started to work as a cook's assistant in a restaurant. After having worked in the restaurant for a year, she left the job and opened her own food-vending stall. Yaa did not discuss her life in Bangkok, but chose instead to focus on her life at the present. Yaa found that Koh Samui provided her with a better financial situation and a better lifestyle, without having to be a sex worker. It allowed her to do things that she could not do when she was in Bangkok, like spending time with her daughter. She could even take extended time off during the low tourist season to go and visit her daughter and her family. Last year Yaa's daughter came during her school vacation to visit her and help in the food stall. She also found that she had more time to do personal things like go to a temple to make merit that was something she did not even think about when she was living in Bangkok. Koh Samui had allowed her to regain her self-esteem.

Nat

Nat, who was twenty-four years old when I spoke with her, had been working in a 'girlie-bar' on Lamai Beach. She moved from Khon Kaen Province in the Northern part of Thailand to Koh Samui, two years before. The main reason she had moved to the island was that she saw many people in her hometown that had a better economic situation and living conditions because of having a *farang* husband. All of the people she knew had found their *farang* husbands in major tourist destinations like Bangkok, Pattaya, Phuket or Koh Samui. This made these places her dream financial destinations. One day she was offered the opportunity to follow a woman from her village to Koh Samui. The woman introduced Nat to one of the bar owners on Lamai Beach where she started working as a sex worker. Because Nat kept company with girls who came from the same area, and thus had a similar subculture, local dialect and food, Nat was very comfortable on the island. She stayed with other girls in a house that they rented from the bar owner. Her bar-mates helped her to dress up, to do make up and to speak English. The work was easier than it looked. '*Farang* came here to have fun, and to enjoy, so I was only there to comfort them and to entertain them' Nat emphasizes. The work did not require much knowledge, not even proper English, but good appearance and attitude were necessary. While Nat managed to send home significant amounts of cash working in the sex tourism business, to remain competitive in an increasingly cutthroat business where the girls get prettier and younger, she was forced to spend more and more money on her appearance. She worked as a bargirl from around 5 pm until late at night every day. Her job was to bring in customers and get them to buy alcohol. In order to do this, she would drink and dance with the customers throughout most of the night. If she got lucky, someone would take her out of the bar which meant she would earn extra money to send home and sometimes, if she was really lucky, she would be taken to a nice restaurant for dinner and then to a hotel.

After her first year on the island, one of her bar-mates who she was very close to opened her own bar with the financial support from her '*farang* boyfriend'. Nat moved to the newly opened bar to help her friend. It was then that Nat saw the real potential of working as a bargirl. At that time, her friend, who owned the bar, was talking about marrying the boyfriend and moving to England. Nat was asked to take over the bar business. She saw her life progressing, however not yet to the point that brought her to her ultimate goal – marrying a *farang*. Nat was single when she came to the island and at the time of interview, she was still single. Even though she had many '*farang* boyfriends' in the previous two years, many of whom had given her nice presents which had resulted in her being able to save some money, she neither had the serious relationship she craved for, nor the regular financial support that came with it. She knew instinctively that when she owned the bar, her finances would be more stable, but she was still hoping to marry a *farang* like her friend, and either move to a foreign country or return to her hometown to live there permanently, just like other 'normal' women in her village. She said 'I don't know what is going to happen in the future, but if other girls can have a *farang* and move overseas then why not me!'.

8.4 Sex tourism: Koh Samui and women's identities

The development of sex tourism on the island illustrates changes similar to those of other forms of tourism on Koh Samui, such as the development of valueless agricultural land into thriving tourist sites (see Chapter 6). The commercial sex infrastructure has transformed the backstage of the beachfront into a touristic area. Thus, the beachfront is reserved for hotels and resorts and along the beach road, there are shops and bars. It required only little for landowners to transform their land into a sex business area: a small plot of land and a small amount of capital investment enabled those who were small landholders or those who were disadvantaged compared with the capitalists (see Chapter 7) on the island, to join in the growth of tourism. One of the landowners on Lamai Beach who turned his property into a number of bar units for rent, explained that the profits from investments in this section were easier, larger and faster.

From the perspective of sex business management, starting a commercial sex venture, particularly a 'girlie-bar', is not complicated. Since much of the infrastructure for bars already exist. They only have to pay a small amount of rent for the facilities. One of the bar owners in the busy sex business area on Lamai Beach explained that she had paid only 300,000 *baht* during a three year key contract in addition to the 5,000 *baht* for the monthly rental. After her initial outlay, she only needed to invest in some music equipment and fridges for drinks. As soon as the bar opened, girls who wanted work would turn up spontaneously. Such 'easy' nature of establishing a sex tourism business, seen from a purely business perspective, reinforced the expansion and boom of sex tourism

180

establishments significantly. It therefore also stimulated the process of touristization on Koh Samui. Similar to the process of Bangkok's industrialization and urbanization that attracted people from rural areas into the city (Askew 2002), tourism-urbanization on Koh Samui, especially sex tourism has caused people, mostly women, to migrate to the island (the tourist destination). Thus, the implication of tourism development upon Koh Samui's modernization and urbanization is inextricably linked to women in the island's modern history.

Moreover, the power of tourism and its development in a 'Thai context' resulted in a transformation of various practices connected to sexuality and women's status. In this respect, tourism and most importantly sex tourism, shapes the gender landscape on Koh Samui. To address the representation of the competing gender identities, I argue that the depiction of sex tourism on Koh Samui is slanted toward gender. Of course, tourism development affects various aspects of different sexual relations and social life, but the sex industry draws large numbers of migrants, mostly women, into the area. In other words, one critical factor in shaping the island's gender landscape is the immigration of sex workers to Koh Samui. Within this context therefore, the island's modernizing economy brought with it the patterns of a sex-dominated work. Furthermore, as sex tourism plays a crucial part of tourism development on Koh Samui, the appearance and socializing of sex workers is an important aspect of the island's modernity and urbanization. The notion of sex tourism, with its focus on respectability and fashion of women on Koh Samui, has resulted in 'a city of women' (Askew 2002: 257). Askew notes that;

> The critical facilitator of women's transition into the world of sex work is the subculture formed around women's friendship networks, collective coping strategies and mutual socialisation. While women clearly have to cope with adjustments and problems alone, both at the individual psychological level and an interpersonal level with customers, it is critical that we appreciate the collective dimension of prostitution as a women world. Women commonly advise newcomers about the explicit and cheeky forms of behaviour required of their work. Women literally learn to *perform* the trade in the company of other women: they learn how to make body contact, to wink seductively, and to speak a smattering of English. More experienced women often introduce their neophyte friends to male

customers whom they know and trust as farang chai di (foreigner with good heart) or farang nissai di (foreigner with good character).

(Askew 2002: 270; the italic is original)

The 'girlie-bar' is a typical place that seeks to build a particular image of sex workers and their womanhood. It is a pattern of materialistic socializing, and of performative and symbolic activity (McDowell 1996). Accordingly, bar girls are presented as a commodity exemplar for the sex trade, embodying the life of an urban dweller being modern and beautiful (*than samai*) that has become a central aspect of Thai's commodification sex discourse (Van Esterik 2000). They appear to be the complete opposite of their complicated real background. In fact, the sex workers are a combination of having a pretty appearance, charming, friendly and fun personality, and possessing a happy, smiling and positive attitude. Within the sex tourism space, experienced women become the epitome of appropriate sex worker behavior, as they are a compendium of sexual knowledge. This 'packaged knowledge' is passed from experienced to inexperienced girl on an informal basis (see Nat's story). This is reflected in the fundamental transformation of women into sex workers by making them comfortable with their womanhood, and 'being a woman'. The girls' similar cultural backgrounds, education, and most importantly, their core understanding of the world, serves as the foundation for their friendships. As in the case of Nat, who spends most of her time in the company of girls who come from the same area and thus share a dialect and food, she seems very comfortable in the bar atmosphere.

Furthermore, most sex workers on the island share some sort of 'negative' social identity in terms of both their finances and their role in society. This makes it easy for women who enter into the sex business to develop friendships and to become part of the group. The sex tourism space therefore unites desperate women who act in solidarity and create a sense of group commonality of loving-kindness and compassion. Thus, while sex workers are increasingly excluded from non-sex-tourism society life, a new style of community develops in their sex tourism space. In foreign-oriented sex tourism, a number of things are particularly striking about the women's self-identity. For example, sex workers on Koh Samui often refer to the economic opportunities: quick cash and a lump sum are the opportunity (e.g. Pen, Yaa and Nat). Although, some literature paints sex works as shameful (Jackson and Cook 1999, for example), these women (and perhaps men as well) see it as a way to provide financial support to and enhance the well-being of their families. In other words, while working in the sex business is perceived as 'bad karma' (Van Esterik 2000), it provides those sex workers with greater autonomy with which to support their families. Subsequently, the money they provide their families with makes them feel as though they are 'dutiful daughters' (Ekachai 1990; Phongpaichit 1982).

The connection between sex tourism and women's status in Thai Buddhist society is complex. While sex work is a result of 'bad karma', sex tourism provides for women financially and gives them time to attend merit at temples. Sex workers are 'aware' of their evil life (*chew it beep*), and are convinced of the need to make merit to insure a better rebirth. In a vicious circle, however, the only means they have to raise money to make merit is through prostitution' (Fieldwork 2005). This is not a judgment. Sex workers are struggling with the circle of 'bad karma' and perceive sex tourism as a sensitive way out of this cycle. Sex tourism is connected to the long-standing social values of being 'bad girls', given to the role of females once they are prostitutes (see Van Esterik 2000 about the Thai perceptions on 'bad girls' and 'good girls'). To return to their villages and start a family is a dream of many women, especially of sex workers. However, society generally undermines respect of sex workers by painting them as irrational and unacceptable wives and mothers. For instance, the Chiang Mai Empower Group's campaign (2003; see Appendix I) reflects them in a non-sex-tourism space as 'bad mothers', 'irresponsible' and 'evil wicked women'.

Optimistically, sex tourism helps women to progress socially. Van Esterik (2000: 170) summarized that 'they can hope to catch a foreign male who accepts that their immoral practices are for moral reasons – to support their poverty-stricken families'. Thus, sex tourism serves as a space for encounters between sex workers and potential future 'boyfriends'. In this case, sex tourism is not only conceived of as being financially beneficial to the life of women, but also as of fundamental importance to their success in restoring their identity as wife and mother. In addition, as I discussed previously, tourism development does not affect all genders or social groups with the same intensity. While sex tourism has shaped some women's identities on Koh Samui, the new generation of local elites, both princes and princesses, are in command of managing their tourism businesses and making them more profitable. The gap between these two groups (princesses and sex workers) could not be wider. The local elite's successes are based on their families existing wealth and their long-existing powerful networks between their kin and local politicians. Thus, their identities lead to the appropriate positions in terms of social and economic class. Women in other social classes also benefit from Koh Samui tourism development to a certain extent, as their encounters with the tourism industry result in less manual work than women of previous generations.

8.5 Sex tourism: a changing fortune for Thai sex workers on Koh Samui?

The sex workers' stories discussed in this chapter present the possibility of the emotional and internalized empowerment of woman in sex work, which should not be separated from the sex worker's restructured identity. This identity is a combination of the individual's gender, sexuality and changing social status. Thus, it seems that sex tourism can be a place where women are presented with opportunities. Along with the negative impact of sex tourism such as HIV or co-dependence on *farang* men, there are also benefits to be gained for female sex workers far beyond the economic sphere. It is certainly not my intention to support the sex industry or to wish other women to seek opportunities through sex tourism. My intention is rather to point out why some women become sex workers and how they keep their dignity while performing their work. Sex tourism on Koh Samui provides a space of hope for women to build their own character as wife and mother, unlike local-client prostitution, which is limited. Thus, the emotions and dilemmas of women's identities as posed by sex tourism are primarily reflected in their concerns of having more freedom, and of their social, and economic position. As Cohen (1996: 253-4; emphasis in original) notes, 'the women working with *farangs* are in many respects the 'elite' among the prostitutes: they earn significantly more than those working with Thais, enjoy greater independence, and are rarely controlled by pimps or pushed into prostitution against their will'. Moreover, with the 'one-customer-one-girl' rule in Thailand's sex tourism space (Askew 2002), the encounter of sex workers and foreign clients enables the development of romantic relationships. In this respect, an open-ended sex worker-foreign client contact (Cohen 1996) could possibly develop into a romantic girlfriend-boyfriend relationship, which could become long term and might even end in marriage in some cases. With their new social status, the women could be accepted back to the village in accordance with the tolerance that Buddhist teaching inculcates (Keyes

1984). Therefore, it is the hope of marrying a *farang* that enables women to escape life as a sex worker.

The negotiation of re-building self-identity is a challenge, as is the language barrier. However, sex workers on Koh Samui at least have a chance to negotiate. The links between gender and power need to be emphasized. In accordance with Tucker's (1999) research study in Goreme, it is a misunderstanding to accept the relationships 'in favour of the [only] men [*farang*]'. Tucker (1999: 201) notes that;

> 'I have viewed the relationships as processes throughout which the expectations and power of each partner are constantly negotiated. Looking at how the relationships begin in the fun and playful realm of the tourist sphere, and following them through to longer-lasting relationships and marriage, allows us to see the choices and strategies of both the men and women involved.'

Sex tourism thus allows sex workers to use this space to renegotiate their own identity, which is reflected in the number of women who have had the opportunity to move out of this business to find a new family within other cultures. Therefore, sex tourism in Thailand is often a space of hope for Thai sex workers as it can provide a *passport to re-identity*. Nevertheless, the bar women on Koh Samui, similar to others in Thailand's major tourist destinations, are considered an attraction for some and tolerated by Thais who take a different 'moral' view of prostitution. Regardless of individual perception with the concept of sex tourism in Thailand, sex work is work and should be understood from this perspective.

8.6 Summary

The 'girlie-bar' is essentially a typical place that builds a particular image of sex workers and their womanhood as being a combination of having a pretty and charming appearance, a friendly and fun personality, and happy, smiling, positive attitudes. It is, in a way, a pattern of modernizing womanhood in the space of sex work. Such life opportunities that tourism provides for the Thai bar workers have been rarely considered in the literature due to its perceived 'inappropriateness', the stereotyping of moral issues.

Through the traditional power and knowledge that comes from the networks in which sex-workers operate, there are also remarkable, often hidden nuances to be discovered through a contextualized approach. Too little is known about sex workers' attitudes to their work. My argument based on my observations and conversations is that the women focus on their optimistic attitudes towards the social and economic opportunities achievable through sex work on Koh Samui. While the discussion in this study is not intended to support the sex industry or to wish other females to look for opportunities through sex tourism, it is suggested to consider a different perspective when studying the sex tourism industry in order to fully understand its massive development. Since they are already working in the 'oldest business there is', the sex industry, sex work should be accepted as work. Moreover, most importantly, 'sex workers are people who must be treated as equals within society' (Chiang Mai Empower Group, 2003). In other words, they should be allowed to live with dignity and to progress in their future. It is an opportunity for life.

CHAPTER 9

CONCLUSION: POSITIONING HISTORY, TOURISM AND KOH SAMUI

9.1 Introduction

This chapter locates the research context within the aim, summarizes the findings and returns to the larger picture by presenting the implications of the research findings. The aim of this thesis was to develop and apply the concept of tourism history research by examining a tourist destination's change and adaptation over time. The study focused on examining the tourism history as a theoretical concept by applying it to the case of tourism development on Koh Samui, Thailand. This thesis therefore proposed an analytic framework of tourism history and discussed its value for a tourist destination's analysis. Koh Samui constituted the case study as a reference point to better illustrate specific issues relating to the research argument. This included an inquiry of the validity of the analytic tool, and involved linking the historical approach (and its perspectives) with tourism studies. The thesis examined Koh Samui societal change and adaptation during its tourism period by considering the implications of tourism development from the perspective of tourism history. The thesis focused on the interactions between history and tourism on Koh Samui. Thus, the thesis's objectives focused on the characters and processes of change of Koh Samui society. The case study was chosen due to 1) the distinctive character of the destinations' historical period (pre-tourism period and tourism period); 2) my familiarity with the place and prior knowledge of the site; and 3) adding to Cohen's (1996) study on tourism development on Koh Samui, one of the very first studies of tourism development in the area. Drawing on existing literature and other case studies, and introducing new conceptual perspectives, the thesis developed a theoretically informed foundation for examining the role of historical perspective to tourism studies – the tourism history approach. Issues relevant to tourism history were considered as such analysis provided an understanding of the diverse changes associated with tourism development over time (Walton 2005).

The conceptual framework presented in Figure 1.1 formed the thesis approach as it linked the historical perspective with tourism studies (Chapter 2), tourist destination development theory (Chapter 3) and the concept of the tourism period (Chapter 2). Methodologically (Chapter 4), the research aim and objectives were obtained through a qualitative research approach using ethnography and oral history methods (observation and participation; in-depth interview and oral history; as well as map survey techniques). Following Duval's (2004) notion, the thesis has emphasized the need 'to be conscious of the larger historical processes that have shaped the very performance, culture or attribute under scrutiny' (2004: 58). By examining the broader issues of the interactions between a tourist destination and tourism, and focusing on how history and culture of a tourist destination at both local level and national level were a great influence of a tourist destination development, the significant potential of using the tourism history approach to study a tourist destination development is emphasized. In essence, the framework in Figure 1.1 formed the basis for understanding how Koh Samui society's historical and cultural legacies, along with Thai history, has influenced past and present development patterns of Koh Samui as a tourist destination.

The examination of the relationship between history and tourism in the literature, discussed in Chapter 2, illustrated that the perspective of tourism history was significant. Specifically, by adopting a tourism history perspective in analyzing the data, it was confirmed that studying the historical implications of tourism at a destination was *beyond* describing the issues of tourism impacts simplistically. The empirical information about the shifting historical period, physical landscape, social configuration, and the issues of Thai gender on Koh Samui have been examined in order to present *change* and *adaptation* of Koh Samui society. The empirical material discussed in the previous four chapters (Chapters 5, 6, 7, and 8) emphasized the suitability of using the tourism history approach to understand a tourist destination comprehensively. Therefore, the framework in Figure 1.1 provided the basis to show how tourism has taken place; what changes tourism has brought and how; how life at home in relation to the family and the neighborhood has changed; and how those who are directly associated to tourism have adapted to live with it.

A range of qualitative research techniques (observation and participation; in-depth interview and oral history; map survey) was used to facilitate the gathering of the research data. However, some aspects of the research process were accompanied with difficulties.

These being, my position as the researcher in relationship to the research site, as discussed in Chapter 4; the marginal amount of longitudinal statistical data; the sensitivity of undertaking research in a commercial business environment, and privacy issues to receive information about real business ownership, as discussed in Chapter 6 to name a few. Working within those constraints a picture of Koh Samui society during its tourism development period was constructed. Therefore this research advances theoretical knowledge on utilizing the tourism history approach. It also reveals knowledge on understanding the implications of tourism on the society of Koh Samui. The identification of the tourism periodization in the process of Thailand's modernization and the emphasis on the Thai tourism system builds on the thesis' contribution to knowledge.

9.2 Tourism History and Koh Samui society

The focus of Objective One was to develop the framework, approach and theoretical conception of tourism history with particular focus on Koh Samui society. To achieve this objective, the relationships between history and tourism were discussed in order to understand Koh Samui society by grouping Koh Samui society into two historical periods – the pre-tourism period and the tourism period. These diverse relationships were discussed by considering that tourism development is an on-going process, which is part of the larger globalization process. Thus it may actually not be too dissimilar to other periods of conventional Thai history such as colonialism or nationalism. It is interesting to note that tourism has not 'totally' changed Koh Samui society in terms of social and political structure (Chapter 5). From the thesis's perspective, the touristization period of Koh Samui society, from the 1970s to the time of my fieldwork (2007), is a homogenized idiosyncratic period in which Koh Samui socialization is characterized by significant tourism experiences. In this respect, for most locals on Koh Samui who are aged fifty or older, the touristization period has made a significant change in their lives and the lives of their families. It has not only meant the move from a rural society to an increasingly urbanized one, but also to urbanization with a tourism-oriented focus. Whether or not these people understand the concepts of 'touristic transformation' (Cohen 2001) or the 'touristification' of their home (Picard 1996), they have been witness to the whole process of tourism development which has heavily influenced Koh Samui society over time. They have seen a process of transformation from a *traditional livelihood* (pre-industrial, rural, agrarian or agriculturally organized) to a *tourism livelihood* (service industry, capitalist, urban, business oriented).

In the Koh Samui context, and due to the ups and downs of the agricultural market in previous decades, members of Koh Samui society had a lot of experience from which to draw upon as people devised alternative ways of making a living. For many this made the acceptance of tourism development an easy choice. Through the process of tourism industrialization on the island, people on Koh Samui began to realize that they were gaining economic benefits from the tourism industry, especially when compared to their previous agricultural orientation and to other non-tourism regions in Thailand. Tourism was not only seen as a major blessing for the locals but also ultimately contributed to the pride of being an island local (Chapters 6, 7). This thesis's finding reflected Macleod (2004), Maiava (2001) and Tucker (2003)'s concerns that although rapid tourism development affected change of local experiences, socio-spatial and social-culture, local people are capable of managing their problems and needs. For locals, they are not *static position* to tourism development. In fact, they have abilities and flexibilities to change and to adapt with any situation in order to cope with tourism development. However, their capabilities to change and to adapt towards tourism industry are not the same depending upon their individual historical and cultural background. Described in this thesis is how the combined environment and history of Koh Samui have played a large role in creating the tourism boom evident today. The conclusion of this description corresponds with Stonich (2000) in that by providing insights and evidence of the characteristics of its culture, norms and values, we are adding to the understanding of how tourism influences a tourist destination. Moreover, Cole (2008) also concedes that examining the interaction between tourism and a tourist destination needs to understand the destination's cultural values and ideologies, including how it is constructed, practiced and transformed. Therefore, this thesis addresses the tourism history approach as the importance of taking a place's historical and cultural legacies along with rapid tourism growth of the place into a study of tourist destination development.

9.3 Tourism, historical, and cultural legacies of Koh Samui society

At the time of Thailand's modernization, Bangkok's centralized system affected the local elite's viewpoints, status, livelihood and social organization (Chapter 5). With an educational reform in Thailand, an urban middle class developed on Koh Samui that was a crucial factor in dealing with the future of its development (Chapters 6, 7). Educated people who had migrated from Bangkok to Koh Samui taught about the value of urbanization, how to appreciate development and provided insight into the future of the island. Although in the beginning these migrants may not have understood what tourism development meant to their future or even how modernization would affect their society, they were dissatisfied with their isolation and lack of urbanity. Thus, people on Koh Samui supported the development of self-identity and the construction of a practicable modern identity towards tourism-urbanization. Importantly, the people of Koh Samui who were educated in Bangkok or overseas returned to the island when the island's potential for development was already known. Therefore, from a local perspective the aim was to urbanize Koh Samui's locality with continuous development, which would then lead the locals to take control of the next stage of change and progress. Chapter 6 presented a physical landscape-based discussion as one of the ways in which Koh Samui has been located within the tourism context. The focus was to present the areas of differences between the agricultural practices and the tourism system that have encouraged tourism growth. In essence, it shows how the physical land (and landscape) on Koh Samui provides an excellent framework for representing the values and different interests of agrarians and tourism developers. This, in turn, somewhat reflects Young's (1983) notion of 'touristization'. Moreover, the thesis presented Koh Samui's physical landscape as a different appropriation of significant tourism activities.

In addition to the representation of the place and space on Koh Samui, tourism development has had implications for the island's cultural landscape. In accordance with Thai values, the traditions of Koh Samui society reflect patriotism, ties to a village and family customs, love of study, tolerance of others and an emphasis on spiritual life and Buddhist cosmology (Chapter 5, Chapter 6, Chapter 7, and Chapter 8). In other words, the Thai modernization process simultaneously and considerably influenced the norms of the island - Buddhism, the monarchy and the central Thai language. Specifically, hierarchy, status, personal loyalty, tolerant social etiquette and social stratification in terms of gender, age, education and family prestige are the norm and value of Thai traditional practices - a worldview that provides fundamental support of Koh Samui's culture to the present day. Moreover, the teaching of Buddhism and modern education provides people on Koh Samui with a certain way of behaviour, rules, norms and practices. The Thai bureaucracy with Bangkok administration, coupled with Chakri dynasty is another factor shaping the life of the island. Such cultural traditions are common to an agricultural society, to peasants in the countryside and to scholars who are absorbed in the Buddhist culture. Despite the agricultural revolution (cash crops), the foundations of socio-cultural practices on Koh Samui remained mainly rural and agricultural. However, this cultural core is not static – instead it has changed and continues to change (Cole 2008; Tucker 2003; Picard 1996; Crick 1994). Koh Samui, as a part of Thailand's agricultural civilization, was an agricultural society and its culture and society was that of a village. The research findings have shown that precisely this special social organization constituted an important source of strength by which the island survived socially.

From the 1970s onwards, however, Koh Samui entered a new era: the tourism development period. Its culture and society, previously based on farming with century-old techniques, could no longer fulfill the function that it once had. Many forms of behavior and many elements of the spiritual culture, which could be adapted to the demands of life in the past, were no longer practicable in many circumstances. New forms of survival had to be established for the requirements of today's tourism development. Many changes occurred in Koh Samui society, and tourism has had an important involvement with nearly all these processes. Therefore, as Koh Samui enters into a modernized society, the study of tourism development on Koh Samui must acknowledge the local desire as being a stereotypical process of globalization. It is important to note that Thainess is a broader national identity. It is very much a nation-construct, whether we are agreeing with it or not, and it is perceived to be stable, authentic, static and a timeless entity. Thai culture, before the existence of the modern Thainess, had a long history of interaction with alien cultures, which resulted in changes and adaptations along the national history. In this respect, Thailand, with its many traditions, cultures and values has been interacting with the influences and demands of outside cultures, which have been built upon each other over time and have contributed to the Thai identity. The Thai identity as discussed in Chapter 5 has made many significant contributions to the development of the island's socio-cultural identity. In addition, as discussed in Chapter 6, and illustrated in Chapters 7 and 8, the modern Koh Samui society indicated an emergence of new forms of society because of tourism's driving force. Similarly to Askew's (2002) studies of Bangkok, Koh Samui developed its own societal and cultural patterns, renovating and revitalizing them through the influences and demands of nation culture along with the absorption of new cultural elements from tourism migrants and tourists.

9.4 Tourism and process of change of Koh Samui society

The focus of Objective Three was to explore the character and process of change of Koh Samui society. To accomplish this task, the island's transformations generated by the advancement of tourism and social change were examined using notions of pre-existing culture, livelihood, landscape and development of the island as benchmarks. Although the initial tourism development into the area represented an exploration stage, appropriate government policies and an influx of outsider investments led to backpackers becoming familiar in the 1970s. This was followed by hotel and resort construction at the end of the 1980s. Considering Butler's tourist lifecycle this means that starting from the 1980s, tourism on Koh Samui became the dominant economic sector. Capacity limitations became heightened, but to the expense of local ownership. The small scale of tourism activities at the beginning indicated local involvement. Tourism was still at a very low level until the end of the 1980s, at which point Koh Samui opened the airport, resulting in increased rates of growth. With the introduction of the airport, the island's fast economic growth led to the next development stage. Since then, Koh Samui has attained its 'development stage' in Butler's evolutionary model, partly due to massive investments from outsiders. These movements were significant factors in the island's overall societal evolution.

For the locals, significant benefits from tourism development appeared during the post-airport era (since the 1990s), when tourism offered considerable opportunities for earning a better income. With the increasing importance of tourism on the island's economy, by the 2000s tourism became the island's dominant industry with outside investment bringing high levels of growth. This was due to tourism offering primary income to people that had not encountered foreigners before. A real boom occurred in the 2000s, with an influx of outside capital creating the possibility of the island remaining at the development stage: noticeably higher rates of growth were present, many at international standard. Also, it is very important to consider that while Thailand's overall economy was still recovering from its economic depression of 1997, the 2004 Tsunami on the west coast of Thailand actually brought boom to Koh Samui's (on the east coast) tourism economy. Multi-million dollar land developments continue to be planned by international hotel chains (Chapter 5), including the upgrade of existing tourism businesses (Chapter 6). Almost immediately several international hotel chains such as Bayan Tree, for instance, began construction. Moreover, Marriot Renaissance replaced the local-owned hotel called Buriraya Resort and Spa. Such power shift was characteristic of the general tourism development patterns (of ownership) on Koh Samui. From a historical perspective this suggests that the island is still in the development stage; the growth of tourism enterprises, and significant capital investment are indicative of this, both for local and foreign owners. However, it is clear that some forms of discernible evolutionary process do occur on Koh Samui; investment patterns change and the carrying capacity limit will be reached soon. Such growth-based tourism development produces stresses, which has consequences for the islands' environmental, social, and political state, but also for the visitation experience.

The shifting of the principal market on Koh Samui illustrates the ability to articulate the value of the island in terms of destination development. What is most apparent is that by the next decade (2010s), international hotels such as Banyan Tree and Sheraton on Lamai Beach, Conrad on Pang Ka Beach (the west side of the island) and Dusit Thani on Charngmon Beach are expected to have begun operation. The construction of these international hotels is seen as an indicator of the increasing investments into the island's tourism industry. Butler (1980: 8) states that increasing investments by 'external organizations, particularly for visitor accommodations indicates the 'development' stage of the destination'. With increasing investments in tourist accommodations, it can be argued that Koh Samui is still *in fashion*, and creating a range of opportunities for the standardized, severely packaged and mass marketed tourists.

Concerning the destination development on Koh Samui, Westerhausen (2002) states that backpackers have shifted away from the island to other destinations because of the tourism boom significantly since the beginning of the 1990s. In this respect, the period of the 1990s is a decade of mass tourism on Koh Samui, which was characterized by 'an

194

unprecedented building boom' (Westerhausen 2002: 201). Consequently, if viewed from the backpacker market segment alone, Koh Samui's tourist market could be seen as having stagnated according to Butler's tourist lifecycle theory. However, the boom of tourism on the island resulted, on a political level, from the central government in Bangkok reorganizing the island local government administrative procedures and managing and overseeing what was becoming a substantial influx of capital (Tambon Municipality of Koh Samui 2003). Along with massive investments from both national and local governments for tourist infrastructure, multi-million corporations invested in tourist facilities. Both were instrumental in introducing a 'new market development stage' of mass tourism. Therefore, depending on the aspect of analysis, it should not be forgotten that Koh Samui has a somewhat different tourist area lifecycle pattern.

In addition, in the face of the massive tourism-growth-driven development and the attraction of the economic benefits, people on Koh Samui now know how to make the most of the tourism industry. This occurs between place and activities, people and culture, and between both different cultures and the Thai culture as well as between the latter's traditional and modern components. Consequently, negotiation has resulted in what Koh Samui society had become today. These negotiations included changes in land ownership, practice and production, increased individualism and economic roles and professional entrepreneurial behavior. However, there is no clear direction as to where the negotiation will lead Koh Samui society. So far, people on Koh Samui are able to manage negotiations and handle the new forms of culture. The outcome of this thesis concurs with that of Tucker (2003): local people are not 'passive victims' to tourism development, rather, they *enjoy* the tourism development process and develop strategies to *benefit* from tourism opportunities. In fact, the people on Koh Samui are capable of showing initiative in gathering up what is good and progressive from the newcomers. For example, tourism has turned valueless land into a veritable goldmine, created a tourism-related class that has replaced the traditional agriculture-related social system, and provides opportunities for those of all classes. Those in the lower classes have been able to move to a higher class, such as tourism entrepreneurs. Tourism has provided significant opportunities for women, including those who work in the sex tourism field (Chapters 7 and 8). Tourism has also created a major distinction in the lifestyles amongst different generations on Koh Samui, most significantly for the elite young generation that has returned home, along with inward migrants. Domestic tourism has involved a Bangkok-centered metropolitan culture, reflected in urban tastes and a manipulation of the standard Thai dialect. This represents the present and points to some of the changes in the future.

Furthermore, the thesis's finding also revealed the differentiation between constructing Koh Samui local identity during its tourism development period and Thailand national identity during the country modernization process. As the national identity is very much a national-construct, particularly when the nation was facing the Western colonial powers in the nineteenth century (Chapter 5), Koh Samui along with other tourist destinations nationally, is now experiencing fundamental change without any particular identity-focused direction. In fact, Koh Samui is handling its fundamental change in terms of coping and negotiating its new identity on an individual level without the benefit of any national direction. Particularly, with the Thailand modernization process, Koh Samui has gained its values from existing national social and cultural identities, which were influenced by hierarchy, status, personal loyalty, tolerance, social etiquette and social stratification in terms of gender, age, education and family prestige. With tourism development, on the other hand, people on Koh Samui, similarly to Tucker's (2003) finding that tourism reshapes locals' activities, businesses and the role of different genders, became strong in preponderance of entrepreneurship. Moreover, the predominance of women in the tourist landscape as discussed in Chapter 6, 7, and 8 indicates their high status gained through tourism as opportunity, freedom and independence (Macleod 2004; Tucker 2993; Yasmeen 2002). Therefore, female participation in tourism seems to turn the stereotypical gender notion of mobility (that women are less free and mobile than men) on its head.

Cohen (1996: 213) once described the situation on Lamai Beach as: '[t]he under-capitalized local owners of bungalow-resorts do not possess the means for a drastic expansion and improvement of their facilities.' This was true at the beginning of the tourism development on the island, and also for families who could not cope with the competition from tourists and tourism workers once Koh Samui moved into the 'development stage' of Butler's evolutionary model. However, only within the past three decades Koh Samui's physical environment and historical culture have contributed to the island's rise of tourism wealth. Even though all developments on the island have not only come from local people, they have added important parts to the islands' tourism growth. In other words, Koh Samui is listed among the world's top tourist destinations, with a new generation of locals now contributing and benefiting from significant expansion and improvement of the Koh Samui's tourism industry. Despite this tourism development, Because of the overall foundation of the Thailand modernization process, the local response to tourism has been spontaneous and endogenous. On Koh Samui locals interpret opportunities and respond to them in an active process of negotiation. This thesis argues that some people, such as the new middle-class groups on Koh Samui like Nee and Sak (Chapter 6), or others involved in tourism entrepreneurship like Jit, Pong, Joy and Som (Chapter 7), and people in the sex tourism industry like Pen, Yaa, and Nat (Chapter 8) are all presently striving to create, to the best of their ability and by participation and consensus, a material tourism that is complementary to their social position.

9.5 Times have changed: the Thailand modernization process and the Koh Samui tourism period

This research provides connections to the phenomena (process of tourism development), the place (Koh Samui), the periods (agricultural period and tourism period) and the consequences (modern society of Koh Samui in its tourism period). Throughout the thesis, Koh Samui served as a venue for the formulation of concepts from an academic, tourism historical perspective by studying changes in a rural destination over time. Chapter 5 has shown that the way to epochal change in the history of Koh Samui has been opened through the island's *reactions* to tourism. More precisely, it was a consequence of a series of reactions, through inter-linkages between tourism growth and the island's physical and social change. The findings presented in Chapters 5, 6, 7 and 8 illustrated such tourism history of Koh Samui society.

Throughout Koh Samui's history there have been two major events that resulted in center-periphery interaction between Koh Samui and the Thai system. These are the Thailand modernization process in the nineteenth century and the global tourism process beginning in the 1970s. The effects of the two major encounters – inner-colonialism (Thailand modernization process) and tourism (global tourism process) – are quite different for Koh Samui society. The government, as outlined in Chapter 5, introduced a system of political administration and a cultural model of the society that was almost completely standardized at the time. The process was intended to insert the practice of

Thainess and connect the island, along with other regions, to the national society. Consequently, the island's original people and customs established some forms of local collaboration. Tourism is introduced as a means of change. Koh Samui, before exposure to the West through tourism, had already been in the midst of *change* through penetration by the country's influences. However, such relatively marginal change had not been capable of generating transformative energies. Regardless of the state reformation, which became the foundation of the island's society in terms of its cultural values and ideologies, and with Thai identity making a significant contribution to the building of a life on the island, Koh Samui remained a poor, agricultural society that relied mostly on its natural resources (Chapter 5). Moreover, Chapters 6 and 7 gave background to the Thai modernization process, and how these implications paved the way in the growth and development of particular groups within Koh Samui society. The Thai modernization process provided the basis for the cultural traditions of Koh Samui society, which in turn has benefited the ensuing generations, particularly the 'princes and princesses' of the island, by providing them with the means to cope and easily adapt to change.

The contemporary model of Koh Samui identity and the system of power and status distribution originates from these early forms of collaboration. In this regard, Koh Samui found itself in the process of Thailand's transformation during the country's modernization process. Importantly, the critique of the Thai modernization process discussed in this thesis is not new to Thai studies. The point made here is that as presented in Chapter 5 although Koh Samui finds itself in the modernization transformation process shared by the rest of Thailand, the island is a relative latecomer to Thai history. Before tourism development took place on Koh Samui, the island's relationship to Thai history was merely through marginalizing processes, both in the stark forms of regional politics and in representational terms compared to other regions. Even though the island had an isolated marginal character, that character had been shaped through national history involving reformation issues. The process of Koh Samui's urbanization, with the growth of non-agricultural activities such as the tourism industry and services goes hand-in-hand with the gradual shrinking of the agricultural economy. As an economy in transition, the very foundation and roots of the island's economy are being transformed, with a measurable effect on its society, education, wealth and culture. Consequently, Chapters 5 and 7 have shown that the position of Koh Samui within Thai society has not been entirely peripheral, particularly when it is exclusively defined from an economic aspect. Seen from a symbolic economic perspective, as considered in Chapters 6 and 7, it appears that Koh Samui society has been an active co-producer of its own social stature and has secured a number of specific privileges for itself. Thus, it is necessary to emphasize that some of the most distinctive and dramatic transformations in Koh Samui society have been the result of specific historical encounters with newcomers or new ideas.

In the modern society of Koh Samui, encounters with outsiders during its tourism period have resulted in significant shifts of what has become an episode of reconstructing the local society. Therefore, the position of Koh Samui within the wider Thai society has changed continuously during the time of its tourism development. As discussed in Chapter 5, Koh Samui has been shaped by its touristization, in line with national tourism strategies. Consequently, over three decades, from a coconut plantation Koh Samui transformed into a tropical paradise. From a backpacker destination to a massive tourist market, Koh Samui's geography, society and culture have experienced a marked transformation. Therefore, tourism has become a unique and major factor in such 'evolution' of the physical environment and society on Koh Samui. In this regard, Koh Samui has a distinctive touristization period, which serves as one of the most significant issues in the modern society of the island. The transformation from a traditionally agricultural society and the process of the assimilation of tourism development presents the most important mechanisms and conditions for Koh Samui modernity. The finding of the thesis reflects Duval's (2004) suggestion that when researching Koh Samui society, it is important to recognize the constitution of the national history and culture to the subject of the island's distinctive cultural traditions and its economic and social progress in modern times. Therefore, studies of social change on Koh Samui society need to pay attention to shifts in the distribution of the overall Thai social constructions.

In addition, it is important to understand people's pasts, as in Cole's (2008) study, in order to comprehend how their present confrontations may result in a new identity. Moreover, by putting the knowledge of the past into a present and a broader context, a better understanding of the current situation may develop. Koh Samui today, just as with other places, interacts and reacts with its past in the process of shaping its future. The identity that results from this process may remain the same or nearly the same or it may be very different. As presented in Chapter 7, the younger generation of the local elite might move out of their traditional social class. However, their education, financial situation and family ties still somehow identify them as a modern form of the local elite – the 'princes and princesses' of the island. As Duval (2004: 58) points out, 'one needs to be conscious of the larger historical processes that have shaped the very performance, culture or attribute under scrutiny'. Thus, placing Thailand's historical and cultural legacy within the tourism system has resulted in a better understanding of modern Koh Samui society and how it has changed during the touristization period - a crucial perspective to consider as it shows the linkages between changes on Koh Samui, the tourism period and the process of Thailand modernization as a whole. Following Walton's (2005) suggestion, understanding the historical process of location will provide significant outcomes in the study of tourism development. This thesis proposes that tourism periodization, specifically on Koh Samui, provides an alternative way to look at Thai history and the country's 'center-periphery' relations in Thai tourism studies. Tourism history of Koh Samui should explore beyond the analysis of the current situation of the industry and the destination. Only then will it add to an understanding of how a destination changes due to its current tourism development.

9.6 The thesis contribution to tourism studies

This thesis explored tourism on Koh Samui in a wider Thai tourism context. By doing so, the research focused on tourism internally (Cole 2008). Tourism and Koh Samui was the focus in order to contribute to the knowledge of tourism studies, particularly Thai tourism studies – as a way of learning about and understanding tourism in Thailand. For example, the discussion of the evolution of relations between Koh Samui and Thailand revealed unusual effects on Koh Samui during the critical stage of its transition to a touristic system. The existing relations between Koh Samui and Thailand during the Thai modernization process and major tourism development stage, recognize the place of Koh Samui within Thailand history (Chapter 5). From this point of view contemporary Koh Samui society stems from these Thai interconnections, particularly within the island's tourism period. This study adds to an understanding of Thailand government relations and their influences in the region. Pre-tourism identity and that of the tourism period therefore cannot be completely separated, as the former had a hand in shaping the latter, at least to some degree. This suggests that traditional perceptions of Koh Samui society have not remained unaffected by the major encounter of tourism in the island's more recent society. Rather Koh Samui has achieved a complete process of social development, which is orientated to tourism industrialization and modernization. The implications of the development of Koh Samui's tourism industrialization, as illustrated in Chapters 6, 7 and 8, represent the path of the socio-economic development on the island during the tourism period. In recent years, the trend of urbanization on Koh Samui has taken place in a rapid and powerful way. It has influenced the tourism space for production, consumption and the reproduction of tourism-related activities. The thesis draws on these concerns to show how Koh Samui society has changed significantly because of its tourism development. In other words, as presented in the Figure 9.1, Koh Samui society during its tourism period is the product of the combinations of 1) the Thailand historical and cultural legacies; 2) the Thailand tourism development system; 3) Koh Samui tourism development; and 4) the Thai identity, particularly during the Thailand modernization process.

Figure 9.1: The Koh Samui context

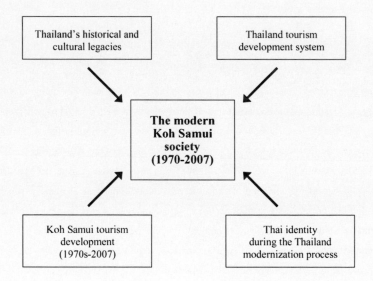

Subsequently, to understand Koh Samui as a subject of research is to understand not only the island itself but to build up a better understanding of Thailand tourism as well. Moreover, as studying modern Koh Samui society, the island's history and the cultural

201

interaction must be examined within the context of Thailand as a whole. Experiences of different cultures have existed in what is now Thailand in terms of developing the national culture, society, ethnicity and way of life. Clearly, to study the distinctive Koh Samui society cannot be done without a detailed study of both traditional and modern Thailand. In addition, Koh Samui presents a place for tourism economic accumulation and investment. It has constructed its place into one single unit of tourism business. It is a place of tourist spectacle and entertainment as well as a place of ordinary people, their lives and survival. Thus, through the documentation and interpretation of the role of Koh Samui in defining tourism as an analytical change of the society, culture and landscape, this thesis presents insights into modern Thailand because of the tourism modernization processes. The thesis considers the general implications of tourism on Koh Samui society, and thus contributes to the understanding of broader social change concepts in Thailand developmental studies.

9.7 Concluding Remarks

Tourism and Koh Samui's modernization are seen variably equated in this thesis with the *concomitant* changes on Koh Samui, if not all, being directly connected to the presence and persistence of tourism. Therefore, tourism is a subject of Koh Samui's historical periodization for the purposes of analyzing modern Koh Samui society. Thus, it can be argued that the tourism periodization marking the 'modern' society of Koh Samui is really a marking of history that represents modernizing influences on the island. While the thesis proposes that the internal changes from the integration of tourism development on Koh Samui are certainly worth of further study, more research is also needed in the area of Koh Samui's local government and its local political systems. With such research we would have a clearer view of how local governments react to or handle pressure from tourism. Particularly on the issue of identity, it would be interesting to study local government's policies in order to understand whether Koh Samui's local government concerns with identity-focused towards tourism development. In addition, while this thesis focuses on how locals react and their perceptions of tourism development, more research is needed in the area of tourists' reactions and their perception to tourism development on Koh Samui. Understanding such matters in more detail would help Koh Samui to achieve sustainable management of the island as it opens up and moves towards global tourism integration.

In summary despite all the physical, socio-cultural and gender changes that have happened on Koh Samui because of tourism, the culture of the pre-tourism period constituted an important part of the development during its tourism period. All major changes and variations during this period are reactions to the island's historical and cultural legacies. Therefore, to study changes of tourism, one needs to take the *history* of the place into serious consideration. From a conventional historical perspective, tourism is unlike Western colonialism in the nineteenth century in terms of its influence on the nation's environmental, political and social change. However, it has a similar influence on the micro level, and particularly on the regional level. Moreover, the reaction towards Western colonialism during that time was in the form of national unity within a set period, while the reaction towards tourism is based on individuality and is set within different timeframes. While Thailand deals with Western colonialism as a single place, the reaction to tourism is different from place to place. Importantly, if tourism is recognized as *one* 'major' significant social event, a collective close-up analysis of local tourism development from different regions would contribute to the understanding of overall Thai society during the Thailand touristization period. The challenges facing Koh Samui will most probably grow with more development and further pushing of tourism growth. The industry is the main factor in reaching growth targets of the island. For this reason, we must carefully evaluate and analyze these trends taking place in Koh Samui, and particularly consider the islands' external tourism development relations. Even more importantly, we must analyze the changes that are taking place in the world's tourism industry.

BIBLIOGRAPHY

Abbott, J., 1995, 'Community Participation and its relationship to community development,' *Community Development Journal*, 30(2): 158-168

Afolayan, A.A., 2001, Issue and challenges of emigration dynamics in developing countries, *International Migration*, 39(4): 5-40

Agarwal, S., 1994, 'The resort cycle revisited: implications for resorts', Pp. 194-208, in C.P. Cooper and A. Lockwood, (eds.), Progress in Tourism, Recreation and Hospitality Management (Vol. 5), London, Belhaven

Agarwal, S., 1997, 'The resort cycle and seaside tourism: an assessment of its applicability and validity', *Tourism Management*, 18(2): 65-73

Agarwal, S. 2002, 'Restructuring seaside tourism: the resort lifecycle', *Annals of Tourism Research*, 29(1): 25-55

Andrew, T. ed., 2000, *Civility and Savagery: Social Identity in Tai States*, Surrey, Curzon Press

Antaseeda, P., 2002, Trouble in paradise, *Bangkok Post*, June 21, 2002

Apostolopoulos, Y., 1996, Introduction: Reinventing the sociology of tourism, Pp. 1-12, in Y. Apostolopoulos, S. Leivadi and A. Yiannakis, (eds.), *The Sociology of Tourism: theoretical and empirical investigations*, London, Routledge

Apostolopoulos, Y., Leivadi, S. and Yiannakis, A., (eds.), 2002, *The Sociology of Tourism: Theoretical and Empirical Investigations*, London, Routledge

Apostolopoulos, Y. and Gayle, D.J., 2002, 'From MIRAB to TOURAB? Searching for sustainable development in the Maritime Caribbean, Pacific, and Mediterranean,' Pp.3-14, in Y. Apostolopoulos and D.J. Gayle, (eds.), *Island Tourism and Sustainable Development: Caribbean, Pacific, and Mediterranean Experiences*, Praeger Publisher, Westport

Askew, M., 2002, *Bangkok: place, practice and representation*, London, Routledge

Askew, M., 2003, 'The cultural factor in rural-urban fringe transformation: land, livelihood, and inheritance in western Nonthaburi', Pp. 287-322, in F. Molle and T Srijantr, (eds.), *Thailand's Rice Bowl: Perspectives on agricultural and social change in the Chao Phraya Delta,* Bangkok, White Lotus

Ateljevic, I. and Doorne, S., 2000, 'Staying within the fence: lifestyle entrepreneurship in tourism', *Journal of Sustainable Tourism*, 8(5): 378-392

Ayala, H., 1991, 'Resort hotel landscape as an international megatrend', *Annals of Tourism Research*, 18: 568-587

Baecharoen, I., 2000, *Impacts of Religious Tourism in Thailand*, unpublished Master of Tourism Thesis, Department of Tourism, University of Otago, Dunedin

Baffie, J., 2003, 'Ethnic groups in the central plain of Thailand: the setting of a mosaic', Pp. 37-76, in F. Molle and T Srijantr, (eds.), *Thailand's Rice Bowl: Perspectives on agricultural and social change in the Chao Phraya Delta*, Bangkok, White Lotus

Bale, J. and Smith, D.D., 1988, *Tourism and Development in the Third World*, Routledge, London

Bangkok Airway 2002, *Samui Airport*, http://www.bangkokair.com

Bangkok Post, May 10, 1998

Bangkok Post, October 6, 1998

Bangkok Post, March 16, 1999

Bangkok Post, August 3, 1999

Bangkok Post, July 21, 2002

Banks, A., 2003, Autobiography and cultural geography: Using personal experience to form research, Pp. 88-90, in A. Blunt, P. Gruffudd, J. May, M. Ogborn and D. Pinder, (eds.), *Cultural Geography in Practice*, New York, Oxford University Press

Baker, C and Phongpaichit, P., 2005, *A History of Thailand*, Cambridge, Cambridge University Press

Barme, S., 2002, *Woman, Man, Bangkok: Love, Sex, and Popular Culture in Thailand*, Rowman & Littlefield Publishers, Inc., Lanham

Barnes, H.E., 1962, *a History of Historical Writing*, New York, Dover Publications, Inc.

Barnett, H.G., 1983, 'Learning about culture: reconstruction, participation, administration 1934-1954, Pp. 157-174, in G.W. Stocking, Jr., (ed.), *History of Anthropology, Volume 1: Observers Observed: Essays on Ethnographic Fieldwork*, Wisconsin, the University of Wisconsin Press

Belsky, J., 2004, 'Contributions of qualitative research to understanding the politics of community ecotourism,' Pp. 273-291 in J. Phillimore and L. Goodson, (eds.) *Qualitative Research in Tourism*, Routledge, London

Berkhofer, R.F., 1969, *A Behavioral Approach to Historical Analysis*, New York, The Free Press

Boissevain, J. (ed.), 1996, *Coping With Tourists*, Oxford, Berghahn Books

Boonsirichai, M., 2002, Tourists' Perceptions of Samui Island, Thailand, as a tourist destination, Unpublished Master of Science Degree, University of Wisconsin-Stout

Boribal, B. and Griswold, A.B., 1950, Sculpture of Peninsular Siam in the Ayutthya Period, *Journal of the Siam Society*, 38/2: 1-60

Brown, J.M., 1985, *From Ancient Thai to Modern Dialects: and other writings on historical Thai linguistics*, Bangkok, White Lotus

Bruner, E.M., 1986, 'Experience and its expressions,' Pp.3-30, in V.W. Turner and E.M. Bruner, (eds.), *The Anthropology of Experience*, Chicago, University of Illinois Press

Bruner, E. M., 1991, Transformation of self in tourism, *Annals of Tourism Research*, 18: 238-250

Bunnag, Taj., 1977, *The Provincial Administration of Siam 1892-1915*, Kuala Lumpur, Oxford University Press

Burke, P., 1991, 'Overture: the new history, its past and its future,' Pp.1-23, in P. Burke, (ed.), *New Perspectives on Historical Writing*, Oxford, Polity Press

Burn, W.L. 1968, 'Politic Under Reform,' Pp. 112-122, in W.H. Heahl, Jr. (ed.), *The Reform Bill of 1832: Why not Revolution?*, New York, Holt, Renehout and Winston

Burns, P. 2001, 'Brief encounter; Culture, tourism and the local-global nexus,' In S Wahab and C. Cooper (eds.), *Tourism in the Age of Globalization*, London, Routledge

Butler, R.W., 1980, 'the concept of a tourism area cycle of evolution: implications for management of resources,' *Canadian Geographer*, 24: 5-12

Butler, R.W., 1993, 'Tourism development in small islands: past influences and future directions,' Pp.71- 91, in D.G. Lockhart, & D. Drakakis-Smith, and J. Schembri, (eds.), *The Development Process in Small Island States*, Routledge, London

Butler, R.W., 2006a, 'The concept of a tourist area cycle of evolution: implications for management of resources,' Pp. 3-12, in R.W. Butler, (ed.), *The Tourism Area Life Cycle Vol. 1: Applications and Modifications*, Cromwell Press, Clevedon

Butler, R.W., ed., 2006b, *The Tourism Area Life Cycle Vol. 1: Applications and Modifications*, Cromwell Press, Clevedon

Carr, E.H., 2001, *What is History? With a New Introduction by Richard J. Evans*, Hampshire, PALGRAVE

Carter, H., 1995, *The Study of Urban Geography; Fourth Edition*, London, Arnold

Castells, M., 1983, *The city and the grassroots: a cross-cultural theory of urban social movements*, Berkeley, University of California Press

Chang, T.C., & Milne, S., & Fallon, D., & Pohlmann, C., 1996, Urban heritage tourism: the global-local nexus, *Annals of Tourism Research*, 23(2): 284-305,

Chatrudee, T., 2002, Resort Islands Growing Thirsty, *Bangkok Post*, 2002, 10 May

Cheater, A.P., 1987, 'The anthropologist as citizen: the diffracted self?,' Pp. 164-179, in A. Jackson (ed.), *Anthropology at Home*, New York, Tavistock Publications

Chiangmai News, 27th November 2004

Chon, K.S. and Singh, A., 1994, Environmental challenges and influences on tourism: the case of Thailand's tourism industry,' Pp. 81-91, in C.P. Cooper and A. Lockwood, (eds.), *Progress in tourism, recreation and hospitality management,* (Vol. 6), Chichester, John Wiley

Clifford, H., 1990, *Further India: Being the story of exploration from the earliest times in Burma. Malaya, Siam, and Indo-China,* White Lotus, Bangkok

Cohn, B.S., 1987, *An Anthropologist among the Historians and Other Essays,* Delhi, Oxford University Press

Cohen, E. 1982, 'Marginal paradises: bungalow tourism of the islands in Southern Thailand,' *Annals of Tourism Research,* 9, Pp. 189-228

Cohen, E., 1988, Authenticity and commoditization in tourism, *Annals of Tourism Research,* 15(3): 371-386

Cohen, E., 1989, Primitive and remote, Hill Tribe Trekking in Thailand, *Annals of Tourism Research,* 16(1): 30-61

Cohen, E., 1996, *Thai Tourism: Hill tribes, islands and open-ended prostitution,* Collected Papers, Bangkok, White Lotus

Cohen, E., 2000, *The Commercialized Crafts of Thailand: Hill Tribes and Lowland Villages,* collected articles, Surrey, Curzon Press

Cohen, E., 2001, Thailand in 'Touristic Transition', Pp. 155-175, in P. Teo, T.C. Chang and K.C. Ho, (eds.), *Interconnected Worlds: Tourism in southeast Asia,* Amsterdam, PERGAMON

Cohen, E., 2004, *Contemporary Tourism: Diversity and change,* Amsterdam, ELSEVIER

Cohn, B.S., 1971, *India: the Social Anthropology of a Civilization,* in D.M. Schneider, Series Editor of Anthropology of Modern Societies Series, New Jersey, Prentice-Hall, Inc.

Cohn, B.S., 1987, *An Anthropologist among the Historians and Other Essays*, Delhi, Oxford University Pressb

Cole, S., 2008, *Tourism, Culture and Development: Hopes, dreams and realities in East Indonesia*, Clevedon, Channel View Publications

Colic-Peisker, V., 2004, 'Doing Ethnography in 'One's Own Ethnic Community,' Pp. 82-94, in L. Hume and J, Mulcock, (eds.), *Anthropologists in the Field: Cases in Participant Observation*, New York, Columbia University Press

Collingwood, R.G., 1959, 'The historical imagination,' Pp. 66-84 in H. Meyerhoff, (ed.), *The Philosophy of History in Our Time: an Anthology*, New York, Double Anchor Books

Conlin, M.V. and Baum, T., 1995, 'Island tourism: an introduction,' Pp.3-13, in M.V. Conlin and T. Baum, (eds.), *Island Tourism: Management, Principles and Practice*, John Wiley & Sons Ltd., West Sussex

Cooper, C., 1992, 'The lifecycle concept and strategic planning for coastal resorts,' *Built Environment*, 18: 57-66

Cooper, C. and Jackson, S., 1989, 'Destination area lifecycle: the Isle of Man case study,' *Annals of Tourism Research*, 16(3): 377-398

Crick, M., 1994, *Resplendent Sites, Discordant Voices: Sri Lankans and International Tourism*, Switzerland, Harwood Academic Publishers

Croce, B., 1959, 'History and chronicle,' Pp. 44-57, in H. Meyerhoff, (ed.), *The Philosophy of History in Our Time: an Anthology*, New York, Double Anchor Books

Croy, W.G. and Walker, R.D., 2003, 'Rural tourism and film – issues for strategic regional development, Pp.115-133, in D. Hall, L. Roberts and M. Mitchell, (eds.), *New Directions in Rural Tourism*, Hants, Ashgate

Danto, A.C., 1985, *Narration and Knowledge*, New York, The Columbia University Press

Davies, C.A., 1999, *Reflexive Ethnography: a Guide to Researching Selves and Others*, London, Routledge

209

Delamont, S., 1995, *Appetites and Identities: an Introduction to the Social Anthropology of Western Europe*, London, Routledge

Denzin, N.K. and Lincoln, Y.S., 2000, 'Introduction: the discipline and practice of qualitative research', Pp. 1-28, in N.K. Denzin and Y.S. Lincoln (eds.), *Handbook of Qualitative Research*, 2nd ed, Sage Thousand Oaks, California

Di Benedetto, C. A. and Bojanic, D.C., 1993, 'Tourism area life cycle extension', *Annals of Tourism Research*, 20: 557-570

Diller, A. 1991, 'What Makes Central Thai a National Language?', Pp. 87-132, in C.J. Reynolds, (ed), *National Identity and Its Defenders: Thailand, 1939-1989*, Victoria, The Publications Officer Centre of Southeast Asian Studies Monash University

Douglas, N., 1997, 'Applying the life cycle model to Melanesia,' *Annals of Tourism Research*, 24(1): 1-22

Doxey, G.V., 1975, A causation theory of visitor-resident irritants; methodology and research inferences. *Sixth Annual Travel Research Conference* (pp. 195-198), San Diego, CA September 8-11

Dragadze, T., 1987, 'Fieldwork at home: the USSR,' Pp. 154-163, in A. Jackson (ed.), *Anthropology at Home*, New York, Tavistock Publications

Duval, D.T., 2004, 'Cultural tourism in postcolonial environments: negotiationg histories, ethnicities and authenticities in St. Vincent, Eastern Caribbean,' Pp. 57-75, in C.M. Hall and H. Tucker, (eds.), *Tourism andPostcolonialism: Contested discourses, identities and representations*, London, Routledge

Dymond, D., 1982, *Writing Local History: a Practical Guide,* London, Bedford Square Press/ NCVO

Echtner, C.M. and Jamal, T.B., 1997, The disciplinary dilemma of tourism studies, *Annals of Tourism Research*, 24(4): 868-883

Ekachai, S., 1990, *Behind the Smile: Voice of Thailand*, Bangkok, Thai Development Support Committee

Ekinsmyth, C., 2002, 'Feminist cultural geography', Pp. 53-65, in P. Shurmer-Smith, (ed.), *Doing Cultural Geography*, London, Sage Publications

Ekinsmyth, C. and Shurmer-Smith, P., 2002, 'Humanistic and behavioural geography', Pp. 19-28, in P. Shurmer-Smith, (ed.), *Doing Cultural Geography*, London, Sage Publications

Ellen, R.F., ed., 1984, *Ethnographic Research: a guide to general conduct*, London, Academic Press Ltd.

Elliott, J., 1983, 'Politics, powers, and tourism in Thailand, *Journal of Tourism Research*, 10: 377-393

Elliott, J. 1997, *Tourism: politics and public sector management*, London, Routledge

Eng, L.A., 1998, 'Some experiences and issues of cross-cultural fieldwork in Singapore,' Pp.98-115, in P.L.P. Huen, & J.H. Morrison and K.C. Guan, (eds.), *Oral History in Southeast Asia: Theory and Method*, Singapore, Institute of Southeast Asian Studies

Engerman, D., 1994, A research agenda for the history of tourism, towards an international social history, *American Studies International*, 32, 3-31

Evans, R.J., 2001, 'Introduction,' Pp. ix-xlvi, in E.H. Carr, (ed.), *What is History? With a New Introduction by Richard J. Evans*, Hampshire, PALGRAVE

Evans, R.J., 2002, 'Prologue: what is history? – now,' Pp. 1-18, in D. Cannadine, (ed.), *What is History Now?*, Macmillan, Palgrave

Fadzillah, I, 2004, 'Going beyond 'the west' and 'the rest': conducting non-western, non-native ethnography in northern Thailand,' Pp. 32-45, in L. Hume, and J. Mulcock, (eds.), *Anthropologists in the Field: Cases in Participant Observation*, New York, Columbia University Press

Fagence, M., 2003, 'Tourism and local society and culture', Pp. 55-78, in S. Singh, D.J. Timothy and R.K. Dowling, (eds.), *Tourism in Destination Communities*, Oxon, CABI Publishing

Fairclough, N., 1989, *Language and Power*, London, Longman

Featherstone, M. (ed.), 1990, *Global Culture: Nationalism, Globalization and Modernity*, London, Sage

Flood, E.T. 1969, 'The 1940 Franco-Thai Border Dispute and Phibuun Songkraam's Commitment to Japan,' *Journal of Southeast Asian History* 5(2): 304-325

Fordham, G., 1994, 'Participant observation and language learning,' Pp. 9-36, in M. Crick and B. Geddes, (eds.), *Research Methods in the field: ten anthropological accounts*, Victoria, Deakin University Press

Foster, D.M. and Murphy, P., 1991, 'Resort cycle revisited: the retirement connection,' *Annals of Tourism Research,* 18: 553-567

Ganguly-Scrase, R., 1994, 'The self as research instrument,' Pp. 37-58, in M. Crick and B. Geddes, (eds.), *Research Methods in the field: ten anthropological accounts*, Victoria, Deakin University Press

Gasset, J.O.Y., 1959, 'History as a system,' Pp. 57-64, in H. Meyerhoff, (ed.), *The Philosophy of History in our time: an anthology*, New York, Double Anchor Books

Gentilcore, D., 2005, 'Anthropological approaches,' Pp. 49-70, in G. Walker, (ed.), *Writing Early Modern History*, London, Hodder Arnold

Getz, D., 1992, 'Tourism planning and destination life cycle,' *Annals of Tourism Research,* 19: 752-770

Giddens, A., 1991, *Modernity and Self Identity*, Cambridge, Polity Press

Girling, J.L.S., 1981, *Thailand: Society and Politics*, Ithaca, Cornell University Press

Gmelch, G., 2003, *Behind the Smile: the working lives of Caribbean Tourism*, Bloomington, Indiana University Press

Goldman, M., 1972, 'Franco-British Rivalry Over Siam, 1896-1904,' *Journal of Southeast Asian Studies,* III(2): 210-228

Goldsmith, A., 1996, *The Island: paradise in Koh Samui*, Tauranga, New Zealand

Goodman, J., 1997 'History and anthropology', Pp. 783-804, in M. Bentley, (ed.), *Companion to Historiography*, London, Routledge

Green, R., 2005, Community perceptions of environmental and social change and tourism development on the island of Koh Samui, Thailand, *Journal of Environmental Psychology*, 25(1): 37-56

Gross, R., 1993, *Buddhism after Patriarchy*, Albany, State University of New York Press

Hall, C.M., 1994, 'Gender and economic interests in tourism prostitution: the nature, development and implications of sex tourism in South-east Asia, Pp. 142-163, in V. Kinnaird and D. Hall, (eds.), *Tourism: A Gender Analysis*, Chichester, John Wiley & Sons

Hall, C.M., 1997, *Tourism in the Pacific Rim: development, impacts and markets, 2nd edition*, Melbourne, Longman

Hall, C.M., 2004, 'Reflexivity and tourism research: situating myself and/with others,' Pp. 137-155, in J. Phillimore and L. Goodson, (eds.) *Qualitative Research in Tourism*, Routledge, London

Hall, C.M. and Page, S., (eds.) 2000, *Tourism in South and Southeast Asia: Issues and Cases*, Oxford, Butterworth Heinemann

Hall, C.M. and Page, S.J., 2002, *The Geography of Tourism and Recreation: Environmental, Place and Space*, London, Routledge

Hall, C.M. and Tucker, H., 2004, 'Tourism and postcolonism: an introduction,' Pp. 1-24, in C.M. Hall and H. Tucker, (eds.), *Tourism and Postcolonialism: Contested discourses, identities and representations*, London, Routledge

Hammersley, M., 1992, *What's Wrong with Ethnography?*, London, Rutledge

Hammersley, M. and Atkinson, P., 2007, *Ethnography: Principle in practice, third edition*, London, Routledge

Hanna, S.P. and Del Casino Jr. V.J., 2003, Introduction: tourism spaces, mapped representations, and the practices of identity, Pp. ix-xxvii, in S.P. Hanna and V.J. Del Casino Jr. (eds.), *Mapping Tourism*, Minneapolis, University of Minnesota press

Hantrakul, S., 1983, *Prostitution in Thailand*, Clayton, Victoria, Monash University, Center for Southeast Asian Studies

Harrison, D., 1992, *Tourism & the Less Developed Countries*, London, John Wiley & Sons Ltd.

Hastrup, K. 1987, 'Fieldwork among friends: ethnographic exchange within the Northern civilization,' Pp. 94-108, in A. Jackson (ed.), *Anthropology at Home*, New York, Tavistock Publications

Haug, F., 1987, *Female Sexualization*, London, Verso

Hawkins, D.E. and Holtz, C., 2001, 'Environmental policies and management systems related to the global tourism industry,' Pp.261-289, in S. Wahab and C. Cooper, (eds.), *Tourism in the Age of Globalisation*, Routledge, London

Haywood, K.M., 1986, Can the tourist area cycle of evolution be made operational?, *Tourism Management*, 7(3): 154-167

Haywood, K.M., 2006, 'Evolution of tourism areas and the tourism industry,' Pp. 51-70, in Pp. 3-12, in R.W. Butler, (ed.), *The Tourism Area Life Cycle Vol. 1: Applications and Modifications*, Cromwell Press, Clevedon

Henige, D., 1982, *Oral Historiography*, London, Longman

Herbert, D.T. and Matthews, J.A., 2004, 'Introduction,' Pp. 163-170, in J.A. Matthews and D.T. Herbert, (eds.), *Unifying Geography: Common heritage, shared future*, London, Routledge

Herbert, S., 2000, 'For ethnography,' *Progress in Human Geography*, 24(4): 550-568

Higham, J., 2000, 'Thailand: prospects for a tourism-led economic recovery,' Pp. 129-143, in C.M. Hall and S. Page, (eds.), *Tourism in South and Southeast Asia: issues and cases*, Oxford, Butterworth-Heinemann

Hovinen, G.R. 2002, 'Revisiting the destination lifecycle model,' *Annals of Tourism Research,* 29(1): 209-230

Huen, P.L.P., Morrison, J.H., and Guan, K.C., (eds.), 1998, *Oral History in Southeast Asia: Theory and Method*, Singapore, Institute of Southeast Asian Studies

Hume, L. and Mulcock, J., 2004a, 'Introduction: Awkward spaces, productive places,' Pp. xi-xxvii, in L. Hume and J, Mulcock, (eds.), *Anthropologists in the Field: Cases in Participant Observation*, New York, Columbia University Press

Hume, L. and Mulcock, J., (eds.) 2004b, *Anthropologists in the Field: Cases in Participant Observation*, New York, Columbia University Press

Inglis, F., 1993, *Cultural Studies*, Oxford, Blackwell

Intarakomalyasut, N. 2001, 'Amazing but not for long', *Bangkok Post*, 2 July 2001

Ioannides, D., 1992, 'Tourism development agents: the Cypriot resort cycle', *Annals of Tourism Research*, 19(4): 711-731

Ioannides, D., 2003, 'The economics of tourism in host communities', Pp. 37-54, in S. Singh, D.J. Timothy, and R.K. Dowling (eds.), *Tourism in Destinaiton Communities*, Oxon, CABI Publishing

Ioannides, D. & Apostolopoulos, Y. and Sonmez, S., 2001, 'Searching for sustainable tourism development in the Insular Mediterranean,' Pp. 3-22, in D. Ioannides, Y. Apostolopoulos, and S. Sonmez, (eds.), *Mediterranean Islands and Sustainable Tourism Development: Practices, Management and Policies*, London, Continuum

Iredale, D., 1974, *Local History Research and Writing: a Manual for Local History Writers*, Leeds, The Elmfield Press

Isvilanonda, S. and Hossain, M., 2003, 'Dynamics of rice farming in the Chao Phraya Deltaa: a case of study of three villages in Suphan Buri province, Pp. 109-124, in F. Molle and T., Srijantr, (eds.), *Thailand's Rice Bowl: Perspectives on agricultural and social change in the Chao Phraya Delta,* Bangkok, White Lotus

Jackson, A., 1987a, 'Reflections on ethnography at home and the ASA,' Pp. 1-15, in A. Jackson, (ed.), *Anthropology at Home*, London, Tavistock Publications Ltd

Jackson, A., 1987b, (ed.), *Anthropology at Home*, London, Tavistock Publications Ltd

Jackson, P.A., 1989, *Buddhism, Legitimation and Conflict: the political functions of urban Thai Buddhism*, Singapore, Institution of Southeast Asian Studies

Jackson, P.A. and Cook N.M., 1999, (eds.), *Genders & Sexualities in Modern Thailand*, Silkworm Books, Chiang Mai

Jafari, J. and Aaser, D., 1988, 'Tourism as the subject of doctoral dissertation,' *Annals of Tourism Research* (15): 407-429

Jamal, T.B. and Getz, D., 1995, 'Collaboration theory and community tourism planning,' *Annals of Tourism Research*, 22(1): 205-217

Jamieson, W., 2001, *Defining Urban Destination Management, Community Tourism Destination Management: Principles and Practice*, Canadian Universities Consortium, Urban Environment Management Project, Bangkok, Asian Institute of Technology

Jariyasombat, P., 1998, 'Samui flourishes amid recession: hoteliers report heavy bookings', *Bangkok Post*, October 6, 1998

Jarujitiphan, P., 1993, '*Impact of tourism development on Samui Island's economy and education, (Phon Ka Top Khong Kan Tong Teaw Tho Saad Ta Kit Lae Kan Sook Sa),*' unpublished Doctoral Thesis, Srinakharinwirot University, Bangkok, Thailand

Jenkins, C.L., 1997, 'Impacts of the development of international tourism in the Asian region,' Pp.48-64, in F.M. Go and C.L. Jenkins, (eds.), *Tourism and Economic Development in Asia and Australasia*, Cassell, London

Jenkins, K., 2003, *Refiguring History: New Thoughts on an old Discipline*, London, Routledge

Jordanova, L., 2000, *History in Practice*, London, Arnold

Kabilsingh, C., 1991, *Thai Women in Buddhism*, Berkeley, Parallax Press

Kabilsingh, C., 1997, 'Present situation of women in Buddhism,' Pp. 257-275, in S. Virada and S., Theobald, (eds.), *Women, Gender Relations and Development in Thai Society*, Chiangmai, Women's Studies center, Faculty of Social Science, Chaing Mai University

Kanjanaphan, A., 2000, 'Ideology and methodology in local history: cultural perspective,' (*Naew Kwam Kid Lae Wi Ti Sook Sa Pra Wat Ti Sat Tong Tin Ney Tang Wat Tha Na Tum*), *Journal of Institution Cultural Art Research*, 1(2), Pp. 17-32

Keane, M., 2000, 'Rural tourism and rural development,' Pp.107-122, in H. Briassoulis and J. Straaten, (eds.), *Tourism and the Environment: Regional, Economic, Cultural and Policy Issues*, Dordrecht, Kluwer Academic Publisher

Kearns, R. A., 2000, 'Being there: research through observing and participating,' Pp. 103-121, In I. Hey, (ed.), *Qualitative Research Methods in Human Geography*, Victoria, Oxford University Press

Keyes, C.F. 1984, 'Mother or mistress but never a monk: Buddhist notions of female gender in rural Thailand', *American Ethnologist*, 11 (May): 223-241

Khongmuangphet, K., 1988, 'From the West to the East; Following the Route of the Villagers Along the Krabi Shore' *(Chaak tawan tok su tawan ook taam senthaang chao ban fang thale krabi)*, *Muang Boran*, 14(3): 51-58

Killick, A.P., 1995, The penetrating intellect: on being white, straight, and male in Korea, Pp. 76-106, in D. Kulick and M. Willson, (eds.), *Taboo: Sex, Identity and Erotic Subjectivity in Anthropological Fieldwork*, London, Routledge

Kim, W.B., 1997, 'Culture, History, and the city in East Asia,' Pp. 17-39, in W.B. Kim, & M. Douglass, & S. Choe, and K.C. Ho, (eds.), *Culture and the City in East Asia*, Oxford, Clarendon Press

King, B.E.M., 1997, *Creating Island Resorts*, Routledge, London

King, R., 1993, 'The geographical fascination of islands,' Pp.13-37, in D.G. Lockhart, & D. Drakakis-Smith, and J. Schembri, (eds.), *The Development Process in Small Island States*, Routledge, London

King, V., 1999, *Anthropology and Devleopemnt in South East Asia; Theory and Practice*, Oxford, Oxford University Press

Kitahara, A., 2003, 'Lan Laem from 1980-1996: profile of a rice growing village in Nakhon Pathom province, Pp. 267-286, in F. Molle and T. Srijantr, (eds.), *Thailand's Rice Bowl: Perspectives on agricultural and social change in the Chao Phraya Delta*, Bangkok, White Lotus

Koh Samui Community Magazine, 2004, Thambon Municipality, Koh Samui,

Koh Samui Community Magazine, 2005, Thambon Municipality, Koh Samui

Koh Samui Community Magazine, 2007, Thambon Municipality, Koh Samui

Kontogeorgopoulos, N., 1998, 'Accommodation employment patterns and opportunities,' *Annals of Tourism Research*, 25(2): 314-339

Krongkaew, M., 1995, *Thailand's Industrialization and its Consequences*, New York, St. Martin's Press

Kulick, D. and Willson, M. (eds.), 1995, *Taboo: Sex, Identity and Erotic Subjectivity in Anthropological Fieldwork*, London, Routledge

Ladkin, A., 1999, 'Life and work history analysis: the value of this research method for hospitality and tourism,' *Tourism Management*, 20(1): 37-45

Ladkin, A., 2004, 'The Life and Work History Methodology: A discussion of its potential use for tourism and hospitality research,' Pp. 236-254, in J. Phillimore and L. Goodson, (eds.) *Qualitative Research in Tourism*, Routledge, London

Larcom, J., 1983, 'Following Deacon: the problem of ethnographic reanalysis, 1926-1981,' Pp. 175-195, in G.W. Stocking, Jr., (ed.), *History of Anthropology, Volume 1: Observers Observed: Essays on ethnographic fieldwork,* Wisconsin, the University of Wisconsin Press

Law, J., 2000, On the subject of the object: Narrative, technology, and interpellation, *In Configurations*, 8(1), 1-29

Lefebvre, H. 2004, *The Production of Space*, Nicholson-Smith, D. (trans.), Malden, Blackwell

Li, L. and Zhang, W., 1997, 'Thailand: the dynamic growth of Thai tourism', pp. 286-303, in F.M. Go and C. L. Jenkins, (eds.), *Tourism and Economic Development in Asia and Australasia*, Cassell Imprint, London

Limanonda, B., 1995, 'Families in Thailand: beliefs and realities,' Special Issue: Families in Asia: Beliefs and Realities,' *Journal of Comparative Family Studies*, 26(1): 67-82

Lockhart, D.G. & Drakakis-Smith, D. and J. Schembri, (eds.), 1993, *The Development Process in Small Island States*, Routledge, London

Lockhart, D.G., 1993, 'Introduction,' Pp.1-9, in D.G. Lockhart, & D. Drakakis-Smith, and J. Schembri, (eds.), *The Development Process in Small Island States*, Routledge, London

Lofgren, O., 1987, 'Deconstructing Swedishness: culture and class in modern Sweden,' Pp.74-93, in A. Jackson (ed.), *Anthropology at Home*, New York, Tavistock Publications

Lyttleton, C., 2000, Endangered Relations: Negotiating Sex and AIDS in Thailand, Amsterdam, Harwood Academic Publishers

Maanen, J.V., (ed.), 1988, *Tales of the Field: on writing ethnography*, Chicago, University of Chicago Press

Maanen, J.V., (ed.), 1995, *Representation in Ethnography*, California, Sage

MacCannell, D., 1976, *The Tourist*, London, Macmillan

MacCannell, D. 1992, *Empty Meeting Ground – The Tourist Paper*, London, Routledge

Macleod, D.V.L., 2004, *Tourism, Globalisation and Cultural Change: as Island Community Perspective*, Clevedon, Channel View Publications

Mahidol University, 1997, *A Review Study on the Tourism Development Plan for the Upper Southern Region: Chumporn, Ranong, Suratthani, Nakornsrithammarat,*

Pattalung, Trang, Pang-Nga, and Krabi, Faculty of Environment and Resources Studies, Bangkok

Maiava, S., 2001, *A Clash of Paradigms: Intervention, Response and Development in the South Pacific*, Aldershot, Ashgate Publishing Limited

Maitheson, A. and Wall, G., 1982, *Tourism: Economic, Physical and Social Impacts*, London, Longman

Markandya, A. and Richardson, J., 1992, *The Earthscan Reader in Environmental Economics*, London, Earthscan Publications Ltd.

Marwick, A. 2001, *The New Nature of History: Knowledge, Evidence, Language*, Chicago, Lyceum Books.

McCrady, D.G., 2006, *Living with Strangers: the Nineteenth-Century Sioux and the Canadian-American Borderlands*, Lincoln, University of Nebraska Press

McCullagh, C.B., 2004, *The Logic of History: Putting Postmodernism in Perspective*, London, Routledge

McDowell, L., 1996, 'Spatializing feminism: geographical perspective,' Pp. 28-44, in N. Duncan, (ed.), *Body Space: Destabilizing Geographies of Gender and Sexuality*, London, Routledge

McKercher, B. and du Cros, H. 2002, *Cultural Tourism: the partnership between tourism and cultural heritage management*, New York, The Haworth Hospitality Press

Mettarikanon, D., 1983, 'Prostitution and Thai Government Policy 1868-1960' (*Sopheni kap naiyobai rathaban thai ph'o s'o 2411-2503)*, unpublished Master Thesis, Chulalongkorn University, Bangkok, Thailand

Meyer, W., 1988, *Behind the Mask: toward a transdisciplinary approach of selected social problems related to the evolution and context of international tourism in Thailand*, Saarbrucken, Verlag Breitenbach

Meyerhoff, H., 1959, 'History and philosophy: an introduction,' Pp.1-25 in H. Meyerhoff, (ed.), *The Philosophy of History in Our Time: an Anthology*, New York, Double Anchor Books

Miller, P., 1998, 'Canada's model forest program: the Manitoba experience,' Pp.135-152, in J. Lemons, & L. Westra, and R. Goodland, (eds.), *Ecological Sustainability and Integrity: Concept and Approaches*, Kluwer Academic Publishers, Dordrecht

Mills, M.B., 1995, 'Attack of the widow ghosts: gender, death, and modernity in Northeast Thailand', Pp. 244-273, in A. Ong and M.G. Peletz, (eds.), *Bewitching Women, Pious Men: Gender and Body Politics in Southeast Asia*, Berkeley, University of California Press

Mills, M.B., 1999, *Thai Women in the Global Labor Force: Consuming desires, contested selves*, New Brunswick, Rutgers University Press

Molle, F and Srijantr, T., (eds.), 2003a, *Thailand's Rice Bowl: Perspectives on agricultural and social change in the Chao Phraya Delta*, Bangkok, White Lotus

Molle, F and Srijantr, T., , 2003b, 'Introduction', Pp. 1-9, in F. Molle and T, Srijantr, (eds.), *Thailand's Rice Bowl: Perspectives on agricultural and social change in the Chao Phraya Delta*, Bangkok, White Lotus

Molle, F. and Srijantr, T, 2003c, 'Between concentration and fragmentation: the resilience of the land system in the Chao Phraya Delta', Pp. 77-108, in F. Molle and T Srijantr, (eds.), *Thailand's Rice Bowl: Perspectives on agricultural and social change in the Chao Phraya Delta*, Bangkok, White Lotus

Morris, R.C. 2000, *In the Place of Origins: modernity and its mediums in Northern Thailand*, Durham, Duke University Press

Morrison, J.H., 1998, 'A global perspective of oral history in Southeast Asia,' Pp.1-16, in P.L.P. Huen, J.H. Morrison and K.C. Guan, (eds.), *Oral History in Southeast Asia: Theory and Method*, Singapore, Institute of Southeast Asian Studies

Mulder, N., 2000, *Inside Thai Society: religion, everyday life, change*, Chiang Mai, Silkworm Books

Nartsupha, C. and Chanikornpradit, P., 2003, 'The Economic History of the Village on the East Coast of Southern Thailand', Pp. 3-14, in A. Nozaki and C. Baker, (eds.), *Village Communities, States, and Traders: essays in honour of Chatthip Nartsupha*, Bangkok, Thai-Japanese Seminar and Sangsan Publishing House,

Nash, D, 1989, 'Tourism as a form of imperialism', Pp. 37-52, in V. Smith, (ed.), *Hosts and Buests: The Anthropology of Tourism (2nd edition)*, Philadelphia, University of Pennsylvania Press

Nash, D., 1996, *Anthropology of Tourism*, Oxford, Pergamon

Nash, D. and Smith, V.L., 1991, 'Anthropology and tourism,' *Annals of Tourism Research*, (18): 12-25

National Economic and Social Development Board office of the Prime Minister, *Thailand National Economic and Social Development Plans*, Bangkok, Thailand

Ngaosyvathn, M., 1995, 'Buddhism, merit making and gender; the competition for salvation in Laos,' Pp. 145-160, W. J. Karim, (ed.), *'Male' and 'Female' in Developing Southeast Asia*, Oxford, Berg Publishers

O'Connor, S. J., 1986, 'Introduction', in The Archaeology of Peninsular Siam: *Collected Articles from the Journal of the Siam Society 1905-1983*, Bangkok, The Siam Society

Overton, J., 1999, 'Sustainable development in the Pacific Islands,' Pp.1-15, in J. Overton and R. Scheyvens, (eds.), *Strategies for Sustainable Development: Experiences from the Pacific*, University of New South Wales Press, Sydney

Panya, O., 1995, Change from within: adaptation and self-determination in three rural communities of Northeast Thailand 1900-1992, Unpublished Doctoral thesis, Department of Geography, Victoria University of Wellington, Wellington

Papatheodorou, A., 2004, Exploring the evolution of tourism resorts, *Annals of Tourism Research*, 31(1): 219-237

Parnwell, M.J.G., 1993, 'Environmental issues and tourism in Thailand', Pp. 286-302, in M. Hitchcock, V.T. King, and M.J.G. Parnwell, (eds.), *Tourism in South-East Asia*, London, Routledge

Parnwell, M.J.G., (ed.), 1996, *Uneven Development in Thailand*, Avebury, Aldershot

Paviagua, A. 2002, 'Urban-rural migration, tourism entrepreneurs and rural restructuring in Spain', *Tourism Geographies*, 4(4): 349-371

Pearce, P., Moscardo, G. and Ross, G., 1996, *Tourism Community Relationships*, Oxford, Pergamon

Peleggi, M. 2007, *Thailand: the worldly Kingdom*, London, Reaktion

Petkaew, P., 2003, 'The Process of Change in Social, Culture and Economy: the case study of Koh Samui, Surathani' (*Kan Plean Plang Taang Sung Kom Whaathanatham Laae Sethakit: Sooksa Koranee Koh Samui Chanwat Surathani*), Surathani, Ratjaphat Surathani

Phillimore, J. and Goodson, L., 2004, 'Progress in qualitative research in tourism: epistemology, ontology and methodology,' Pp. 3-29, in J. Phillimore and L. Goodson, (eds.) *Qualitative Research in Tourism*, London, Rutledge

Phiriyarangsan, S. and Phongpaichit, P., (eds.), 1992, 'The Middle Class and Democratization in Thailand' (*Chonchan Klang Bon Krasae Pratchathipatai Thai*), Bangkok, Political Economy Center, Chulalongkorn University and Freideric Ebert Foundation

Phongpaichit, P., 1982, *From Peasant Girls to Bangkok Masseuses*, Geneva, International Labour Office

Phongpaichit, P. and Baker, C., 1995, *Thailand, Economy and Society*, Kuala Lumpur, Oxford University Press

Phongpaichit, P. and Baker, C., 1996, *Thailand's Boom!*, New South Wale, Allen & Unwin

223

Phongpaichit, P. and Chiasakul, S., 1993, 'Service,' Pp. 151-171, in P.G. Warr, (ed.), *The Thai Economy in Transition*, Cambridge, Cambridge University Press

Phongphit, S. and Hewison, K., 2001, *Village Life: Culture and Transition in Thailand's Northeast*, Bangkok, White Lotus Press

Picard, M., 1995, 'Cultural Heritage and tourism capital: cultural tourism in Bali', in M. Lanfant, J. Allcock and E. Bruner, (eds.), *International Tourism – Identity and Change*, London, Sage

Picard, M., 1996, *Bali: Cultural Tourism and Touristic Culture*, Singapore, Archipelago Press

Picard, M. and Wood, R., 1997, *Tourism, Ethnicity, and the State in Asian and Pacific Societies*, Honolulu, University of Hawaii Press

Pirenne, H., 1959, What are historian trying to do? Pp.87-99 in H. Meyerhoff, (ed.), *The Philosophy of History in Our Time: an Anthology*, New York, Double Anchor Books

Pongponrat, K., 2007, Community Participation in Local Tourism Development Planning in Thailand: a case study of Koh Samui, Surat Thani Province, Unpublished Doctoral of Philosophy Degree, Asian Institute of Technology, Bangkok, Thailand

Priestley, G. and Mundet, L., 1998, 'The post-stagnation phase of the resort cycle', *Annals of Tourism Research*, 25(1): 85-111

Prins, G., 1991, 'Oral history,' Pp. 114-139, in P. Burke, (ed.), *New Perspectives on Historical Writing*, Oxford, Polity Press

Qu, H. and Zhang, H.Q., 1997, 'The projection of international tourist arrivals in East Asia and the Pacific,' Pp. 35-47 in F.M. Go, and C.L. Jenkins, (eds.), *Tourism and Economic Development in Asia and Australasia*, London, Cassell Imprint

Rangsiwararuk, K., 2003 'Samui', (*Samui ti ruk*), Nonthaburi, TBK Media Publishing

Ray, H.P., 1998, *The Winds of Change: Buddhism and the Maritime Links of Early South Asia*, Delhi, Oxford University Press

Reynolds, B.E., 1990, 'Aftermath of Alliance: the Wartime Legacy in Thai-Japanese Relation,' *Journal of Southeast Asian Studies*, 21(1): 66-87

Reynolds, C.J. (ed.), 1991, *National Identity and Its Defenders: Thailand 1939-1989*, Victoria, Monash University

Reynolds, C.J., 1991a, 'Introduction,' Pp. 1-40 in C.J. Reynolds (ed.), *National Identity and Its Defenders: Thailand, 1939-1989*, Victoria, Monash University

Reynolds, C.J. (ed.), 1991b, *National Identity and Its Defenders: Thailand, 1939-1989*, Victoria, Monash University

Reynolds, C.J. 2006, *Seditious Histories: contesting Thai and Southeast Asian Pasts*, Singapore, Singapore University Press

Redclift, M., 1994, 'Sustainable development: economics and the environment,' Pp.17-34, in M. Redclift and C. Sage, (eds.), *Strategies for Sustainable Development: Local Agendas for the Southern Hemisphere*, West Sussex, John Wiley & Sons

Richards, G. and Hall, D., 2000, 'The community: a sustainable concept in tourism development?,' Pp. 1-13, in G. Richards and D. Hall, (eds.), *Tourism and Sustainable Community Development*, London, Rutledge

Richter, L.K., 1993, 'Tourism-policy-making in South-East Asia,' Pp. 179-199, in M. Hitchcock, & V.T. King, and M.J.G. Parnwell, (eds.), *Tourism in South-East Asia*, London, Routledge

Richter, L.K., 1999, 'The politics of heritage tourism development: emerging issues for the new millennium,' Pp.108-126, in D.G. Pearce and R.W. Butler, (eds.), *Contemporary Issues in Tourism Development*, London, Rutledge

Robertson, R. 1990, Mapping the global condition: Globalization as the central concept, in M. Featherstone (ed.), *Global Culture: Nationalism, Globalization and Modernity*, London, Sage

Robinson, M. & Evans, N. and Callaghan, P., (eds.), 1996, *Tourism and Culture: Towards the 21st Century Conference Proceeding*, Newcastle, University of Northumbria

Rouhomaki, O., 1999, *Fishermen No More?: Livelihood and environment in Southern Thai maritime villages*, Bangkok, White Lotus

Russo, A.P. and Segre, G., 2009, 'Destination models and property regimes: an exploration,' *Annals of Tourism Research*, 36(4): 587-606

Ryan, C. and Aicken, M., (eds.), 2005, *Indigenous Tourism: the commodification and management of culture*, Amsterdam, ELSEVIER

Ryan, C. and Crotts, J., 1997, 'Carving and tourism: a Maori perspective,' *Annals of Tourism Research*, 24(4): 898-918

Ryan, C. and Hall, C.M., 2001, *Sex Tourism, Marginal People and Liminailities*, London, Routledge

Samudavanija, C., 1987, 'Political History,' Pp. 1-40, in S. Xuto (ed.), *Government and Politics of Thailand*, Southeast Asian Studies Programme, Institute of Southeast Asian Studies, Singapore, Oxford University Press

Samui Community Newspaper, Vol. 2, Issue 7, 15 February – 15 March 2007,

Samui Explorer, February 2006

Sasidharan, V., and Thapa, B., 2002, 'Sustainable coastal and marine tourism development: a Hobson's choice?,' Pp.93-112, in Y. Apostolopoulos and D.J. Gayle, (eds.), *Island Tourism and Sustainable Development: Caribbean, Pacific, and Mediterranean Experiences*, Westport, Praeger Publisher

Satayanuruk, A., 2005, 'History for communities: new direction for studying history' *(Pra wat ti sat pher chumchon: tid tang mai khang kan suk sa pra wat ti sat)*, Bangkok, TRF

Schliesinger, J., 2001, *Tai Group of Thailand: Volume 2, Profile of the Existing Groups*, Bangkok, White Lotus

Schneider, D.M, 1971, 'Editorial foreword,' Pp. vii-viii, in B.S. Cohn, D.M., *India: The Social Anthropology of a Civilization*, in D.M. Schneider, Series Editor of Anthropology of Modern Societies Series, New Jersey, Prentice-Hall, Inc.

226

Scholte, J. 1997, 'Identifying Indonesia,' Pp. 21-44, in M. Hitchcock and V. King, (eds.), *Images of Malay-Indonesia Identity*, Oxford, Oxford University Press

Schultz, P., 2003, *1,000 Places to See before You Die: a traveler's life list*, New York, Workman Publishing

Schwartz, R., 1997, *Pleasure Island, Lincoln*, University of Nebraska Press

Selby, M. and Morgan, N.J., 1996, 'Reconstruing place image: a case study of its role in destination market research,' *Tourism Management*, 17(4): 287-294

Shaw, G. and Williams, A.M., 2004, *Tourism and Tourism Spaces*, London, SAGE Publications

Shurmer-Smith, P., 2002(a), 'Marx and after', Pp. 29-40, in P. Shurmer-Smith, (ed.), *Doing Cultural Geography*, London, Sage Publications

Shurmer-Smith, P., 2002(b), 'Poststructuralist cultural geography', Pp. 41-51, in P. Shurmer-Smith, (ed.), *Doing Cultural Geography*, London, Sage Publications

Sillitoe, P. and Bicker, A., 2004, 'Introduction: hunting for theory, gathering ideology,' Pp.1-18, in A. Bicker, P. Sillitoe and J. Pottier, (eds.), *Development and Local Knowledge*, London, Rutledge

Singh, T.V., 1989, *The Kulu Valley: Impact of tourism development in the mountain areas*, New Delhi, Himalayan Books

Sirisaard, S. 2001, 'An investigation of resident's perception of social impacts tourism Pattaya,' Unpublished Master of Tourism Thesis, Department of Tourism, University of Otago, Dunedin

Sithiratbut, U., 1983, Monthon Isan and its Historical Significance, unpublished Master of History Thesis, Chulalongkorn University, Bangkok

Sivaraksa, S., 1991, 'The Crisis of Siamese Identity,' Pp. 41-58, in C.J. Reynolds (ed.), *National Identity and Its Defenders: Thailand, 1939-1989*, Victoria, Monash University

Skinner, G.W., 1957, *Chinese Society in Thailand: An Analytical History*, New York, Ithaca

Small, J., 1999, 'Memory-work: a method for researching women's tourist experiences', *Tourism Management*, 20(1): 25-35

Small, J., 2004, 'Memory-work, Pp. 255-272, in J. Phillimore and L. Goodson, (eds.) *Qualitative Research in Tourism*, Routledge, London

Smith, M.K., 2007, *Tourism, Culture and Regeneration*, Oxfordshire, CABI

Smith, R., 1991, Beach resorts: A model of development evolution, *Landscape and Urban Planning*, 21: 189-210

Smith, R. A. 1992, Beach resort evolution: implications for planning, *Annals of Tourism Research*, 19: 304-322

Smith, V.L., 2004, 'Foreword,' Pp. xv-xvi, in J. Phillimore and L. Goodson, (eds.), *Qualitative Research in Tourism*, London, Routledge

Sofield, T.H.B., 2001, 'Globalisation, tourism and culture in Southeast Asia,' Pp. 103-120 in P. Teo & T.C. Chang and K.C. Ho, (eds.), *Interconnected World: Tourism in Southeast Asia*, Amsterdam, Pergamon

Somswasdi, V. and Theobald, S., (eds.), 1997, *Women, Gender Relations and Development in Thai Society*, Chiangmai, Women's Studies center, Faculty of Social Science, Chaing Mai University

Son, N.T. & Pigram, J.J. and Rugendyke, B.A., 2002, 'Tourism development and national parks in the developing world: Cat Ba Island National Park, Vietnam,' Pp.211-231, in D.G. Pearce and Butler, R.W., (eds.), *Contemporary Issues in Tourism Development*, Routledge, London

Soonthornwanit, C., 1996, 'Studying on Local History' (*Kan Sook Sa Pra Wat Ti Sat Tong Tin*), *Journal of Humanity and Social Science*, Narasuen University, (December): 18-24

Southern Thailand Cultural Encyclopedias, 1986, Volume I

Srijantr, T, 2003, 'Agrarian transformations in the Chao Phraya Delta: a case study in tambon Thung Luk Nok, Pp. 110-125, in F. Molle and T Srijantr, (eds.), *Thailand's Rice Bowl: Perspectives on agricultural and social change in the Chao Phraya Delta,* Bangkok, White Lotus

Stanfield, J.H., 1987, 'Life history analysis and racial stratification research', *American Behavioral Scientist*, 30(4): 429-440

Steinberh, D.J. (ed.), 1987, *In Search of Southeast Asia: A Modern History*, Honolulu, University of Hawaii Press

Stephen, J.Z., (n.d.), *Buddhist Education under Prince Wachirayan Warorot*, Ann Arbor, University Microfilms International

Stonich, S.C., 2000, *The Other Side of Paradise: Tourism, conservation, and development in the Bay Islands*, New York, Cognizant Communication Corporation

Stott, P. 1991, 'Mu'ang and Pa: Elite views of nature in a changing Thailand,' Pp. 142-154, in M. Chitakasem and A. Turton, (eds.), *Thai Constructions of Knowledge*, London, School of Oriental and African Studies, University of London

Strathern, M., 1987, 'The limits of auto-anthropology,' Pp. 16-37, in A. Jackson, (ed.), *Anthropology at Home*, London, Tavistock Publications Ltd

Sunstein, B.S. and Chiseri-Strater, E., 2002, *Fieldworking: Reading and Writing Research (second edition)*, Boston, Bedford/St. Martin's

Swarbrooke, J., 1999, *Sustainable Tourism Management,* New York: Cabi Publishing.

Szuster, B.W., & Molle, F., & Flaherty, M., and Srijantr, T, 2003, 'Socio-economic and environmental implications of inland shrimp', Pp. 177-194, in F. Molle and T Srijantr, (eds.), *Thailand's Rice Bowl: Perspectives on agricultural and social change in the Chao Phraya Delta,* Bangkok, White Lotus

Tambon Municipality of Koh Samui, 2001, *The Five-Year Development Plan*, Koh Samui, Municipality of Koh Samui

Tambon Municipality of Koh Samui, 2003, *The Five-Year Development Plan*, Koh Samui, Municipality of Koh Samui

Tambon Municipality of Koh Samui, 2004, *The Five-Year Development Plan*, Koh Samui, Municipality of Koh Samui

Tambon Municipality of Koh Samui, 2006, *The Five-Year Development Plan*, Koh Samui, Municipality of Koh Samui

Tambon Municipality of Koh Samui, 2007, *The Five-Year Development Plan*, Koh Samui, Municipality of Koh Samui

Tambon Municipality of Koh Samui, 2008, *The Five-Year Development Plan*, Koh Samui, Municipality of Koh Samui

Tanabe, S. and Keyes, C.F., 2002a, 'Introduction,' Pp. 1-39, in S. Tanabe and C.F. Keyes, (eds.), *Cultural Crisis and Social Memory: Modernity and Identity in Thailand and Laos*, Honolulu, University of Hawaii

Tanabe, S. and Keyes, C.F. (eds.), 2002b *Cultural Crisis and Social Memory: Modernity and Identity in Thailand and Laos*, Honolulu, University of Hawaii

Tantiwiramanond, D. and Pandey, S. R., 1987, 'The Status and Role of Thai Women in the Pre-modern Period: a Historical and Cultural Perspective', *Sojourn*, 2(1): 125-149

Tantiwiramanond, D. and Pandey, S. R., 1997, 'New opportunities or new inequalities: development issues and women's lives in Thailand, Pp. 83-136, in S. Virada and S. Theobald, (eds.), *Women, Gender Relations and Development in Thai Society*, Chiangmai, Women's Studies center, Faculty of Social Science, Chaing Mai University

Tejapira, K., 2002, 'The postmodernisation of Thainess,' Pp. 202-227, in S. Tanabe and C.F. Keyes, (eds.), *Cultural Crisis and Social Memory: Modernity and Identity in Thailand and Laos*, Honolulu, University of Hawaii Press

Terwiel, B.J., 1991, 'Thai Nationalism and Identity: popular themes of the 1930s,' Pp. 133-156, in C.J. Reynolds (ed.), *National Identity and Its Defenders: Thailand, 1939-1989*, Victoria, Monash University

Thompson, P., 1978, *The Voice of the Past: Oral History*, Oxford, Oxford University Press

Tighe, A.J. 1986, The arts/tourism partnership, *Journal of Travel Research*, 24(3): 2-5

Timothy, D.J. and Boyd, S. W., (eds.), 2003, *Heritage Tourism*, Harlow, Prentice Hall

Thailand Development Research Institute, 1994, *Thailand Development Research Institute Quarterly Review*, Bangkok

Thailand Development Research Institute, 1996, *Thailand Development Research Institute Quarterly Review*, Bangkok

Thailand Development Research Institute, 2000, *Thailand Development Research Institute Quarterly Review*, Bangkok

Thongsuk, S., 2006, Samui's past and future – can the island be saved?, *Community: insights into island life*, December 2006

Tosun, C. 2002, 'Host perceptions of impacts: A comparative tourism study,' *Annals of Tourism Research*, 29(1): 231-253

Tooman, L.A.,1997, 'Applications of the life-cycle model in tourism,' *Annals of Tourism Research,* 24(1): 214-234

Tourism Authority of Thailand 1980, *Thailand Tourism Statistical Report 1980*, Bangkok, Tourism Authority of Thailand

Tourism Authority of Thailand, 1985, Prepared by Environmental and Resources Management Department, Thailand Institute of Scientific and Technological Research (August 1985), *Master Plan for Tourism Development of Ko Samui/ Surat Thani*

Tourism Authority of Thailand 1994, *Thailand Tourism Statistical Report 1994*, Bangkok, Tourism Authority of Thailand

Tourism Authority of Thailand, 1997, *Annual Report 1997*, Bangkok, Tourism Authority of Thailand

Tourism Authority of Thailand, 1998, *The Action Plan Formulation for Rehabilitation of Tourism Attractions at Ao Plang-Nga, Krabi, Phuket, and Ko Samui Surrounding: Final Report*, Bangkok, TAT

Tourism Authority of Thailand, 2001, *Annual Report 2001*, Bangkok, Tourism Authority of Thailand

Tourism Authority of Thailand, 2002, *Statistical Report 2002*, Bangkok, Tourism Authority of Thailand

Tourism Authority of Thailand, 2004, Tourism Performance 1990-2001, http://www.tatnews.org/about-tat/celebrating.asp/ (Access on 8 February 2004)

Tourism Authority of Thailand, 2007, *Statistical Report 2007*, Bangkok, Tourism Authority of Thailand

Tourism Authority of Thailand, 2010, Tourist arrivals in Thailand 1998-2007, http://www2.tat.or.th/stat/web/static_index.php (Access on 16 May 2010)

Tourism Organization of Thailand, Pacific Consultants International, Tokyo and Design 103 Limited (March 1979), *Master Plan and Feasibility Study Tourism Development of Phuket*

Towner, J., 1988, 'Approaches to tourism history,' *Annals of Tourism Research* (15): 47-62

Towner, J., and Wall, G., 1991, 'History and tourism,' *Annals of Tourism Research* (18): 71-84

Towner, J., 1996, *An Historiography Geography of Recreation and Tourism in the Western World, 1540-1940*, Chichester, John Wiley

Tribe, J., 1997, The indiscipline of Tourism, *Annals of Tourism Research*, 24(3): 638-657

Tribe, J., 2001, Research paradigms in the tourism curriculum, *Journal of Travel Research*, 39: 442-228

Tucker, H, 1999, 'Living with Tourism: tourism, identity and change in a village in central Turkey', unpublished Doctoral Thesis, University of Durham, Scotland

Tucker, H., 2002, 'Welcome to Flintstones-Land: contesting place and identity in Goreme, Central Turkey', Pp. 143-159, in S. Coleman and M. Crang, (eds.), *Tourism: between Place and Performance*, New York, Berghahn

Tucker, H., 2003, *Living with Tourism: Negotiating Identities in a Turkey Village*, Routledge, New York

Van Esterik, P., 2000, *Materializing Thailand*, Oxford, BERG

Vansina, J., 1961, *Oral Tradition: A Study in Historical Methodology*: translated by H.M. Wright, 1965, London, Routledge & Kegan Pual

Vansina, J., 1985, *Oral Tradition as History*, London, James Curry

Vaughn, L. 2006, *Writing Philosophy: A Student's Guide to Writing Philosophy Essays*, New York, Oxford University Press

Vickery, M. 1970, 'Thai Regional Elites and the Reforms of King Chulalongkorn,' *Journal of Asian Studies*, 29(4): 863-882

Vivian, J., 1992, 'Foundations for sustainable development: participation, empowerment and local resource management,' Pp.50-77, in D. Ghai and J.M. Vivian, (eds.), *Grassroots Environmental Action: People's Participation in Sustainable Development*, Routledge, London

Wahab, S. and Cooper, C. 2001a, Tourism, globalization and the competitive advantage of nations, in S. Wahab and C. Cooper, (eds.), *Tourism in the Age of Globalization*, London, Rutledge

Wahab, S. and Cooper, C. (eds.), 2001b, *Tourism in the Age of Globalization*, London, Rutledge

Wahnschafft, R., 1982, Formal and informal tourism sectors: a case study in Pattay, Thailand', *Journal of Annals of Tourism Research*, 9: 429-451

Waldren, J. 1996, *Insiders and Outsiders: Paradise and Reality in Mallorca*, Oxford, Berghahn Books

Walters, M. 1995, *Globalization*, London, Routledge

Walton, J.K, 1997, Taking the history of tourism seriously, *European History Quarterly*, 27: 573-581

Walton, J.K., 2005, 'Introduction', Pp. 1-18, in J.K. Walton, ed., *Histories of Tourism: representation, identity and conflict*, Clevedon, Channel View Publications

Walton, J.K., 2009, 'Histories of tourism', Pp. 115-129, in T. Jamal and M. Robinson (eds.), *The SAGE Handbook of Tourism Studies*, Los Angeles, SAGE

Wangpaichite, S. 1996, *The Approach to Ecotourism in Thailand*, Bangkok, Srinakharinwirot University

Warr, P.G., (ed.), 1993, *The Thai Economy in Transition*, Cambridge, Cambridge University Press

Waters, M. 1995, *Globalization*, London, Routledge

Wells, K. E., 1975, *Thai Buddhism: Its Rites and Activities*, Bangkok, Suriyabun Publishers

Wesseling, H. 1991, 'Overseas history,' Pp.67-92, in P. Burke, (ed.), *New Perspectives on Historical Writing*, Oxford, Polity Press

Westerhausen, K., 2002, *Beyond the Beach: An Ethnography of Modern Travellers in Asia*, Bangkok, White Lotus

White, H., 1981, 'The value of narrativity in the representation of reality,' Pp. 1-23, in W. Mitchell, (ed.), *On Narrative*, Chicago, University of Chicago Press

White, H., 1989, 'Figuring the nature of the times deceased: literary theory and historical writing,' Pp.19-43, in R. Cohen, (ed.), *The Future of Literary Theory*, New York, Routledge

White, H., 1990, *The Content of the Form; narrative, discourse and historical representation*, Maryland, The Johns Hopkins University Press

Wilkinson, P. 1989, 'Strategies for Tourism in Island Microstates', *Annals of Tourism Research*, 16: 153-177

Wilkinson, P.F., 1997, *Tourism Policy & Planning: Case Studies from the Commonwealth Caribbean*, New York, Cognizant Communication Corporation

Williamson, P. and Hirsch, P., 1996, 'Tourism development and social differentiation in Koh Samui,' Pp. 186-203, in M.J.G. Parnwell, (ed.), *Uneven Development in Thailand*, Avebury, Aldershot

Winichakul, T., 1994, *Siam Mapped: a history of the geo-body of a nation*, Silkworm Books, Chiang Mai

Wisansing, J., 2004, Tourism planning and destination marketing: towards a community-driven approach: a case of Thailand: unpublished Doctoral Thesis, Lincoln University, New Zealand

Wishart, D., 2002, 'The selectivity of historical representation,' *Journal of Historical Geography*, 23(2): 111-118

Wong, P.P., 1993, 'Island tourism development in Peninsular Malaysia: environmental perspective,' Pp.83-97, in PP. Wong, (ed.), *Tourism Vs Environment: the Case for Coastal Areas*, Dordrecht, Kluwer Academic Publishers,

World Tourism Organization, 2004, Tourism Enriches: A Global Communications Campaign for Tourism. Retrieved 30 August, 2005, from http://www.world-tourism.org/newsroom/campaign/menu.htm

Wyatt, D. 1969, *The Politics of Reforms in Thailand*, New Haven, Yale University Press

Wyatt, D. 1982, *Thailand: A Short History*, New Haven, Yale University Press

Wyatt, D. 1994, *Studies in Thai History*, Chiang Mai, Silkworm Books

Yasmeen, G., 2002, 'Nurturing, gender ideologies, and Bangkok's foodscape', Pp. 147-166, in S. Sarker and E. Niyogi De, (eds.), *Trans-Status Subjects: Gender in the Globalization of South and Southeast Asia*, Durham, Duke University Press

Young, B., 1983, Touristization of traditional Maltese fishing-farming villages: a general model, *Tourism Management*, 4(1): 35-41

Zack, S.J., 1977, Buddhist Education under Prince Wachirayan Warorot, PhD Dissertation, Cornell University, Ann Arbour, UMI

Appendix I

The campaign of the promotion of the rights and opportunities of sex workers by the Chaing Mai Empower Group

Because we work in the sex industry...

Because to many people what we do is more important than who we are,

And our work is called dangerous and we are exploited,

And society doesn't accept our work but we are expected to work,

And our work is outside the law,

And if we get raped it's no big deal it's our job,

And if we get bashed we deserve it,

And if we raise our voices we're loud mouthed bitches,

And if we like our work we're nymphos [sic],

And if we don't like our work we're helpless victims,

And if we love women it's because we are sexually perverse,

And if we go to the doctor we're diseased and dirty,

And if we don't we're a danger to society,

And if our kids live with us we're obviously bad mothers,

And if we have our family care for our kids we're irresponsible,

And if we stand up for our rights we're ruining the nation's image and name,

And if we don't fight for our rights we're too lazy to be bothered,

And if we have sex for free we're worthless tramps,

And if we charge for our work we're nothing but whores,

And because we try and find safe work tools but men try not to use them,

And if we are pregnant and have an abortion, we're evil wicked women,

And because society won't accept us but accepts all those who profit from us,

And lots and lots....

And lots of other reasons

We call for acceptance that sex work is work

And sex workers are people who must be treated as equal within society

(empowerChiang Mai 2003)

Source: The original campaign sign for sex workers' rights and opportunities from EmpowerChiang Mai group.

Appendix II

The voice of the empowerment group on the legislation of prostitution on the 27th November 2004

Most of you will have seen us working in bars, karaoke bars, massage parlours or brothels. We sell drinks, sing [and] entertain clients while they drink, play snooker, dance and some of us sell sex. It seems everybody has an opinion on who we are, why we work and what we want.

… However, it was clear to us that many academics and non-sex worker groups are continuing to quote old and often inaccurate information about us. Most of us are women. Most of us are single mothers and the main supporters of our extended families. We are blood donors and voters. We are good Buddhists and take our religious responsibilities seriously. We worry about social issues like youth violence, drug use and the environment. We are active in our communities caring for others. We contribute to the economy via sales tax and tourism promotion. We participate in social and medical research. We eat, we sleep, we do housework, we dream. We are Thai, hill tribe, and we are from other countries in the region. Like all workers we work to provide a good life for our families and ourselves. Most of us have had many other jobs like cooking, waitressing [sic], laundry, sewing or running small businesses. Sex work is not the last resort but rather that job that we have chosen because it offers us the best opportunities.

Source: The Chiangmai News (27th November 2004)

Appendix II

the voice of the empowered ... an of the legisla...
November 2004

Most of you will have seen us working in bars,
hotels. We sell drinks, sing [and] entertain customers and some of us sell sex. It seems everybody...
why we work and what we mean.

... However, it was clear to us that many understa...
remaining to quote old... and often I sometimes...
women. Plenty of us are single mothers and...
families. We are blood donors and voters. We...
religious responsibilities seriously. We worry...
violence, drug use and the environment. We are...
for others. We contribute to the economy via sal...
participate in social and medical research. We...
dream. We are Thai, hill tribal, and we are from...
all workers we work to provide a good life for...
us have had many other jobs, like cooking, w...
running small businesses. Sex work is not the best...
have chosen because it offers us the best opportuni...

Source: The Chiangmai News

Lightning Source UK Ltd.
Milton Keynes UK
UKOW051906250712

196566UK00001B/47/P